ORIGINS OF THE FRENCH
WELFARE STATE

This is the first comprehensive modern analysis of public and private welfare in France, which offers a deeply researched explanation of how France's welfare state came to be and why the French are so attached to it.

The author argues that France simultaneously pursued two different paths toward universal social protection. Family welfare embraced an industrial model in which class distinctions and employer control predominated. By contrast, protection against the risks of illness, disability, maternity, and old age followed a mutual aid model of welfare. The book examines a remarkably broad cast of actors that includes workers' unions, employers, mutual leaders, the parliamentary elite, *hauts fonctionnaires*, doctors, pronatalists, women's organizations – both social Catholic and feminist – and diverse peasant organizations. It also traces foreign influences on French social reform, particularly from Germany's former territories in Alsace-Lorraine and Britain's Beveridge Plan.

PAUL V. DUTTON is Assistant Professor of European History, Northern Arizona University, Flagstaff.

NEW STUDIES IN EUROPEAN HISTORY

Edited by
PETER BALDWIN, University of California, Los Angeles
CHRISTOPHER CLARK, University of Cambridge
JAMES B. COLLINS, Georgetown University
MIA RODRIGUEZ-SALGADO, London School of Economics and Political
Science
LYNDAL ROPER, Royal Holloway, University of London

This is a new series in early modern and modern European history. Its aim is to publish outstanding works of research, addressed to important themes across a wide geographical range, from southern and central Europe, to Scandinavia and Russia, and from the time of the Renaissance to the Second World War. As it develops the series will comprise focused works of wide contextual range and intellectual ambition.

Books in the series

ORIGINS OF THE FRENCH WELFARE STATE

The struggle for social reform in France 1914–1947

PAUL V. DUTTON

CAMBRIDGE
UNIVERSITY PRESS

PUBLISHED BY THE PRESS SYNDICATE OF THE UNIVERSITY OF CAMBRIDGE
The Pitt Building, Trumpington Street, Cambridge, United Kingdom

CAMBRIDGE UNIVERSITY PRESS
The Edinburgh Building, Cambridge CB2 2RU, UK
40 West 20th Street, New York, NY 10011-4211, USA
477 Williamstown Road, Port Melbourne, VIC 3207, Australia
Ruiz de Alarcón 13, 28014 Madrid, Spain
Dock House, The Waterfront, Cape Town 8001, South Africa

http://www.cambridge.org

© Paul V. Dutton 2002

First published 2002

Printed in the United Kingdom at the University Press, Cambridge

Typeface Baskerville Monotype 11 / 12.5 pt.   *System* LaTeX 2$_\varepsilon$ [TB]

A catalogue record for this book is available from the British Library

ISBN 0 521 81334 4 hardback

For Shelby

Contents

Figures

Tables

Acknowledgments

This book would not have been possible without the aid and inspiration of many teachers, colleagues, and friends. I would like to thank Allan Mitchell for his incisive evaluations and unstinting support of this study when it was hatched as a doctoral dissertation at the University of California, San Diego. Allan quite literally opened many archive doors for me in Paris and saw to it that the benefits of his prodigious work, at least in a small way, were bestowed upon me. I am also grateful for the encouragement and advice of Elinor Accampo, Cheryl Koos, Rachel Fuchs, Martha Hildreth, John Marino, and Pamela Radcliff. They helped me to see the topic in broader terms than I would have otherwise. At Johns Hopkins, I would like to thank David Calleo, Ilya Prizel, and Kendall Myers whose enthusiastic renderings of interwar Europe prompted my own fascination.

In Paris, my debts run to many. I would like to thank Patrick Fridenson for pointing the way to new sources and inviting me to attend his seminar on French industrial enterprises at the Ecole des Hautes Etudes en Sciences Sociales. I would also like to thank Jean-Claude Chesnais for his invaluable advice and hospitality. Jean-Claude introduced me to Pierre Laroque, who graciously invited me to his home when a strike made an interview difficult at his government office. For this morning of reflections, so late in his life, I thank Pierre Laroque. I am also indebted to numerous staff members at archives and libraries in Paris, Bar-le-Duc, Chartres, Metz, and Rodez. These include Françoise Blum at the Musée Social; Madame Duvigneau of the Archives Départementales de la Moselle; Francine Gilère of the Archives Nationales; Albert Guyot at the Caisse d'Allocations Familiales de la Moselle; Jean-Claude Jolly of the Archives de l'Assemblée Nationale de France; Corinne Lehmann of the Alliance Nationale/Population Avenir; Agnès Nicolay of the Syndicat Général des Entrepreneurs du Bâtiment et des Travaux Publics de la Moselle; and Madame Villeroil of the Caisse d'Allocations Familiales de

Paris. At the Caisse Nationale des Allocations Familiales, I am indebted to Director Philippe Steck and Historian Jean-François Montes for their interviews, as well as to Madame Guibet of the Service de Documentation for uncovering the *procès-verbaux* of Comité Central des Allocations Familiales.

Financial support is always worthy of praise. Grants from the University of California, San Diego Department of History, and a Laura and John Galbraith Fellowship supported a year-long research sojourn that launched the study. Subsequent trips and valuable release time from teaching were made possible by the Institut Français de Washington and the Office of the Associate Provost for Research and Graduate Studies at Northern Arizona University.

I have previously published portions of the book. I would like to acknowledge the University of Chicago Press for its original publication of "An Overlooked Source of Social Reform: Family Policy in French Agriculture," *Journal of Modern History* 72 (June 2000): 375–412, and Oxford University Press for its original publication of "French Versus German Approaches to Family Welfare in Lorraine, 1918–1940," *French History* 13 (December 1999): 439–463. The anonymous readers of these articles helped to shape my thinking about family welfare and therefore made an important contribution to this book.

Lastly, I owe the greatest thanks to my best friend and wife, Shelby Reid, whose confidence sustained me throughout the project. To her, I dedicate the book.

Abbreviations

CAFM	Caisse d'Allocations Familiales de la Moselle
CAPS	Commission d'Assurance et de Prévoyance Sociales
CCAF	Comité Central des Allocations Familiales
CCRP	Caisse de Compensation de la Région Parisienne
CFTC	Confédération Française des Travailleurs Chrétiens
CGPF	Confédération Générale de la Production Française
CGT	Confédération Générale du Travail
CGTU	Confédération Générale du Travail Unitaire
CHAAPS	Commission de l'Hygiène, de l'Assistance, de l'Assurance et de la Prévoyance Sociales
CNFF	Conseil National des Femmes Françaises
CNN	Congrès National de la Natalité
CNR	Conseil National de la Résistance
CSAF	Commission Supérieure des Allocations Familiales
CSN	Conseil Supérieur de la Natalité
FMT	Fédération Mutualiste du Travail
FNMCA	Fédération Nationale de la Mutualité et de la Coopération Agricoles
FNMF	Fédération Nationale de la Mutualité Française
FNSEA	Fédération Nationale des Syndicats d'Exploitants Agricoles
GIMM	Groupe des Industries Métallurgiques, Mécaniques et Connexes de la Région Parisienne
GIRP	Groupe des Industries de la Région Parisienne
HCP	Haut Comité de la Population
ILO	International Labor Organization
MRP	Mouvement Républicain Populaire
PCF	Parti Communiste Français

SFIO	Section Française Internationale Ouvrière
UCSAF	Union Centrale des Syndicats des Agriculteurs de France
UFCS	Union Féminine Civique et Sociale
UFSF	Union Française pour le Suffrage des Femmes
UIMM	Union des Industries Métallurgiques et Minières
UNSA	Union Nationale des Syndicats Agricoles

Introduction

On a rainy December morning in 1995 Pierre Laroque gazed out the window of his apartment on Paris' Avenue Victor Hugo and contemplated the snarled traffic below. France's greatest strike since May 1968 had paralyzed the city's metro trains and buses, causing a morass of automobiles on streets throughout the metropolis. Strikers' wrath was aimed at a government plan to trim the welfare state that Laroque had done so much to create. The plan, authored by President Chirac's first prime minister, Alain Juppé, sought modest reductions in benefits as part of a larger package to halt welfare spending deficits. Yet the public-sector unions – supported by a significant portion of the populace – viewed "le plan Juppé" as but a first step in the dismantling of France's generous system of social protections. I had come to interview Laroque about the 1930s and his years at the Conseil d'Etat. He seemed pleased with my interest in the interwar period, perhaps because he had grown weary of the recent media inquiries that focused on his better known role as the founding director of social security after 1945. France had just marked the fiftieth anniversary of its postwar welfare state and Laroque, quite inescapably, had been the subject of numerous television and newspaper interviews.[1] The passing media attention and the strike appeared to have put him in a reflective mood, with a regard for a longer view of France's welfare state that I had come to discuss and which this book attempts to illuminate.[2]

Laroque deservedly holds the title of "father" of the French welfare state. But his reforms cannot be compared with Bismarck's creation of

---

[1] Laroque was principal author of the *ordonnance* of 4 October 1945, which is popularly seen as the birth of *sécurité sociale*. Laroque died in 1997. For a general overview, see Jean-Jacques Dupeyroux, *Sécurité sociale*, eighth edition (Paris: Editions Dalloz, 1994); John Ambler (ed.), *The French Welfare State: Surviving Social and Ideological Change* (New York University Press, 1991); François Ewald, *L'Etat providence* (Paris: Grasset, 1986); Jean-Pierre Dumont, *La Sécurité sociale toujours en chantier: histoire, bilan, perspectives* (Paris: Editions ouvrières, 1981); Pierre Laroque (ed.), *The Social Institutions of France* (New York: Gordon and Breach, 1983).

[2] Author's interview with Pierre Laroque, Paris, 2 December 1995.

illness, accident, disability, and retirement insurance for German workers in the 1880s. Similarly, although he is sometimes referred to as the
"French Beveridge," Laroque could not achieve a systematic rationalization of social welfare in France comparable to what Beveridge envisioned
for Britain in the 1940s.[3] Such a massive restructuring was impossible in
France because of well-entrenched social programs that dated from the
interwar and Vichy years. This study examines the origins and development of the most important social welfare initiatives of the twentieth century prior to 1945, namely family allowances (*allocations familiales*) and social insurance (*assurances sociales*). Together they determined the essential
nature of the welfare state that was launched after the Second World War.

Today's *sécurité sociale* owes its complex mélange of alphabet-soup taxes
and benefits, semi-public institutions and, above all, its specialized professional funds to the varied beginnings and evolution of family welfare
and social insurance between 1914 and 1947. Some scholars have argued that this complexity and the relatively late and limited success of
systemic unification make France an exception among European welfare
states. But exceptions may only be perceived in reference to a notion of
normality, which is usually assigned to Britain, Germany, and Sweden,
and based primarily on measures of political modernization and economic development.[4] These studies underscore the tardiness of French
developments in areas such as unemployment insurance, which was not
introduced until 1958. However, they do not adequately appreciate the
derivations of France's myriad programs that have incrementally led to
a welfare state of remarkable generosity and durability. Indeed, French
social spending bucked the economic downturn of the 1970s and went
on to surpass both Germany and Britain during the 1980s, attaining
Scandinavian proportions as a percentage of gross domestic product by
1989.[5]

---

[3] On Britain, see Geoffrey Finlayson, *Citizen, State, and Social Welfare in Britain, 1830–1990* (Oxford
University Press, 1994). On Germany, see Young-Sun Hong, *Welfare, Modernity, and the Weimar State,
1919–1933* (Princeton University Press, 1998); David F. Crew, *Germans on Welfare. From Weimar to
Hitler* (Oxford University Press, 1998); and Allan Mitchell, *The Divided Path: The German Influence on
Social Reform in France after 1870* (Chapel Hill, NC: University of North Carolina Press, 1991).
[4] Peter Flora and Jens Alber, "Modernization, Democratization, and the Development of Welfare
States in Western Europe," in Peter Flora and Arnold Heidenheimer (eds.), *The Development of
Welfare States in Europe and America* (New Brunswick, NJ: Transaction, 1981), pp. 37–80; Hugh
Heclo, *Modern Social Politics in Britain and Sweden: From Relief to Income Maintenance* (New Haven, CT:
Yale University Press, 1974).
[5] According to the International Labor Organization 1989 spending on social insurance, income
maintenance, and family welfare measured 35.9 percent of GDP in Sweden, 28.4 percent in
Denmark, 21.2 percent in Norway, 27.1 percent in France, 22.7 percent in West Germany, 17.3
percent in the United Kingdom and 12.2 percent in the United States. See *The Cost of Social Security:
Fourteenth International Inquiry, 1987–1989* (Geneva: ILO, 1996), pp. 73–75.

Perceptions that the development of French social welfare lagged behind other major European countries may be linked to the term "welfare state." As we will see, the diverse family welfare programs and social insurance protections that France enjoys today grew out of employer initiatives and private mutual aid societies. In the case of family welfare, employer programs constituted the bulk of expenditures and were largely outside of the state's purview until 1932 when the government mandated that all employers pay family allowances. Yet even after this legislation, employers closely guarded their prerogatives over administration, excluding the state from control of this important social program. Similarly, mutual aid societies, which were in essence private health insurance clubs, became the essential organs of the country's first social insurance law in 1930. When legislation required workers to enroll in social insurance funds, private mutual aid societies captured the vast majority of these compulsory enrollees. Thus, the central role of employer initiative and private actors relegated state officials to oversight functions that poorly befits the title of "welfare state." Yet this fact should not diminish our appreciation of France's sophisticated family welfare and social insurance systems between the world wars. Only through an accurate reckoning of these largely private and highly decentralized efforts at social protection can we fully understand the social democracy that exists in France today.

The tendency to privilege evidence of direct state control in the examination of social policy has been accentuated by previous treatments of family welfare. Several of the most extensive studies of family allowances focus their attention on the politics of France's pronatalist and social-Catholic familial movements.[6] French family policy has thus become a field unto itself, hindering a comprehensive analysis of the interaction between family welfare and social insurance. This study integrates its examination of employers' family allowance practices and the contemporaneous battles over social insurance. In so doing, we find that employers used their highly evolved institutions of family welfare in an attempt to derail legislation on compulsory social insurance. Indeed, during the mid-1920s the *grand patronat* envisioned a wholly employer-controlled system of social welfare. Many large industrialists had long been interested in perfecting their paternalistic practices in order to

---

[6] Jean-Claude Chesnais, "La politique de la population française depuis 1914," in *Histoire de la population française*, vol. IV, Jacques Dupâquier (ed.) (Paris: Presses Universitaires de France, 1988), pp. 181–231; Robert Talmy, *Histoire du mouvement familial, 1896–1939*, 2 vols. (Paris: Union Nationale des Caisses d'Allocations Familiales, 1962); Dominique Ceccaldi, *Histoire des prestations familiales en France* (Paris: Union Nationale des Caisses d'Allocations Familiales, 1957).

pacify labor unrest and build loyalty among their workers.[7] Large-scale institutional collaboration in the payment of family allowances put paternalistic control of workers within reach of medium-sized and even small employers. This option proved highly attractive to employers as the financial burden of social insurance became apparent. An examination of family policy alongside social insurance thus permits a full valuation of employer initiatives as an interactive element in France's evolving welfare institutions.

Consideration of family welfare beside social insurance is also imperative because of their varying distributional characteristics. Family allowances redistributed income away from households without dependent children to those where young children were present, irrespective of a worker's wealth or income.[8] In contrast, the redistribution of income effected by social insurance aligned much more closely with class divisions. Social insurance taxes were levied as a percentage of wages on workers and employers, yet most benefits were substantially the same, irregardless of worker premiums. Thus, highly paid workers subsidized their lower-paid comrades whose payroll deductions were insufficient to cover the cost of their benefits. This aspect of social insurance evoked little controversy when the program was initially launched in the 1930s because compulsory participation was limited primarily to the industrial working class. However, when efforts to universalize social insurance moved to the fore after 1945, the class character of its redistributional effects became highly contentious. Meanwhile, family welfare practices created an iniquitous distribution of resources according to gender. Employers required that recipients of family allowances hold the status of *chef de famille* (head of household), a legal designation that was often denied to a woman as long as she was married, even if she had been abandoned or constituted the sole breadwinner for her children. Hence a complete picture of the inequities and redistributional character of social policy according to class and gender cannot be drawn without a comparative consideration of family welfare and social insurance.

---

[7] Susan Pedersen, *Family, Dependence, and the Origins of the Welfare State: Britain and France, 1914–1945* (Cambridge University Press, 1993). Also see Gérard Noiriel, "Du 'patronage' au 'paternalisme': la restructuration des formes de domination de la main-d'œuvre ouvrière dans la métallurgie française," *Le Mouvement Social* 144 (July–Sept. 1988), 19–35; Donald Reid, "Industrial Paternalism: Discourse and Practices in 19th-Century French Mining and Metallurgy," *Comparative Studies in Society and History* 27:4 (Oct. 1985), 579–607.

[8] Jean-Pierre Jallade, "Redistribution in the Welfare State: An Assessment of French Performance," in Jallade (ed.), *The Crisis of Redistribution in European Welfare States* (Stoke-on-Trent, UK: Trentham Books, 1988), pp. 221–253.

THE INDUSTRIAL AND MUTUAL MODELS AND THEIR CONTEXT

French family welfare and social insurance conformed to contrasting models of welfare protection which led to strikingly different outcomes. Mutual aid societies served as the model for social insurance while industrialists' family allowance institutions became the archetype for family welfare. The adoption of mutual aid societies as the principal vehicle for the implementation of social insurance proved largely successful. The inherent flexibility of the mutual model and the mutual movement's widespread political popularity permitted the creation of a compulsory social insurance system of approximately nine million workers by 1939. However, the choice of the mutual model also proved fateful for France's postwar welfare state. The creation of a "mutualized" social insurance system immortalized decentralization along occupational lines. In contrast to the relative success and enduring influence of the mutual model, the industrial model of family welfare suffered from internal contradictions and a popular aversion to employer control. These difficulties prompted extensive state-directed reforms, beginning in the late 1930s. The reformers of 1945 continued the rationalization begun under the late Third Republic by assuring, for example, the democratic governance of family welfare institutions. However, the administration of family welfare remained separate from social insurance because of the differing models and unique interwar evolutions of the two programs. In order to fully appreciate the significance of the mutual and industrial models to the construction of France's welfare state, several contextual issues that confronted social reformers in France and elsewhere in Europe must be considered.

The battle between liberty and obligation was the most evident struggle in the creation of the French and other European welfare states.[9] This was principally an ideological struggle between the defenders of *laissez-faire* liberalism and the diverse forces of socialists, social Catholics, and solidarists, who favored varying levels of state intervention to promote the common welfare. Liberal thought, which stood upon the tenet of individual initiative, dominated French social policy making after the Restoration of 1815. As a result, the nineteenth century witnessed a widespread acceptance of *assistance* to the helplessly destitute by state- and Church-run charities, but political leaders rejected as inappropriate any state programs that helped the able-bodied working poor. In the

[9] Henri Hatzfeld, *Du paupérisme à la sécurité sociale, 1850–1940*, second edn (Presses Universitaires de Nancy, 1989).

words of one social reformer at the turn of the century, programs that aided the able-bodied constituted a violation "of the very nature and dignity of man, which are based on his liberty and responsibility."[10] Thus, only when a man had been reduced to the condition of a pauper could he legitimately claim state charity. Otherwise, he should practice *prévoyance*, that is, initiative and prudence to guard himself and his family against the unfortunate consequences of accidents, illness, disability, old age, and unemployment. Women and children who, according to the reigning liberal paradigm, were by nature incapable of possessing the same dignity and rationality, and were legally prevented from exercising the same liberties as men, were not bound by the same limitations on state aid and protection.[11] This is not to suggest that child welfare and aid for poor women were especially plentiful in nineteenth-century France. They were not. Rather it is to indicate that the allocation of welfare resources during the nineteenth century depended on deeply held conceptions of gender which, as we will see, would prove difficult to dislodge long after *laissez-faire* liberalism had ceased to constrain working men's access to welfare benefits. In fact, the most notable late nineteenth-century provocation against the liberal constraints on social welfare bolstered the unequal condition of women in social relations while simultaneously promising working-class men a measure of relief.

A transformation in Church doctrine provided an important contextual factor in the struggle for social welfare. Leo XIII's 1891 encyclical, *Rerum Novarum*, explicitly called on Europe's increasingly powerful industrialists to pay a "just wage." Wages, Leo admonished, should not be decided purely according to the laws of supply and demand nor did the presence of a contract necessarily fulfill an employer's obligation to the notion of justice. Rather, the encyclical defined a just wage according to a gendered model of woman and child dependency according to which earnings were to sustain a sole worker as well as those who relied on him.[12] *Rerum Novarum* fueled a social Catholic movement of

---

[10] M. Lépine, *La Mutualité, ses principes, ses bases veritables* (Paris: 1903), cited by Marcel Porte, *Assurances sociales et traditions mutualistes* (Grenoble: Allier, 1923), p. 5.

[11] Rachel G. Fuchs, *Abandoned Children: Foundlings and Child Welfare in Nineteenth-Century France* (Albany: State University of New York Press, 1984) and *Poor and Pregnant in Paris: Strategies for Survival in the Nineteenth Century* (New Brunswick, NJ: Rutgers University Press, 1992). Also see Elinor Accampo, Rachel Fuchs, and Mary Lynn Stewart, *Gender and the Politics of Social Reform in France, 1870–1914* (Baltimore: Johns Hopkins University Press, 1995). For a survey of the literature on nineteenth-century France, see Philip Nord, "The Welfare State in France: 1870–1914," *French Historical Studies* 18:3 (Spring 1994), 821–838.

[12] "Rerum Novarum," Claudia Carlen, (comp.), *The Papal Encyclicals, 1878–1903* (Wilmington, NC: McGrath, 1981), pp. 241–261.

significant strength in France, thereby clouding the distinction between *laissez-faire* liberals and interventionist socialists. Yet in the eyes of socialists, the social Catholic agenda focused too heavily on appeals to the moral obligation of employers to provide for their workers and thereby abetted the creation of paternalistic regimes under which workers lacked legally prescribed social protections. Nevertheless, *Rerum Novarum* created a narrow political alliance, restricted to welfare concerns, between social Catholics and the interventionist-minded left. For example, social Catholic deputies Abbé Lemire and Paul Lerolle called for a legal mandate on all employers to provide retirement and disability insurance to their male workers as early as 1901.[13] At this time, solidarism, a secular philosophical tendency distinct from socialism and liberalism furnished another platform for state-directed social reform.

Solidarism provided a non-confessional alternative to social Catholicism in the search for social justice. It drew on the thought of Auguste Comte and Alfred J. E. Fouillée, bringing together French philosophical efforts of the late nineteenth century to reconcile moralistic utopianism with materialist conceptions of human nature. In so doing, it sought an accommodation between the purist individualism of liberalism and the collectivist dictates of socialism. According to its principal founder, Léon Bourgeois, solidarist philosophy was needed to achieve the Republic's promise of *fraternité* and to balance the dominant bourgeois conception of *laissez-faire* as the sole criterion of liberty. Bourgeois succeeded in adapting the various strands of solidarist thought into a centrist political platform in 1895 by jettisoning much of its proletarian character. The solidarism of the early twentieth-century Radical party evolved from Bourgeois' creation, offering restrained criticism of the status quo and a gradualist reform program. This platform appealed to the middle class who feared a violent struggle between uncompromising liberals and leftists for control of the Republic.[14] *Rerum Novarum* and solidarism thus permitted Radicals and social Catholics to play critical roles in the struggle between liberals and leftist politicians on questions of social reform. Social Catholics and Radicals also headed France's pronatalist movement, which consistently advocated social policies to stem what they perceived as a crisis of depopulation.

---

[13] Hatzfeld, *Du paupérisme à la sécurité sociale*, pp. 76–77, 98.
[14] J.E.S. Hayward, "Solidarity: The Social History of an Idea in Nineteenth-Century France," *International Review of Social History* 4 (1959), 261–284 and "The Official Social Philosophy of the French Third Republic: Léon Bourgeois and Solidarism," *International Review of Social History* 6 (1961), 19–48.

Pronatalism gained credence well beyond particular parties or religious associations.[15] Unlike solidarism and social Catholicism, each of which were founded on a particular philosophical heritage or religious tradition, the origins of pronatalism lay in a highly refracted view of the social causes and implications of France's demographic circumstances. The largest and most influential pronatalist organizations were found on the right of the political spectrum. They opposed the expansion of women's civil and political rights, supported a tax code that penalized single persons and married couples without children, and called for the enactment of legislation to encourage bourgeois notions of women's domesticity and family values, including criminal penalties for the dissemination of information about birth control.[16] Yet the rightist policy prescriptions of groups such as the Alliance Nationale pour l'Accroissement de la Population Française should not cloud our view of pronatalism's broader significance. That leaders of pronatalist organizations played an important role in imposing a conservative agenda on social reform is indisputable. But their ability to do so arose, in large part, from a popular belief in the country's demographic demise that spanned the political spectrum. Interwar pronatalist propagandists alone could not have produced such a broad consensus on the depopulation crisis. The roots of pronatalism extended much deeper into the French national identity and depended on an essential comparison with "the other" that had not always been prevalent.[17]

There is little doubt that France holds a special place among industrialized countries due to the nature of its demographic transition.[18]

[15] Cheryl A. Koos, "Gender, Anti-individualism, and Nationalism: The Alliance Nationale and the Pronatalist Backlash against the *femme moderne*, 1933–1940," *French Historical Studies* 19:3 (Spring 1996), 699–723; Richard Wall and Jay Winter, "Pronatalism in the Interwar Period in France," *Journal of Contemporary History* 25 (1990), 39–68; Richard Wall and Jay Winter (eds.), *The Upheaval of Work: Family, Work, and Welfare in Europe, 1914–1918* (Cambridge University Press, 1988); Françoise Thébaud, "Le mouvement nataliste dans la France de l'entre-deux-guerres: L'Alliance Nationale pour l'Accroissement de la Population Française," *Revue d'Histoire Moderne et Contemporaine* 32 (1985): 276–301; Richard Tomlinson, "The Politics of 'Dénatalité' during the French Third Republic" (Ph.D. thesis, Cambridge University (1984); Joseph J. Spengler, *France Faces Depopulation, Postlude Edition, 1936–1976* (Durham: Duke University Press, 1979).
[16] Mary Louise Roberts, *Civilization without Sexes: Reconstructing Gender in Postwar France, 1917–1927* (University of Chicago Press, 1994), chs. 4 and 5.
[17] Benedict Anderson, *Imagined Communities: Reflections on the Origin and Spread of Nationalism* (New York: Verso, 1991). Also see Peter Sahlins, *Boundaries: The Making of France and Spain in the Pyrenees* (Berkeley: University of California Press, 1989).
[18] The theory of demographic transition posits that the relationship between industrialization and fertility is inverse: industrialization raises living standards and stimulates a general aspiration toward increasingly greater degrees of comfort, which, in turn, promotes a limitation on childbearing. This theory is opposed by Malthusian theory, which states that economic development

Its fertility decline began relatively early in the nineteenth century and its natural increase fell exceptionally low during the transition period. Indeed, after 1850 French fertility and mortality declined at approximately the same pace and negative population growth prevailed on several occasions during peacetime after 1900.[19] However, in the nineteenth century, news of France's emerging demographic peculiarity failed to elicit alarm. To the contrary, the most critical observers of demographic data of the day, the Economistes, maintained a decidedly Malthusian outlook well into the Second Empire (1852–1870), viewing slow population growth as a beneficial development. In fact, when a lone dissenter, Léonce de Lavergne opined that France's population growth rate "has taken on disquieting proportions . . . indicating serious trouble in the general conditions of society," he faced a scourge of repudiation.[20] In the aftermath of Lavergne's remark, the Economistes reaffirmed their view by declaring that far from being a sign of trouble, slackening population growth corresponded with a positive control of the birthrate, which could lead to better economic circumstances. They reasoned that lower fertility levels signified nothing more than an equilibrium between population and its resources. An observable decline in the birthrate, they insisted, far from being a cause for alarm, represented the emergence of a more favorable balance. As M. E. Legoyt put it: "France is in a privileged situation, having united two modes of enrichment. On the one hand, its revenue is growing while on the other it is tending toward a decrease in expenditures by wisely limiting the costs of its fertility."[21] Malthusian analysis came under stress during the 1860s when Le Play and his journal, *La Réforme Sociale*, argued that an expanding population aided the maintenance of social peace and secured the basic role of the family in society. Yet despite Napoleon III's support for the Le Play school, concern over faltering population growth emerged only in the wake of developments outside France.

---

stimulates fertility, increases the demand for work, and encourages marriage and family formation. Conformity with both theories has been widely observed in Europe. During the initial stages of industrialization, countries have witnessed rapid rises in fertility; subsequent decades brought a demographic transition. See Jean-Claude Chesnais, *The Demographic Transition: Stages, Patterns, and Economic Implications* (Oxford: Clarendon Press, 1992).

[19] *Ibid.*, pp. 221–223. France's relatively early onset of population stagnation during the nineteenth century has also been matched by a similar performance during this century. After a sharp rise in the birthrate immediately after the Second World War, a downward trend resumed by 1950, punctuated only by a brief break in 1972.

[20] *Journal des Economistes* 13 (1857), 226, cited by Yves Charbit, "Les Fondements idéologiques des politiques démographiques en France, 1850–1900," in *La Fécondité dans les pays industrialisés* (Paris: Centre National de la Recherche Scientifique, 1986), 263–272, p. 266.

[21] *Ibid.*, 14 (1857), 362–363, quoted by Charbit, *ibid.*, p. 267.

The Prussian defeat of Austria in 1866 and of France itself in 1870 resulted in a geopolitical view of demographic phenomena that had not been present since the Napoleonic era.[22] Malthusianism, which had predominated two short decades earlier, was displaced by interpretations that dwelt on the relative position of France among its European neighbors. Typical of the new interpretation was Emile Cheyson's contribution to *La Réforme Sociale* in 1891: "The slowdown in French population growth relative to its prolific neighbors is disquieting from the economic, colonial, social, and military points of view. It is a 'national peril' which cannot be ignored."[23] The emerging pronatalist interpretation of France's demographic circumstances contributed to a broader sense of "degeneration" in the late nineteenth century. The notion that France suffered from national decline evolved from what had been a biomedical model. By the end of the century, this clinical model of abnormal individual pathology had made its way into the language of social moralists and was being widely applied to an organic notion of the nation.[24] Pronatalism thus thrived on highly pessimistic views of the national well-being, which had originated in the nineteenth century. Developments between the world wars provided further fuel for the pronatalist cause. The relative strength of Germany's post Great War "baby boom," the stridency of Italian Fascists' family policies, and rise of the Nazi regime after 1933 created an environment in which French pronatalists could reach the apex of their influence. Social reformers of virtually every political camp perceived an amelioration of the "depopulation crisis" as one of their most pressing concerns even if their solutions varied widely. France's perseverance against its demographic nature, which deeply colored the debate over welfare policy during the first half of the twentieth century, serves as a recurrent theme throughout this study.

AIM AND ORGANIZATION OF THE BOOK

The ultimate aim of this book is to explain how social reforms during the first half of the twentieth century shaped the welfare system that emerged after 1945. Within this explanation, I believe, also lies the answer to the question: why are the French so attached to their welfare state?

---

[22] Tomlinson, "The Politics of 'Dénatalité'," p. 2.
[23] *La Réforme Sociale*, 1 June 1896, p. 851, quoted by Charbit, "Les Fondements idéologiques," p. 267.
[24] Robert A. Nye, *Crime, Madness, and Politics in Modern France: The Medical Concept of National Decline* (Princeton University Press, 1984).

Indeed, *la securité sociale*, which is here meant to include the entirety of French social protections and benefits that emerged in the decades after the Second World War, is an intrinsic part of French democracy. It is simultaneously both the agent and evidence of national solidarity. It is "the social" in French social democracy and France's society and politics are unintelligible without an understanding of it.

Social democracy represents an alternative model of democracy to that practiced in the United States where individual liberty and market forces are given a wider berth. Although France is by no means the only social democracy in existence today, its national culture exhibits a unique stridency against the notion that America's present-day political and economic strength justifies an emulation of its social model. This role is not new to the French. Since the late eighteenth century the two nations have often looked critically at each other in search of insights into their own natures and for answers to their own problems.

Although this book lays no claim to be a work on comparative social reform, I believe there are several lessons for Americans in a study of French welfare. I would like to alert the reader to a few of the more poignant cases in advance, but I refrain from commenting on them further, preferring to let each reader draw his or her own conclusions from the French experience. The most obvious case in point is the role of employers in the provision of welfare. Protections and benefits that rely on one's employment (or unemployment) status are endemic in the United States. Employment-dependent programs made up the core of France's family welfare and social insurance programs from the late 1920s until the end of the Second World War. The propensities of this approach to social protection played themselves out in France in a way that I believe bears some relevance to the American case. Also of interest is the French experience with managed health care. Private mutual aid societies, which played a predominant role under France's first national medical insurance legislation during the 1930s, confronted similar criticisms as those faced by today's American health maintenance organizations. Mutual societies sought to contain the cost of diagnosis and treatment by purchasing clinics and hospitals and by instituting tight fee reimbursement schedules. In protest, doctors appealed to legislators and the public in an effort to promote medical practices that they deemed best for the patient. Of course, France's experience with employment-dependent social welfare and the battle between French doctors and medical insurers occurred under vastly differing circumstances than those present in the United States today. Histories cannot offer instant advice for their readers' problems; the temporal and cultural divides are much too great. Nonetheless, I hope readers who are familiar with the tremendous challenges that face American social welfare might gain at least a glimpse of new understanding in the pages that follow.

The book's organization follows the evolution of family welfare and social insurance after 1914. During the Great War, the industrialists who built the family allowance movement took little heed of mutual aid societies and how they might eventually influence social policy. Chapter one thus concentrates on employers' creation of family allowances during and immediately after the First World War. Industrialists worked closely with pronatalists in order to propagate family allowance *caisses* (funds) and together they guarded against state intervention throughout the 1920s. Chapter two takes up the mutual model, its strengths, and its drawbacks as a vehicle for universal social protection. We examine the long history of the mutual movement in the provision of illness and accident insurance to French workers and the mutual movement's relationship to organized labor. Only with this appreciation in place may we analyze the first postwar social insurance bills. Compulsory social insurance in France was motivated by the popularity of a German system, which France had annexed by default in 1918 along with the territories of Alsace-Lorraine. Legislators struggled for eight long years to find a compromise between German-style mandates and what they deemed a more French approach to social welfare that relied on individual initiative, particularly private mutual aid societies.

By the mid-1920s, the *grand patronat* had come to view its control of family welfare as an important asset in the battle against compulsory social insurance. Chapter three explores employers' attempts to use their family allowance *caisses* to derail parliamentary action on social insurance. A deep division between France's socialist and communist trade unions initially bolstered these efforts. Yet chapter four illustrates that the victory of "realists" within the mutual movement by 1926 led to a compromise between mutual leaders and legislators, permitting passage of France's first social insurance law in 1928. The troubled implementation of this legislation, however, especially the strife between mutual societies and doctors, initially offered opponents within the mutual movement a chance to gut the new law. But mutual leaders ultimately moderated their brinkmanship, preferring to maintain their monopoly over an unprecedented, if imperfect, regime of mandatory health insurance. Chapter five returns our attention to family welfare, its tribulations during the Popular Front, and the critical role of the peasantry in shaping France's fledgling welfare state. This theme is continued in chapter six, where we examine several important structural reforms to rural family welfare that were undertaken under Vichy. Also in this chapter we examine the important influence of Lord Beveridge's 1942 plan for social welfare in Britain. The presence of Gaullist planners in London when Beveridge unveiled his proposal sparked considerable controversy among the French and helped shape their postliberation proposals. The book concludes with an examination of the 1945 birth of *la sécurité sociale* in order to analyze the indelible marks that the industrial and mutual models of social welfare, as well as foreign influences, left on France's welfare state.

An industrial model of family welfare

Among the several factors that explain the development of family welfare in the 1920s, none is more important than the social and economic
transformation brought about by the Great War. The war precipitated an
unprecedented state intervention into industrial organization and labor
relations that touched virtually all areas of social policy. Perhaps the most
influential wartime innovation was the system of worker remuneration
known as the *salaire vital*, which explicitly divided the wage between two
basic categories: productive and social use. This chapter analyzes the
salaire vital and its influence on Paris metals employers' postwar adoption
of family allowances as a wage strategy. The growth in industrialists' payment of family allowances functioned in tandem with France's growing
pronatalist movement, which provided both rhetorical ammunition to
employers as well as a popular justification for their policies. The immediate postwar years also witnessed the diffusion of *caisses de compensation*
(equalization funds). These funds served as clearing houses for debts and
credits, and facilitated employers' collective implementation of their new
wage strategy. Once the national scope of the family allowance movement became evident, employers organized a lobby, the Comité Central
des Allocations Familiales (CCAF), whose association with the powerful
Comité des Forges lent it immediate weight in parliamentary circles. The
CCAF eventually played a critical role in guarding against state intervention as well as the geographic extension of employer family allowance
caisses. The post-1918 decade marked a golden age for employers' control
of family welfare. The number and influence of their *caisses* grew well
beyond expectations and operated in near total liberty, unencumbered
by either state regulation or by collective bargaining.[1] The 1930s would
prove much less favorable, but in the 1920s, employers' influence over
worker welfare appeared nearly limitless.

[1] Interview: Aymé Bernard, conducted by Danièle Hanet, Comité d'Histoire de la Sécurité
Sociale, 12 December 1975, Archives Nationales de France, hereafter AN, 37 AS 2.

INDUSTRIAL ORGANIZATION, METALS EMPLOYERS, AND THE *SALAIRE VITAL*

Wartime industrial mobilization played a critical role in the growth of employer-controlled family welfare. Even before the war, the steel industry possessed the most powerful trade associations in France: the Comité des Forges and the Union des Industries Métallurgiques et Minières (UIMM). Dating from the Second Empire (1852–1870) and representing three-quarters of French steel producers, the Comité des Forges maintained order among domestic rivals and defended its members against foreign competition.[2] When the government found itself dangerously unprepared for a long war and in desperate need of an organization that could quickly organize massive increases in industrial production, the Comité des Forges was well positioned to aid the war effort and to simultaneously consolidate its hold over metals production.[3] However, government-created consortia, which were the brainchild of socialist minister of armament Albert Thomas, eventually challenged the Comité des Forges to oversee war-related production. By 1916, consortia administered several sectors of the wartime economy and oversaw the purchase and distribution of raw materials as well as government procurement. In theory, each consortium was responsible to one of the government's executive committees, but in the case of the Consortium of Iron Merchants, substantial power continued to flow from the Comité des Forges, particularly its secretary-general, Robert Pinot.[4]

In addition to national, sector-specific consortia, the government sanctioned the creation of regional consortia in order to coordinate labor and wage policies.[5] In January 1917, UIMM official and industrialist Louis Renault successfully lobbied the government to support a consortium of Paris metals employers. Using his ties with the Comité des Forges and the UIMM as an inducement, Renault succeeded in bringing together hundreds of employers in the Paris region, ultimately forming one of the most important regional employer associations in France: the Groupe des Industries de la Région Parisienne (GIRP). Before the end of the war, the GIRP became the official intermediary for the minister

---

[2] John F. Godfrey, *Capitalism at War: Industrial Policy and Bureaucracy in France 1914–1918* (New York: St. Martin's Press, 1987), pp. 13–17, 221.

[3] Gerd Hardach, "Industrial Mobilization in 1914–1918: Production, Planning, and Ideology," in Patrick Fridenson (ed.), *The French Home Front, 1914–1918* (Providence RI: Berg, 1992), pp. 57–88.

[4] Godfrey, *Capitalism at War*, pp. 225–226.

[5] A shop steward system enabled workers to participate in factory-level discussions, but their influence on planning was nil. See Hardach, "Industrial Mobilization," p. 68.

of armament regarding labor policy. Its delegates were invited to sit with related government study groups and their views were deemed to represent the interests of member firms. Later, on May Day 1920, the GIRP changed its name to the Groupe des Industries Métallurgiques, Mécaniques, et Connexes de la Région Parisienne (GIMM).[6]

The GIRP worked closely with the government to pacify labor unrest during the final year of the war when strikes reached their wartime height. The decree of 17 January 1917 empowered the government to arbitrate wage disputes for all munitions workers. The decree, however, did not put an end to strikes. In fact, the number of strikes in France actually rose from 314 in 1916 to 696 in 1917, as did the number of strikers from 41,409 to 293,810.[7] Popular resentment over wages that failed to keep pace with rising prices, especially in foodstuffs, continued to spur labor unrest.[8] Heavy government borrowing to pay for the war and political leaders' unwillingness to raise taxes meant that tough wage restrictions were needed to attenuate inflationary pressures.[9]

In order to ease wage demands and to avoid a wage-driven inflationary spiral, Charles Picquenard, director at the ministry of labor, and William Oualid, deputy director at the ministry of armament promulgated the *salaire vital*. The *salaire vital* divided the wage into four constituent parts. The first two components, the base wage and merit pay, pertained to the worker's productive capacity. However, the third and fourth portions, a cost-of-living stipend and a family allowance, referred to social circumstances that were unrelated to output. The *salaire vital* thus redefined the wage, by adding to it the social needs of workers. Because different workers had different needs, their remuneration varied even when they furnished identical work. Picquenard and Oualid defined family allowances as "supplementary remuneration, attributed to the worker independently of the value of his work and calculated according to his family responsibilities."[10] Under the *salaire vital*, government arbitrators in wage disputes could target their decisions to achieve the highest overall satisfaction among workers at the least cost.[11]

---

[6] Further pressure from the UIMM increased GIMM membership from approximately 400 in 1920 to 1,009 by the end of 1922. GIMM Annuaires 1920–1922, AN 39 AS 873.

[7] Hardach, "Industrial Mobilization," p. 75.   [8] *L'Humanité*, 21 November 1917.

[9] Tom Kemp, *The French Economy, 1913–1939: The History of Decline* (London: Longman, 1972), pp. 61–62.

[10] William Oualid and Charles Picquenard, *Salaires et tarifs, conventions collectives et grèves: la politique du Ministère de l'Armement et du Ministère du Travail* (Paris: Presses Universitaires de France, 1928), p. 241.

[11] *Ibid.*, pp. 105–108.

Picquenard and Oualid, visionary civil servants that they were, did not create the concept of the *salaire vital* but rather improvised upon earlier efforts to maintain the standard of living of working-class families during wartime. At the time of the *levée en masse* in 1793, soldiers were provided with additional pay for wives, children under twelve, fathers over sixty, and widowed mothers of any age. War allowances (*allocations de guerre*) were abolished at the time of the Restoration, but reemerged in various military and pronatalist legislation under the Third Republic.[12] According to the law of 5 August 1914, pay for mobilized personnel from needy families was supplemented with family allowances paid by the state.[13] Thus, Picquenard and Oualid's innovation of the *salaire vital* pertained less to the nature than to the scope of wartime support for dependent families. They merely followed the logic of total war that had been created by the industrial age. Whereas only those serving under the colors (and a small number of civil servants) had previously been eligible for family allowances, now all munitions workers merited the same benefits as their brothers under arms.

The elaboration of the *salaire vital* struck a blow to those metal workers who advocated equal pay for equal work, a demand that was particularly important for women. Wartime family allowances in private industry were based on the employment of the *chef de famille*. Although a female munitions worker whose husband had been mobilized could continue to receive war allowances from the state (if she did not earn more than five francs per day) she could not attain the status of *chef de famille*.[14] Women whose spouses were not mobilized but employed in a profession where family allowances were not available also went empty-handed. Thus the wartime elaboration of the *salaire vital* complemented industrialists' ongoing reorganization of work and managerial practices to accommodate their new female workers in subordinate positions where wages were lower. This was especially true in metalworking, which was almost exclusively practiced by men before 1914.[15] Women workers constantly

---

[12] André Lebreton, *La Famille et les lois sur les allocations de guerre, les pensions militaires et le pécule* (Saint-Brieuc, 1921), pp. 11, 21–22, 29; André Fonvieille, *Etude critique du régime des allocations aux familles des militaires soutiens indispensables* (Montpellier: L'Abeille, 1919), p. 237.

[13] Ministère de l'Intérieur, Direction du Personnel, *Décrets, arrêtés et circulaires concernant l'application de la loi du 5 août 1914 sur les allocations aux familles des mobilisés* (Melun: Imprimerie Administrative, 1915).

[14] CGT leaders concurred in this policy. Congrès Confédéral de la CGT, *compte rendu*, "Commission supérieure des allocations militaires," July 1918, p. 11.

[15] Laura Lee Downs, *Manufacturing Inequality: Gender Division in the French and British Metalworking Industries, 1914–1939* (Ithaca, NY: Cornell University Press, 1995), chapter 3.

expressed their frustration at being unable to achieve equal pay for equal work due to the employer practice of making minor changes in tasks to create new job descriptions.[16] Equal pay for equal work would become a slogan used by the Confédération Générale du Travail (CGT) against family allowances after the war, but during the war Secretary-General Léon Jouhaux led the union on a path of collaboration that included acceptance of the *salaire vital*.

Family allowances comprised only one aspect of the wartime development of family welfare under employer control. The increased cost of living, especially in centers of war production such as Paris, led minister of armament Thomas to require employers to create housing, cafeterias, stores, and infant day-care centers for the use of their personnel. By October 1917, munitions employers had built 182 factory cafeterias (*restaurants d'usine*), capable of feeding 100,000 workers daily, and 81 stores where supplies could be purchased more conveniently than from other merchants. Shortly before Thomas' departure from his ministry in September 1917, he mandated nursing rooms (*chambres d'allaitement*) for munitions firms employing more than one hundred women between the ages of fifteen and thirty-six. Thomas could impose these requirements because the state was a monopoly customer in the munitions market and because it controlled a scarce supply of skilled workers due to universal conscription. Thomas allocated workers who were recalled from the front in such a way as to increase his leverage on working conditions. In some cases, employers were eager to provide low-cost concessions on working conditions in return for labor peace. Unfortunately, few of the physical modifications that Thomas imposed on employers' plants lasted more than a few months after the Armistice. Employers had always insisted on their provisional character, and once wartime regulation ended, many of these facilities were abandoned.[17]

Employers were adamant about their prerogative to set labor policies in the postwar years. A major strike in the Paris metals sector in May 1918, in which 100,000 workers stayed off the job, alerted employers that the postwar environment would be rife with labor-management conflict. In fact, Picquenard hosted a special conference at the Musée Social in Paris during the summer of 1917 entitled *La Guerre et la vie de demain*

---

[16] See Congrès Confédéral de la CGT, XXVIe Congrès National Corporatif, XXe de la CGT, "Les droits de la femme dans l'économie moderne," *compte rendu*, September 1929, pp. 89–90. Also see Oualid and Picquenard, *Salaires et tarifs*, pp. 108–112.

[17] Aimée Moutet, "Patrons de progrès ou patrons de combat? La politique de rationalisation de l'industrie française au lendemain de la première guerre mondiale," *Recherches*, 32–33 (September 1978), 449–489; Downs, *Manufacturing Inequality*, p. 259.

("The War and the Life of Tomorrow") at which he outlined the potential for heightened worker militancy. Picquenard's analysis paralleled a study conducted by the Syndicat des Mécaniciens, Chaudronniers et Fondeurs de France. Both noted that wages had risen unsustainably during the war due to overtime hours, the replacement of piecework by hourly wages, and state subsidies. Thus, after the war, wages would need to be tamed in order to prevent rampant inflation. The Syndicat offered some solace to its member firms by noting that the rationalization of work that had been achieved during the war would continue to hold down costs. But the Syndicat also counseled employers to maintain and expand their use of the *salaire vital*.[18]

POSTWAR CONDITIONS AND THE INSTITUTION OF FAMILY ALLOWANCES

The spring of 1919 witnessed the explosion of labor unrest that had been predicted by Picquenard and others. The struggle proved critical for the institution of family allowances in the Paris metals industry and prompted employers to strengthen the collusion that the state had instigated among them during wartime. It also decided the fate of wartime cost-of-living stipends and paved the way for employer control of family allowances.

In Paris, strikes began in May 1919 and continued into the summer, with the largest walkout occurring on 4 and 5 June when workers effectively shut down the entire metals industry. 165,000 of approximately 200,000 metal workers struck, blocking factory entrances or protesting in the streets.[19] Under the GIRP's leadership, employers succeeded at limiting the gains of labor, which elevated the status of the GIRP's president, Pierre Richemond, among Paris metals employers. As his status rose, so did his ambitions. Richemond insisted that the GIRP could expand employer collaboration beyond anti-strike management in order to create more efficient labor and wage policies.[20] Richemond's first opportunity to demonstrate the usefulness of expanded collaboration

---

[18] *Information Ouvrière et Sociale* 52 and 53 (1 and 5 September 1918). Also see *Bulletin des Usines de Guerre* 49 (2 April 1917) and George G. Humphreys, *Taylorism in France 1904–1920: The Impact of Scientific Management on Factory Relations and Society* (New York: Garland, 1986). Also see Oualid and Picquenard, *Salaires et tarifs*, pp. 509–519.

[19] Aimée Moutet, "La Rationalisation industrielle dans l'économie française au XXe siècle: étude sur les rapports entre changements d'organisation technique et problèmes sociaux, 1900–1939," thèse de doctorat d'état, Université de Paris I (1984), pp. 261–268.

[20] GIMM "Enquête sur les concessions possibles," May–June 1919, AN 39 AS 914; AN 39 AS 856.

came when workers demanded that the cost-of-living stipend that had been instituted during the war be subsumed into the base wage of the *salaire vital*. The stipend accounted for between 10 and 20 percent of take-home pay. Workers feared that employers might use the Armistice as a pretext to abolish the stipend, claiming its wartime *raison d'être* had expired. Earlier, in November 1917 workers had militated for a closer association between the cost-of-living stipend and the base wage. At that time, the GIRP successfully rebuffed the demand, pointing to the exceptional circumstances produced by the war. The state, they insisted, had created and thus controlled the disposition of the stipend.[21] While this approach prevailed during the war, it assured a subsequent dispute in which employers had little room for maneuver. Increased union militancy and a continued shortage of skilled metal workers appeared to block employers from abolishing the cost-of-living stipend. However, by continuing its distinctive existence within the remuneration system, employers were liable for automatic wage adjustments according to inflation. While this had been the case during the war, there had also been government arbitrators to enforce decisions and industrialists had been assured significant profits from weapons production. Postwar conditions did not offer similar guarantees. Under the inflationary conditions and unstable market that returned to France after the war, metals employers were loathe to accept automatic wage adjustments. Instead, under the leadership of Richemond, employers pursued a third strategy. They conceded the value of the existing cost-of-living stipend by folding it into the base wage, but they vowed to resist any further wage adjustments for inflation. In order to assuage a critical portion of workers, employers instituted generous family allowances.[22]

Paris metals employers' adoption of a wage strategy based on family allowances was also due to outside influences. To be sure, Richemond saw the potential of family allowances earlier than most of his colleagues but transforming the wage practices of hundreds of independent employers could not be accomplished by a single individual or even the weighty GIRP (or GIMM as it became known in May 1920). Richemond and his associates at GIRP, while instrumental in the creation of family allowances, were themselves guided by three developments outside the Paris metals industry. First, during the war, a social Catholic industrialist in Grenoble, Emile Romanet, had invented the *caisse de compensation*, a mechanism that spread the cost of family allowances among employers.

---

[21] *L'Humanité*, 21 November 1917.
[22] GIMM "Grèves et revendications," March–May, 1920, AN 39 AS 915.

Second, the resurgence of the French pronatalist movement provided a rhetoric that proved useful for the spread of allowances. Third, legislation that would have forced employers to pay family allowances acted as a catalyst to voluntary action. Let us consider each of these developments in turn.

In September 1916, Emile Romanet, a manager of the Regis-Joya metalworks in Grenoble, conducted a simple but groundbreaking experiment. He examined the living conditions of eight of his workers, all men, each with different family circumstances. Romanet was struck at the vast difference in quality of life enjoyed by the subjects of his study. Single and married workers without children, he observed, managed fairly well, whereas workers with dependent children under the age of thirteen were much less well off. And fathers of truly large families, containing eight to ten children, lived as if poverty-stricken despite their full-time employment. These findings led Romanet to calculate hypothetical pay bonuses according to family size; he then compared these costs to uniform increases for all workers. Supposing a rise in the cost of living index that would normally result in a 0.80 francs general hike in daily wages, Romanet instead reduced the increase to childless workers and women to 0.60 francs and increased the wage hike for fathers to 0.90 francs. The general wage increase of 0.80 francs resulted in a total daily cost for the company of 3,908.80 francs. The wage hike based on dependent children, however, resulted in a total daily cost to the company of 3,316.20 francs, or 592.60 francs less than the general increase. For Romanet the social Catholic, this simple experiment demonstrated the advantages of family allowances for both needy workers and employers.[23]

Yet for Romanet the industrial manager a vexing problem remained, which would effectively preclude the spread of family allowances. Employing men with children was simply more expensive. A firm that employed relatively more fathers than its competitors would suffer a competitive disadvantage due to higher labor costs. Employers' fear of such a disadvantage would forever contain the institution of family allowances to paternalistic social Catholic employers like Regis-Joya in Grenoble. Further, if the institution did spread, it would discourage the hiring of family men while encouraging the employment of more women, neither of which Romanet wanted to abet. In a breakthrough, the importance of which cannot be underemphasized, Romanet created a *caisse de compensation*.[24] This mechanism served as a clearinghouse through which

[23] Emile Romanet, *Les Allocations familiales* (Lyon: Chronique sociale de France, 1922), pp. 1–5.
[24] Paul Dreyfus, *Emile Romanet: père des allocations familiales* (Grenoble: Arthaud, 1964), p. 78.

employers of a particular region or industry could collectively equalize the costs of dependent children among their personnel. The simplicity of Romanet's innovation greatly contributed to its spread, especially among industrialists whose wages and employment ratios of eligible beneficiaries were not substantially different.[25] The *caisse de compensation* achieved widespread attention just as France entered a two-decade-long period when concerns over depopulation became a well-entrenched feature of public life.

The French public broadly accepted the ethic of pronatalism as a way of dealing with the upheaval and destruction of the Great War. The demographic disaster of the war was obvious. 1.5 million dead, 3 million wounded, and 1.1 million who had suffered a permanent disability. In addition to a widespread perception that France had lost almost an entire generation of potential fathers, a wartime upheaval in traditional gender roles also boosted the appeal of pronatalist organizations. These groups tied French population decline to the erosion of a "domestic ideal" whereby women's proper role lay in bearing and caring for children. France could only safeguard its victory and regain international preeminence through a restoration of the *mère au foyer*. Such views became ubiquitous in the popular press and on the lips of the country's foremost political leaders. From the floor of the Senate in 1919, Georges Clemenceau insisted that, "the Treaty of Versailles does not mention that France pledges to have more children, but it is the first thing that should have been written. For if France renounces large families, you can insert all the beautiful clauses you want in the Treaty . . . taking all artillery from Germany, and France will still be lost because there will not be enough French."[26] Clemenceau's entreaty was but one of many pronouncements by public officials that marked a firing of the pronatalist movement after the war.[27]

The Alliance Nationale pour l'accroissement de la population française constituted the most prominent pronatalist organization. Founded by government statistician Jacques Bertillon in 1896, the Alliance Nationale quickly gained the support of Deputy André Honnorat and physicians Charles Richet and Emile Javal.[28] The development of a

[25] Romanet, *Les Allocations familiales*, pp. 1–5; Georges Maignan, *Les Allocations familiales dans l'industrie et le commerce* (Paris: 1946), p. 32; Oualid and Picquenard, *Salaires et tarifs*, p. 480.

[26] *Journal Officiel*, hereafter *JO*, Débats parlementaires, Sénat, 11 October 1919, pp. 1625–1626.

[27] The premier source on these groups remains Talmy, *Histoire du mouvement familial*, vol. 1, chapters 5–7. Also see Tomlinson, "The Politics of 'Dénatalité'," chs. 5 and 6.

[28] The letter circulated by Bertillon to convoke the Alliance Nationale's first meeting referred to the organization as the "Alliance Nationale pour le relèvement de la population française pour l'egalité devant les impots," Alliance Nationale, Conseil d'Administration, *procès-verbaux*, 12 May 1896.

vibrant pronatalist movement was crucial to the expansion of family allowances in industrial circles *not* because it motivated employers to pay allowances in the first place, but because it supported allowances instead of workers' demands for a universal "family wage." The Alliance Nationale and its supporters in government, the press, and education succeeded in creating a popular perception that paying an individual a family wage was both immoral and dangerous to the economy. In a March 1920 study the Lyon metals group called employers' attention to the dangers of paying a childless worker too much. The report asserted that those without children were not fulfilling their social responsibilities and should not enjoy the same income as parents. Opposed to "equal pay for equal work" on the grounds that it would spur inflation, the authors advocated the continuation and development of the *salaire vital*, which they claimed was "more rational, more human, and more social."[29] Social Catholic industrialists, such as Romanet, made the same argument which in essence declared family allowances to be the solution to inflation: "It is a universally recognized fact that uniform wage increases beget a vicious cycle, aggravating the economic situation. For with each increase in wages, corresponds a parallel and often bigger increase in prices. To the contrary, unequal increases in wages, as in the application of family allowances, is doubly beneficial in reestablishing economic stability: they are less costly for employers and consequently they can lessen the increase in prices that must legitimately be charged on manufactured products."[30] Thus industrial employers benefited from the moralism of the pronatalist movement, melding it with their self-interested economic calculations in order to create a perception that granted credence, even altruism, to a new wage strategy based on family allowances.

By 1920, leaders of the Paris metals group were prepared for action. GIMM President Richemond had been tracking cost-of-living stipends since the end of the war. He had also established contact with industrialists in Isère where Romanet's brainchild *caisse de compensation* was yielding practical results. Moreover, GIMM employers had conducted surveys to ascertain the birthrate of metal workers and their existing family circumstances.[31] Meanwhile the Comité des Forges and the UIMM were mobilizing in favor of voluntary family allowances to

[29] *La Journée Industrielle*, 6 March 1920.
[30] "Exemples d'institutions ou d'organisations sociales existant chez quelques-uns des membres de l'union," *Union Fraternelle du Commerce et de l'Industrie*, Grenoble, no. 1, June 1920, in AN 39 AS 387.
[31] Letter, Keller, Syndicat des Constructeurs Mécaniciens Isère, to Richemond, 21 May 1918; Memo, Villey to Poughon, 4 September 1920, AN 39 AS 837.

head off the possibility of state intervention that would mandate their payment. In March 1919 the secretary-general of the UIMM, Alfred Lambert-Ribot, sent a memo to member associations, including the GIMM, advocating that they create *caisses de compensation* such as that recently founded by Romanet in Grenoble.[32]

Leadership of the metals industry feared passage of a bill sponsored by Radical Maurice Bokanowski, a deputy from the Seine, which would require commercial, industrial, and agricultural employers to join *caisses de compensation*. Bokanowski's bill spelled out specific minimum allowances, instituted mandatory maternity and nursing stipends, and required the payment of bonuses for the birth of each child. The cash value of each of these allowances and the birth bonus would be calculated as a percentage of a worker's wages: the standard family allowance could not fall below 5 percent for the first child and 7.5 percent for each additional child until the age of fourteen. The nursing stipend would be worth 10 percent and a birth bonus fully 66 percent of a worker's monthly wage.[33] The Bokanowski bill presented a major threat to industrialists like Richemond who envisioned family allowances as a flexible instrument that could be used to hold down real wages and divide unions.

To employers' dismay the Bokanowski bill quickly gained broad support in the legislature. This, no doubt, was due to industrialists own pronatalist propaganda in praise of family allowances. Moreover, Bokanowski's proposal appeared to tread as lightly as possible by using employers' existing *caisses de compensation*, and leaving the administration of allowances in employers' hands. Deliberations of the Chamber's Commission d'Assurance et de Prévoyance Sociales (CAPS) on the Bokanowski bill foreshadowed many of the crucial issues that would face the family allowance movement during the next two decades. These included the question of obligation itself, the role of the state, and how to include France's large agricultural sector. In the end, the CAPS charged Victor Jean, a Radical from Bouches-du-Rhône, to draft a favorable report to the Chamber.[34]

After failing to stop the Bokanowski bill in the CAPS, opponents focused their efforts on the Conseil Supérieur du Travail, a consultative body attached to the ministry of labor. Dominated by industrial and

---

[32] Louis Audouin, *Les Caisses de compensation et les allocations familiales dans l'industrie française* (Poitiers: H. Mansuy, 1928), p. 15; Jean Duporcq, *Les Œuvres sociales dans la métallurgie française* (Paris: Université de Paris, 1936), p. 36; Pedersen, *Family, Dependence, and the Origins*, pp. 264–265.

[33] *JO*, Documents parlementaires, Chambre, 24 February 1920, 1920, annexe no. 386, pp. 561–564.

[34] Commission d'Assurance et de Prévoyance Sociales, Chambre, *procès-verbaux*, 12th Legislature, 1919–1924, A13, Dossier 1105, vol. 2, 4 March and 29 April 1921, Archives de l'Assemblée Nationale.

commercial leaders, the Conseil declared that family allowances might be beneficial to working families and increase the birthrate, but the situation did not warrant state action. Further, the Conseil found Bokanowski's requirements far too burdensome for the precarious state of French industry.[35] Although the Conseil Supérieur du Travail played no formal legislative role, its strident opposition to the Bokanowski bill displayed such powerful industrial and commercial opposition to parliamentary action that Victor Jean's report from the CAPS never made it to the Chamber floor for a vote.[36]

Bokanowski had provoked the first interwar legislative battle over the question of state intervention into family welfare. Although his bill would have left administration of allowances in employers' hands, they rejected his attempt to compel allowance payments, especially through a percentage-of-wage method.[37] Once the full force of employer opposition to the legislation became evident, many legislators whose pronatalist pledges had led them to support the legislation, withdrew their support.[38] In return, employers promised a massive but voluntary expansion of family allowances.

FOUNDATION OF THE *CAISSE DE COMPENSATION* DE LA RÉGION PARISIENNE

On 1 March 1920, less than a week after the introduction of the Bokanowski bill, Richemond presided over the constituent assembly of GIMM's *caisse de compensation* in Paris, the Caisse de Compensation de la Région Parisienne (CCRP). Only 87 GIMM members initially enrolled in the CCRP, but enrollment rose as word of the threat of state intervention spread and Richemond invested his own prestige in the project by assuming the CCRP presidency. In order to entice members the CCRP initially set allowances so as not to exceed a quarterly cost of

---

[35] Conseil Supérieur du Travail, 25th session, *compte rendu et annexes*, 16 November 1921, pp. 20–29.

[36] *Tables analytiques des annales de la Chambre des Députés*, 12th Legislature, 1919–1924, Tables de matières (Paris: Imprimerie de la Chambre des Députés), no. 3, p. 570.

[37] Conseil Supérieur du Travail, 25th session, "Rapports sur les allocations familiales, présenté au nom de la Commission permanente," *compte rendu et annexes*, 17 November 1921, pp. 63–71. The author of the Conseil's final report was Léopold Pralon, vice president of the Comité des Forges.

[38] In the elections of 1919, 43 percent of all elected deputies included pronatalist pledges in their *professions de foi* up from 8 percent in 1910. By 1920, 47 percent of all deputies belonged to the Chamber's Groupe pour la protection de la natalité et des familles nombreuses, up from 18 percent in 1911. See Tomlinson, "The Politics of 'Dénatalité'," pp. 330, 338, 340. Also see Commission d'Assurance et de Prévoyance Sociales, Chambre, *procès-verbaux*, 12th Legislature, 1919–1924, A13, Dossier 1105, vol. II, 11 March 1921; Commission du Travail, Chambre, *procès-verbaux*, 12th Legislature, 1919–1924, A73, Dossier 5310, no. 1, 2 January 1922, Archives de l'Assemblée Nationale.

1.2 percent of wages. The CCRP further promised that administration of the *caisse* would cost only one-hundredth of 1 percent of wages.[39] The first allowance schedule paid a flat ten francs for each eligible child. Richemond's gamble that the CCRP would attract sufficient participation among GIMM members proved well placed when heavyweight metals employers André Citroën, Ernest Dalbouze, René Duchemin, Etienne Partiot, and Louis Renault lined up in support. With enrollment climbing past 400 by the fall of 1920, Richemond commented to his colleagues on the CCRP governing board that "introduction of the legislation by Deputy Bokanowski amply justifies the energy we have expended in organizing the *caisse de compensation* and assuring its function before state intervention."[40]

Yet a simple threat of state intervention, as real as it was, could not transform all 1,003 GIMM members into allowance-paying employers. To achieve this, Richemond needed to take his case for a family allowance wage strategy directly to the GIMM membership, which he did at the annual meeting in March 1923. His speech there, delivered during widespread strikes at GIMM plants, provided an unprecedented avowal by an important industrial leader concerning the role of family welfare in industrial wage strategy. Richemond observed that although the cost-of-living index actually fell during the first half of 1921, the corresponding drop in wages was not as great. Therefore, Richemond noted, inflation-adjusted wages were a one-way street where only workers could move forward. He then delivered his main point: "Family allowances permit us to place our comparisons of prewar and postwar wages on a more just and better defined foundation ... You understand then, gentlemen, the precise solution that your governing board proposes. On wages, no uniform changes: if certain individual cases are below average ... then some adjustment can be made on an individual basis, *but there can be no general increases.*"[41] The membership embraced Richemond's appeal. In the spring of 1923 several member firms faced strikes by the Confédération Générale du Travail Unitaire (CGTU) over their refusal to increase wages to keep pace with the rising cost of living. In response, Richemond replaced the original allowance schedule with a progressive scale, raising second- and third-child allowances to 30 and 50 francs respectively, with 80 francs for every fourth and additional child.[42]

[39] CCRP Commission de gestion, *procès-verbaux*, 28 July 1920.
[40] *Ibid., procès-verbaux*, 22 October 1920.
[41] GIMM Assemblée générale ordinaire, *ordre du jour*, 22 March 1923, AN 39 AS 856.
[42] GIMM Assemblée générale extraordinaire, *ordre du jour*, 7 May 1923, AN 39 AS 856.

Percentage of workforce

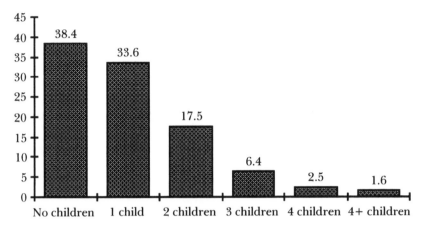

Figure 1   Family circumstance of GIMM personnel. Data derived from Gustave Bonvoisin and Georges Maignan, *Allocations familiales et caisses de compensation* (Paris: Recueil Sirey, 1930), note, p. 192.

Thus, an average male worker with four children whose base and merit wages totaled 400 francs per month, and who had been bringing home an additional 40 francs in family allowances for a total monthly pay of 440 francs, saw his monthly take-home pay rise to 570 francs or about 30 percent. A similar father of nine children enjoyed a raise from 490 francs to 970 francs or about 98 percent. These examples made stupendous propaganda for employers while actually costing them very little. In 1919 the GIMM had conducted a survey of the family circumstances of nearly 100,000 randomly selected workers in order to ascertain the number of children under the age of sixteen present in worker households. The results had revealed that GIMM employers could maintain a highly progressive allowance schedule at relatively little cost in comparison to general wage increases.[43] Figure 1 illustrates the family circumstances of GIMM personnel.

Because most households had no children or only one child, many workers received no raise at all and the total cost to GIMM employers of such a big hike in family allowances totaled only 0.5 percent of wages. While this rise represented more than a 40 percent increase in the CCRP compensation rate (from 1.2 to 1.7 percent of wages), Richemond

[43] Pierre Richemond, "Allocations pour charges de famille et caisses de compensation," *Revue d'Economie Politique*, September–October 1920, 590–606. See especially p. 594.

promised GIMM members that in return their labor relations would be pacified: "This is real help from your personnel's point of view and from the point of view of public opinion and public authorities. It vigorously establishes your generosity as well as the health-promoting and social value of your work and will permit you to successfully resist unjustified demands for general wage increases."[44] By February 1924 virtually all GIMM members were enrolled in the CCRP, presaging Richemond's unanimous reelection as GIMM president.[45] The CCRP armed Paris metals employers with a powerful weapon against worker demands that wages be pegged to rises in the cost of living. If inflation rose, the *caisse* hiked family allowances in order to placate workers with dependent children. Of course, employers paid for these increases, but they did so at less expense than general wage hikes and with the certainty that the load was being equally shared among all producers.

The role accorded to family allowances in the wage strategy of Paris metals employers led to an increased complexity and size of the CCRP. By March 1925 the *caisse* had 1,440 members who employed more than 260,000 workers.[46] In order to administer an organization of this size, the CCRP relied on a body of detailed regulations that categorized the diverse circumstances of employers, workers, and children. The governing board of the CCRP (*commission de gestion*), which was elected each year by the general assembly, served as the ultimate arbiter of conflicts between employers, workers, and the *caisse*. Not surprisingly, CCRP regulations devoted considerable attention to the question of exactly who was eligible to receive family allowances. Employers themselves and their managers were automatically excluded, but "all remaining personnel" were evaluated to ascertain whether they were "the legal representatives of children from whom the right to allowances is born."[47] This phrase permitted employers to insist that the legal beneficiary (*bénéficiare*) of family allowances was not the worker, but his or her child. The worker, in contrast, was designated as the recipient (*attributaire*) of the allowance. In order to qualify as a recipient, a worker had to be a head of household (*chef de famille*) with one or more children. The regulations recognized twelve different types of heads of household.[48]

---

44 CCRP Assemblée générale, *procès-verbaux*, 26 March 1923.
45 GIMM Assemblée générale extraordinaire, *ordre du jour*, 25 February 1924; GIMM Assemblée générale extraordinaire, *ordre du jour*, 28 March 1924, AN 39 AS 856.
46 CCRP Commission de gestion, *procès-verbaux*, 12 March 1925.
47 CCRP *Statuts et Règlement*, Articles 3 and 7 of *Règlement*, AN F22 1536. "All remaining personnel" here includes the categories usually treated distinctively in French: *Ouvriers* and *ouvrières* (generally blue collar), and *employés* and *employées* (generally white collar).
48 *Ibid.*, Article 3.

1. Father
2. Widow
3. Divorced father with custodianship of children
4. Divorced mother with custodianship of children
5. Unmarried father with custodianship of a natural child
6. Unmarried mother of a child not recognized by the father
7. Worker of either sex who has accepted responsibility for orphans from an organization officially registered with the CCRP
8. Mother who provides written proof from her husband's employer that he is not entitled to family allowances
9. Mother who provides written proof that her husband is permanently incapable of work and is not receiving family allowances
10. Mother who has been abandoned by her husband, leaving children
11. Unmarried mother who has been abandoned by the father of her children
12. Ascendants or legal custodians

This list and accompanying regulations demonstrate a traditionally gendered construction of the family and head of household. In contrast to married fathers, married mothers were simply assumed ineligible for allowances unless they could prove otherwise under titles eight through eleven. Further, the *caisse* demanded that married women eligible under title eight resubmit written proof of their continued eligibility every six months. As for abandoned and unmarried mothers, their circumstances had to be certified at their local police station. This requirement meant considerable humiliation and probably discouraged numerous eligible women from gaining access to allowances. Meanwhile, men were simply required to provide a registered birth certificate to their employer for each eligible child.[49]

Additional CCRP policies took aim at the pacification of the labor force. Only particular kinds of absences could occur if workers wanted to collect their full allowance at the end of the month. Tolerated were absences due to sickness, an injury sustained on or off the job, and a serious illness or death in a worker's family. Absence for any other reason meant an automatic reduction in the worker's allowance proportional to missed days.[50] Union activities, work stoppages, and strikes were cause for allowance reductions. Since allowances were calculated on a daily basis once an unexcused absence was recorded, a work stoppage of two hours, which was commonly used by unions to demonstrate their ability to strike without actually having to do so, became a much more costly endeavor

[49] *Ibid.*, Article 22.   [50] *Ibid.*, Articles 6 and 12.

for family allowance recipients. One communist deputy noted that "family allowances are the source of multiple abuses. Some bosses deny them when their workers decide to demonstrate. In effect, within the family itself, it is occasionally the wife who becomes the boss's assistant. She says to her husband 'Don't strike. Don't demonstrate – we'll lose next month's family allowance without which we can't make ends meet. Think of your children!' And the worker goes along and turns yellow, betraying his comrades who are committed to the struggle."[51] The CCRP also delivered allowance checks to the worker's home and made them payable to the person most responsible for childcare, often the mother. Richemond justified this practice by arguing that mothers were more likely than fathers to use the allowance for its intended purpose.[52] On this point he was probably right, but the practice also worked to divide the family in the same way that it divided fathers from their single comrades in the factory. Critics called this practice "an indignity that workers cannot accept. What they want is social solidarity laws, not charity!"[53] Protests from workers' representatives became increasingly common in the postwar years as family allowances grew in proportion to workers' overall take-home pay. Indeed, these protests indicate that within only a few years of its founding, the CCRP achieved considerable success in holding down wages and pacifying the metals workforce. Not surprisingly, family allowances spread quickly beyond the metals sector in the 1920s, encompassing virtually all kinds of industry and large commerce.

EMPLOYERS CREATE A NATIONAL FAMILY ALLOWANCE LOBBY

During the 1920s family allowance *caisses de compensation* proliferated in France's industrial and commercial sectors. Provincial employers were motivated by the same set of social, economic, and cultural factors as the founders of the CCRP. As in Paris, industrialists were usually the founders of provincial *caisses* and their goals were substantially the same: wage restraint, rationalization, labor pacification, and pronatalism. In addition, provincial industrialists benefited from the creation of a national lobby, the Comité Central des Allocations Familiales (CCAF), which aided employers in setting up *caisses* and coordinated national propaganda on their behalf. Table 1.1 lists the 51 *caisses de compensation*

[51] *JO*, Débats parlementaires, Chambre, 22 January 1929, p. 189.
[52] Richemond, "Allocations pour charges de famille et caisses de compensation," p. 598.
[53] *JO*, Débats parlementaires, Chambre, 22 January 1929, p. 189.

Table 1.1. *Caisses de compensation* 1920

Caisse	Firms	Workers employed	Heads of household	Children total benefiting	Paid
Amiens	31	5,820	330	950	51,147
Anger	43	2,000	460	927	30,592
Angoulême	22	1,850	497	854	43,401
Annecy	16	1,386	328	602	56,465
Armentières	19	n/a	314	536	64,411
Beauvais	25	3,690	1,000	1,806	109,213
Blois	23	2,100	545	879	554,512
Bordeaux	31	n/a	599	945	116,066
Caen	31	988	296	541	27,000
Charleville	n/a	n/a	n/a	n/a	n/a
Cholet	16	n/a	740	1,157	125,930
Dieppe	9	2,058	588	1,432	66,494
Dijon	18	3,056	789	1,299	281,983
Elbeuf (t)	47	9,870	2,047	3,409	761,414
Epernay	42	3,516	n/a	1,337	418,000
Epernay (m)	n/a	n/a	n/a	n/a	n/a
La Ferté	10	1,234	223	353	12,200
Grasse	n/a	n/a	n/a	n/a	n/a
Grenoble	n/a	4,888	1,282	2,156	479,417
Le Havre (m)	30	n/a	n/a	n/a	1,200,000
Le Havrie	50	746	210	372	48,000
Lille (t)	71	n/a	910	2,261	165,670
Lille (m)	n/a	n/a	n/a	n/a	612,030
Limoges (m)	14	1,368	308	423	n/a
Limoges (p)	23	4,245	701	1,171	n/a
Lorient	11	500	443	918	3,318
Louvière	50	n/a	400	1,100	n/a
Lyon	217	29,044	7,055	11,742	1,843,002
Lyon (t)	71	9,144	1,247	1,940	324,279
Monluçon	14	7,200	2,020	3,200	347,709
Mulhouse	138	55,400	13,200	23,200	1,698,000
Nancy (m)	23	3,062	n/a	n/a	338,000
Nantes	52	20,395	7,194	12,642	1,275,121
Nevers	21	5,477	1,199	2,032	n/a
Orléans	20	2,708	214	526	52,758
Paris (CCRP)	514	197,179	62,549	68,096	11,444,031
Paris (b)	1,250	n/a	8,135	15,800	1,702,890
Rennes	66	1,752	280	726	56,214
Rodez	n/a	n/a	n/a	n/a	n/a
Roubaix (t)	512	68,000	12,792	20,675	6,800,310
Rouen (t)	112	20,000	5,822	9,635	1,700,968
Saint-Brieuc	n/a	n/a	n/a	n/a	n/a
Saint-Diz (m)	49	11,754	3,550	7,100	1,305,000
Saint-Nic (m)	6	1,063	150	380	117,839
Strasbourg	48	18,000	7,200	20,000	n/a

Table 1.1. (*cont.*)

Caisse	Firms	Workers employed	Heads of household	Children total benefiting	Paid
Thizy (t)	47	7,050	543	1,060	141,700
Toulouse	n/a	n/a	n/a	n/a	n/a
Tours	14	800	187	289	19,100
Troyes	70	15,000	13,553	20,879	832,555
Vienne	69	5,410	1,411	1,879	247,525
Vierzon	n/a	n/a	n/a	n/a	n/a

Notes: t = professional textile *caisse*; m = professional metals *caisse*; p = professional porcelain *caisse*; b = professional building trades *caisse*.
Source: Bureau International du Travail, *Etudes et documents*, Série D, "Salaires et dureé du travail." no. 13, "Les allocations familiales" (Geneva: A. Kundig, 1924), pp. 70–71.

that had been established by the end of 1920 and figure 2 portrays the geographic distribution of *caisses* in 1923.

Also as in Paris, metals employers in the provinces led the founding of *caisses de compensation*. The dynamism of metals industrialists in this regard reflects several compelling factors: their close association with the *salaire vital* under the guidance of the ministries of armament and labor during the war; their exposure to labor militancy and shortages after the Armistice; the superiority of their organizations, especially the Comité des Forges and regional associations such as the GIMM; and their ability to raise revenue to pay the start-up costs that were necessary for *caisses de compensation*.[54] Analogous to GIMM's predominant weight among the membership of the CCRP, the metals industry was the largest sector in the national family allowance movement. By 1928, over half of all industrial and more than one quarter of all commercial wage earners worked for firms affiliated with a *caisse de compensation*.[55] Family allowances were adopted in virtually every region of the Hexagon, especially in traditional metals and mining areas. The lobbying group of the family allowance movement, the CCAF, played an important role in shaping this growth.

In 1936 legal scholar Pierre Mazas explained the motivation behind family allowances as "above all of a moral order, partaking of Christian principles of the essential family wage as described in pontifical encyclicals."[56] This characterization cannot be reconciled with reality.

[54] Interview: Aymé Bernard, Third phase, 19 February 1976, AN 37 AS 2.
[55] VIIIe Congrès National des Allocations Familiales, *compte rendu*, 1928, p. 166.
[56] Pierre Mazas, *Le Fondement de l'obligation aux allocations familiales* (Paris: Recueil Sirey, 1936), p. 29. Mazas was referring primarily to Leo XIII's *Rerum Novarum* of 1891.

Figure 2   Distribution of family allowance *caisses* in June 1923. IIIe Congrès National des Allocations Familiales, *compte rendu*, 1923, preface.

Moral inspiration was a secondary motivation in the creation of the CCRP and the CCAF. No doubt, social Catholicism remained a vibrant tendency in the family allowance movement, yet CCAF meetings revealed pragmatists' dominant role. The nineteenth-century social Catholic origins of family allowances were quickly buried under layers of secular labor-cost calculations and maneuverings to evade state intervention. The circumstances and personalities of the CCAF's founding are particularly helpful in understanding the organization's outlook and the eventual evolution of employers' family welfare programs.

In 1919 two meetings occurred coincidentally in Mulhouse: the annual Congrès National de la Natalité (CNN) and an irregular meeting of industrialists invited by the Société Industrielle de Mulhouse. Among the industrialists were fourteen allowance-paying employers who, upon the suggestion of one of their number, decided to attend portions of the simultaneous meeting of pronatalists. This experience galvanized a desire for further collaboration. The director of the Lyon family allowance *caisse*, Aymé Bernard, volunteered to investigate the possibility of a national organization of *caisses de compensation*. Not surprisingly, Bernard's research led him to contact the Comité des Forges, where the idea received an enthusiastic reception. The secretary-general of the Comité des Forges, Robert Pinot, promised not only to provide office space for the newly created organization in the Comité's own building on Rue Madrid in Paris, he also seconded the services of his bright young assistant, Gustave Bonvoisin. Founding members of the CCAF appointed Bonvoisin director of the new lobby, a post he would hold for over twenty years.

Founders of the CCAF went outside the ranks of the metals industry for the organization's first president. They chose Eugène Mathon, president of the Consortium Textile de Roubaix-Tourcoing and premier advocate of family allowances in the textile industry.[57] This selection immediately lent the CCAF an interindustry character, widening its appeal to other employers. The strategy proved successful. The size and diversity of membership in the CCAF paralleled the growth in number of *caisses* throughout the 1920s. 90 percent of *caisses* became members and more than half of these regularly sent delegations to the CCAF's annual conference, the Congrès National des Allocations Familiales.[58] The choice of Mathon as president, however, proved controversial and ultimately untenable. While Mathon was widely respected among textile manufacturers, many employers took exception to his extreme paternalism. Mathon's Consortium was known for a domineering policy that pressured all of a household's adult members to work for a Consortium firm. If a spouse or child worked elsewhere, for example, the *caisse* reduced the father's family allowances.[59] This policy led to a growing rift between Mathon's Consortium and state officials. In 1923, the dispute spilled onto the floor at the annual CCAF conference when Mathon

---

[57] Interview: Aymé Bernard, Second phase, 17 December 1975, AN 37 AS 2.
[58] CCAF Assemblée générale, *compte rendu*, "Rapport de M. Bonvoisin," 29 May 1933, p. 8.
[59] Pedersen describes the Consortium's conflict with the Ministry of Labor and Church officials. See *Family, Dependence, and the Origins*, pp. 255–261.

exchanged barbed attacks with minister of public health and social insurance, Paul Strauss.[60] Aymé Bernard, who witnessed the confrontation, later expressed ambivalence about Mathon's approach to family welfare and the decision to make him the CCAF's first president: "He was a great Christian, but of an intransigent Christianity . . . You could say his character was a mix of pushiness and progressivism, what one could call paternalism."[61]

Metals industrialist and CCRP Vice President Jacques Lebel replaced Mathon in 1926. The appointment of Lebel to succeed Mathon attests that metals industrialists no longer thought it necessary to fill the CCAF presidency with someone from outside the Comité des Forges clique, and it is unlikely that Mathon, representing textiles, would have agreed on his successor. More importantly, as the decade wore on, CCAF members sought a closer relationship with state officials in order to influence social insurance legislation as well as government plans to require the payment of family allowances. Ministers and their staff, deputies, and senators were always invited to CCAF conferences where they were toasted and pleasantly cajoled on the qualities of appropriate and inappropriate social legislation. Thus Mathon's enmity with state officials, especially the highly regarded Paul Strauss, over the eligibility policies of his Roubaix *caisse* proved too great a liability for the employers' family allowance movement to endure.

In contrast to Mathon's tenure as president, the CCAF's first director, Gustave Bonvoisin, demonstrated an impressive staying power. Criss-crossing the national territory countless times between the wars, Bonvoisin developed an amazing repertoire of arguments for family allowances, distinguishing himself as the mouthpiece *par excellence* of the CCAF.[62] Like Richemond, Bonvoisin appealed to employers' desire to hold down wages, yet he also attracted support for family allowances from a wide swath of the public, including pronatalists, social Catholics, and centrist workers. Bonvoisin effectively targeted his rhetoric according to the audience. When he deemed it appropriate, he raised the specter of Mussolini and then played on public concerns over French depopulation and military impotence. In other circumstances, he recalled Romanet and the social Catholic origins of family allowances, painting them as a noble act in the interest of large families. Elsewhere, his theme was decidedly domestic and secular, tending toward solidarism and the need for

---

[60] IIIe Congrès National des Caisses de Compensation, *compte rendu*, 1923, pp. 63–76.
[61] Interview: Aymé Bernard, Second phase, 17 December 1975, AN 37 AS 2.
[62] Author's interview with Pierre Laroque, 2 December 1995.

Caisses created   Existing *caisses*

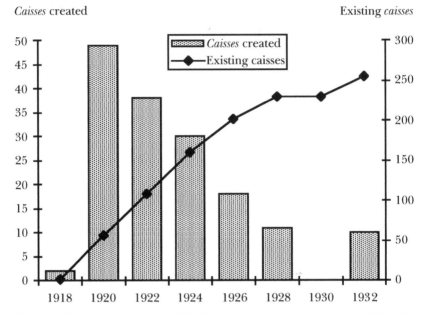

Figure 3   Growth in the number of family allowance *caisses* 1918–1932. Jean Pinte, *Les Allocations familiales* (Paris: Recueil Sirey, 1935), p. 88; Ceccaldi, *Histoire des prestations familiales*, p. 21; Congrès National des Allocations Familiales, *comptes rendus*, 1919–1932.

French of all classes, employers, workers, rich, and poor, to collaborate for a greater France.[63] Figure 3 illustrates the growth in *caisses* over which Bonvoisin presided between 1918 and 1932.

CONCLUSION

The 1920s marked a golden age for employer-controlled family welfare. At decade's end, there were 258 *caisses de compensation*, encompassing over 25,000 employers and 4.17 million wage earners. In addition, many large employers were paying family allowances through their own payrolls, forgoing the advantages of a *caisse* in order to enjoy complete freedom of action.[64] The success of the CCAF proved a turning point

---

[63] For a sampling of Bonvoisin's diverse appeals see the "Conférence faite à la Chambre de Commerce de Paris" (Paris: Arrault, March 1928), pp. 4–9; "*Extrait du Bulletin de la Chambre de Négociants Commissionaires et du Commerce Extérieur*," 1927; IVe Congrès National de la Natalité, *compte rendu*, 1922, pp. 87–88.

[64] Xe Congrès National des Allocations Familiales, "Rapport moral," *compte rendu*, 1930, p. 125. Michelin was perhaps the most notable of these solo allowance-paying employers.

in the development of employer-controlled family welfare. Large-scale collusion, made possible by the *caisse de compensation*, distinguished the development of family allowances from earlier employer paternalism, which generally occurred at the firm level. In effect, industrial and commercial employers had created a national family welfare system that lay completely outside the state's purview. During the immediate postwar years employer-controlled family welfare confined itself to cash benefits for families. But events in parliament soon changed this orientation.

In 1921 the parliament began consideration of legislation to create the country's first compulsory medical, retirement, and disability insurance. Employers opposed social insurance on the grounds that it would drive up labor costs, spur inflation, and render French producers uncompetitive in world markets. State mandated social insurance also appeared to threaten the liberty that employers enjoyed in the administration and payment of family allowances. For some deputies proposed that family allowances be included as one of the benefits under the new social insurance law. In an attempt to thwart such legislation, many employers advocated an expansion of *caisses de compensation* into full-service social welfare institutions. In addition to family allowances, these super *caisses* were to provide medical and disability protections as well as retirement pensions to workers of affiliated employers. Yet while employers waged an increasingly fierce battle against social insurance, which we will examine in chapters three and four, they were not its only opponents. National social insurance also threatened France's mutual aid societies (*sociétés de secours mutuels*). Indeed, the principal dilemma that legislators faced was how to capitalize on the popularity of the voluntary social protections offered by mutual societies while creating a compulsory system that would serve the country's growing industrial centers.

2

A mutual model for social insurance

Creation of compulsory social insurance presented both a danger and an opportunity to France's mutual movement. Danger arose from the possibility that legislators would prefer a centralized and state-administered regime. This scenario would promptly marginalize most mutual societies. For if participation in a state-run system became compulsory and the coverage therefrom sufficient, the appeal of private mutual aid would surely diminish. On the other hand, if the new law placed mutual societies at its center by simply mandating mutual membership, social insurance could present a boon to the mutual movement. Yet this latter possibility, which would appear to be windfall gain, confronted mutual leaders with a doctrinal dilemma. The movement had long embraced voluntarism and rejected state intervention that sought to require individual social protection. Many mutual leaders viewed state-coercion, even if it would increase mutual membership, as an unacceptable adulteration of their principles. They resisted all social insurance legislation and opposed their fellows who cooperated with parliamentary leaders. Indeed, the 1920s debate over national social insurance instigated a fight for control of the mutual movement's leading national association, the Fédération Nationale de la Mutualité Française (FNMF). In opposition to traditionalists, who resisted any form of state mandates, stood a group of what may be termed realists. Realists argued that state-mandated social insurance, if correctly crafted, could save the mutual movement from a peril that loomed just as ominously as a total state takeover of social welfare. They realized that the nation's workforce had entered a transition in which workers without traditional or professional ties to mutualism were gaining the upper hand.

By the early 1920s the mutual movement suffered from inertia. Its origins lay in the broad middle of French society, especially self-employed artisans, their journeymen, shopkeepers, middle-class clerks and other petty bourgeois workers. An increasingly militant and swelling industrial working class, while not wholly outside mutual societies, constituted an aspiring constituency without traditional ties to the movement. Industrial workers' loyalties ran to their unions and allied political parties, whose political clout in parliament rivaled that of the FNMF after the Great War. Not surprisingly then, in the first showdown over social insurance, mutual leaders extolled the movement's great experience and illustrious history in the provision of medical and retirement insurance. These arguments found substantial popular and parliamentary support. However, in order to fully understand the plight of the mutual movement during the battle over social insurance in the 1920s, we must first take a longer look at the institution, its origins, traditions, and wartime experience. This in place, we can turn to the immediate postwar circumstances that brought social insurance to the fore of the legislative agenda and the mutual movement to a crossroads.

MUTUAL AID: A FRENCH TRADITION

In simple terms, mutual societies were voluntarist associations of primarily male breadwinners who sought to protect themselves against the risks of illness and minor accidents. Each member paid an induction and monthly dues, which granted the worker a medical diagnosis and a monetary indemnity in case of incapacitation. A relatively small number of mutual societies also offered retirement pensions. Virtually all guaranteed help with the costs of funeral services and the attendance of fellow members should a malady or accident result in death. These early cooperative associations for social protection boasted a long and sometimes difficult history under several French regimes.

Although mutualists occasionally welcomed state sanction and financial support, they maintained a fundamental belief in individual initiative and prudence (*prévoyance*). One notable mutual leader at the turn of the century remarked that "social insurance would be contrary to the very nature and dignity of man, which are based on his liberty and responsibility."[1] Mutual leaders thus saw their societies as being very different from state- or Church-run charitable assistance for the hopelessly destitute. While the doctrine of self-help and prudence provided a reliable beacon to mutualists before the First World War, the historian is considerably more challenged to elucidate the movement's general

---

[1] M. Lépine, *La Mutualité, ses principes, ses bases veritables*, cited by Porte, *Les Assurances sociales et traditions mutualistes*, p. 5.

structure and operations. This difficulty owes to mutualism's decentralized character and the widely varying practices among its constituent societies.[2] Nevertheless, a brief history of the mutual movement and its prevalent procedures must be sketched in the hope of capturing the salient characteristics of this pivotal player in the evolution of French social protection in the twentieth century.

Mutual leaders commonly identified their practices as far back as classical civilization and traced them directly to the nineteenth century when the movement became distinctly visible from other forms of corporate organization. They pointed to the *collegia tenuiorum* and *collegia funeratitia* of ancient Greece and Rome, which were voluntary associations that collectivized the cost of funeral rituals and burials. After the fall of Rome, they believed, medieval corporations carried the baton of mutual aid, obliging artisans and members of religious orders to render each other support under a wide variety of circumstances. The early modern period witnessed the growth of *compagnonnages*, groups of artisans, usually organized by craft that oversaw not only the rules of production and prices, but also a system of mutual assistance during a member's incapacitation. During the Great Revolution, the Chapelier Law of June 1791 prohibited both religious confraternities and *compagnonnages*. Yet organizations of mutual aid were tolerated during the Napoleonic period (1799–1815).[3] Under the Restoration and through the Second Republic (1848–1852) most mutual societies were local affairs that served a specific profession and depended on a particular benefactor, such as the Church or a regional patron. The size of early nineteenth-century societies usually did not exceed 150 members and were almost exclusively found in urban centers. With the advent of the Second Empire (1852–1870), the societies gained state sanction and subsidies. Napoleon III exacted moneys from the Orléanist family fortune to provide financial help to mutual societies. Also important, the regime granted fee exemptions to mutual societies for burial and civil record keeping. Indeed, Napoleon III adopted the mutual movement as the Empire's favorite vehicle of social welfare. But

---

[2] Several studies have been devoted to specific mutual societies or regions. See Patricia Toucas-Truyen, *Mutualité au sein des populations littorales en Charente-Inférieure, 1850–1945* (Paris: Librairie de l'Inde, 1998); R. Chagny, "La Mutualité française aux XIXème siècle: l'exemple de l'Isère," *Cahiers de l'Institut de Recherches Marxistes*, 33 (1988), 63–84; J.P. Navarro, *La Naissance des sociétés de secours mutuels dans le Tarn* (Union Mutualiste Tarnaise, 1985).

[3] Jean Bennet, *La Mutualité française des origines à la révolution de 1789* (Paris: CEIM, 1981), pp. 42–44; Romain Lavielle, *Histoire de la mutualité* (Paris: Hachette, 1964), pp. 19–36; Conférence de Romain Lavielle, "L'Œuvre de la mutualité et des assurances sociales," Maison de la Mutualité, Paris, 15 March 1944 (Paris: Imprimerie Municipale, 1944), p. 5.

with the bestowal of imperial favor, the Bonapartist regime insisted on the right to appoint mutual society presidents and required societies to register their statutes and membership lists with local government officials. Napoleon even drew up plans to create mutual societies in every town but was stymied by Church resistance to the idea.[4] Due in large part to the emperor's keen interest in mutual aid, many societies flourished, becoming truly multiprofessional associations of 500 adherents or more. An 1864 report noted that mutual societies numbered 5,027 with 714,345 members. This represented a doubling in societies since 1852, when only 2,488 societies attracted a membership of 239,501. Of the membership in 1864, 85,559 were honorary members, that is, adherents who paid dues but did not collect benefits. Their beneficent presence remained critical to the mutual movement's balance sheet throughout the nineteenth and early twentieth centuries. At the end of Napoleon III's reign, mutual membership had surpassed 900,000 members.[5]

The return of republicanism to France in 1871 brought a lifting of government surveillance. This gesture, which appeared to befit the new democratic regime, resulted in only a marginal increase in free (*libre*) societies. Mutual leaders willingly abided the continuation of relatively light government regulations because of the financial advantages afforded to state-authorized societies. Between 1882 and 1902, over one million workers chose state-authorized societies while only 100,000 joined free ones. Thus, while the mutual movement maintained a strong growth rate, its dependence on state subsidies grew apace. As shown in figure 4, by 1902, the Third Republic boasted almost fourteen thousand societies with just over two million members.

Under the Third Republic, secularism eroded the religious affiliations that had been so important among mutual leaders through the Second Empire. This trend was aided by passage of legislation that became known as the Charte de la Mutualité (The Mutual Charter) on 1 April 1898. The Charter provided a legal framework that encouraged mutual society membership and the renovation of society bylaws for state approval. By the turn of the century, the mutual movement had also come

[4] Michel Dreyfus, "Mutual Benefit Societies in France: A Complex Endeavour," *Social Security Mutualism: The Comparative History of Mutual Benefit Societies*, Marcel van der Linden, ed. (Bern: Peter Lang, 1996), pp. 209–224. See especially p. 212.
[5] Bernard Gibaud, *Mutualité, assurances (1850–1914): les enjeux* (Paris: Economica, 1998), pp. 32–42; Allan Mitchell, "The Function and Malfunction of Mutual Aid Societies in Nineteenth-Century France," in Jonathan Barry and Colin Jones (eds.), *Medicine and Charity Before the Welfare State*, (New York: Routledge, 1991), pp. 172–189 and Anatole Weber, *Les Errements des sociétés de secours mutuels*, (Paris: 1913), pp. 16–25, cited by Mitchell, "Function and Malfunction," p. 185.

Number of societies (thousands)　　　　　　　Membership (millions)

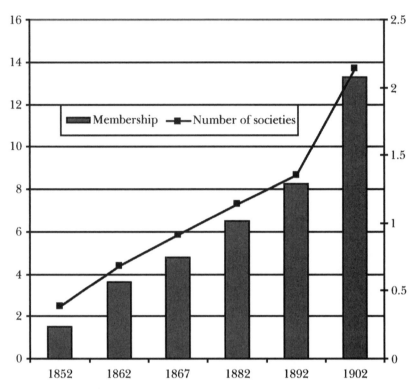

Figure 4　Growth in mutual aid societies and their membership, 1852–1902. Statistics from Anatole Weber, *A travers la mutualité: étude critique sur les sociétés de secours mutuels* (Paris, 1929), p. 29; Yves Guyot, "Les diverses formes de la mutualité," *Journal des Économistes* 72 (1913), p. 8 and *Bulletin du Ministère du Travail* (1922), cited by Georges Weil, *Histoire du mouvement social en France, 1852–1924* (Paris: Alcan, 1924), p. 453.

under the influence of Léon Bourgeois' solidarism. Solidarists rejected both class struggle and economic liberalism. They believed that an active state role in humanitarian and social welfare could alleviate class tension and the revolutionary threat it posed to republican society.[6] Yet, a conversion to republicanism and solidarism did not overturn deeply ingrained practices. In fact, the newly created Charte consecrated one of the movement's most serious limitations as a purveyor of social protection: exclusivity. Article 2 of the 1 April 1898 law stated that "Mutual

[6] Hayward, "The Official Social Philosophy."

aid societies are obliged to guarantee all their participating members the same benefits without distinction other than that which results from premiums paid and inherent risks."[7] The first exclusion permitted by this article, concerning premiums, sprang from the limited ability of societies to afford pension benefits, especially for members who had not contributed for a requisite minimum period. However, the second exclusion, that of risk, bespoke the wide latitude that mutual societies enjoyed in accepting new members as well as cutting benefits to those whose condition threatened the solvency of the association. Indeed, the discretion enjoyed by mutual leaders, which in some cases included breaking their own rules in order to deny admission, hobbled the movement's potential as the basis for a truly national system of social welfare.[8]

Although virtually all mutual societies could boast of democratic proceedings for those within their ranks, their meeting hall doors were shut to wide swaths of the population. Women, immigrant workers, and the chronically ill, were routinely excluded. Women suffered immensely from this exclusion. Most mutual societies preferred to avoid the cost of incapacitation during pregnancy and the risk of death during childbirth. When women succeeded at gaining membership, they were usually prohibited from participating at meetings or membership on the society's governing board. They also suffered lower indemnity rates – by about one third – for missed work because of the disparity in wages between women and men. In 1892, women's clothing manufacturer, Félix Poissineau founded the first maternal mutual society (*mutualité maternelle*) to assure the needs of expecting women and mothers. Numerous honorary members permitted the new mutual society to provide new mothers with four weeks of paid leave to care for their infants directly after birth. Poissineau's maternal mutual society gained wide acclaim and was imitated in several manufacturing centers outside Paris. Although these groupings proved effective at lowering infant mortality rates and promoting the health of working-class women, the movement numbered only 35,000 members by the end of 1910, only a small fraction of working women in need of such services.[9] Moreover, 23,000 of the total 35,000 maternal society members were located in Paris.[10] In fact, a maldistribution of mutual aid in France plagued the movement at large.

---

[7] Porte, *Les Assurances sociales*, pp. 8–9.   [8] Toucas-Truyen, *Mutualité*, p. 278.

[9] Jean Bennet, *Biographies de personnalités mutualistes, XIXe et XXe siècles* (Paris: Mutualité Française, 1987), pp. 361–364.

[10] Mitchell, "Function and Malfunction," p. 184.

In 28,000 of France's more than 36,000 communes, even a young, healthy, financially stable man could not find a mutual society. The movement's nineteenth-century growth expanded services to the major urban agglomerations of Paris, Marseilles, Lyons, Bordeaux, and Lille. But as late as 1910, many departments suffered from an appallingly small number of societies. While 94 percent of urban communes in the department of the Seine had at least one society, less than 5 percent of the communes in Cantal, Corrèze, Corsica, Côtes-du-Nord, and Lozère had a single society.[11] Still in 1923 two-thirds of the communes of rural France remained without a mutual aid society.[12] Indeed, the political elite remained painfully aware that the French mutual movement had not kept up with analogous institutions in other European nations. British friendly societies attracted eleven million members. Germany's obligatory social insurance covered eighteen million and included retirement benefits. Meanwhile, French mutual societies provided security to millions fewer and their ethos was neither charitable nor universal.[13] Artisanal, petty bourgeois, and middle class men constituted its predominant constituency and its leaders clung to the doctrine of voluntary social protection while rejecting many applicants as unsafe risks.

So committed to liberty and choice were mutual leaders that they protested parliament's passage in 1910 of a modest compulsory retirement program for low-income workers. In 1912, when a French court struck down the 1910 legislation's wage withholding provision, which, in practical terms rendered the law nearly useless, mutual leaders breathed a sigh of relief but remained bitter over the less than paramount place that legislators had assigned to them.[14] The shortcomings of the mutual movement – its exclusivity, its maldistribution, and its contentious regard for state intervention – proved to be growing liabilities as production became increasingly industrial. The proletariat participated in mutual societies, but they presented a new kind of member whom the mutual movement was slow to comprehend and accommodate.

In fact, the mutual movement suffered from a rift with France's industrial unions. Although much younger than mutual societies, workers'

---

[11] *Ibid.*, p. 183.
[12] Mutual societies that protected adherents against threats to their crops and livestock were more widespread in the countryside than those which insured against illness, disability, old-age, etc. See Toucas-Truyen, *Mutualité*, p. 277. Also see Philippe Chalmin, *Les Assurances mutuelles agricoles: de la cotise au groupe* (Paris: Economica, 1987).
[13] Léon Bourgeois, *Discours prononcé au banquet offert à M. Mabilleau le 20 décembre 1901* (Paris: 1902), cited by Mitchell, "Function and Malfunction," p. 181.
[14] The law of 5 April 1910, known as Retraites Ouvrières et Paysannes (ROP). See Bernard Gibaud, *De la mutualité à la sécurité sociale: conflits et convergences* (Paris: Editions Ouvrières, 1986), p. 97; Lavielle, *Histoire de la mutualité*, pp. 70–74.

unions also traced their heritage to early modern *compagnonnage*. Both movements achieved a national scope at almost precisely the same moment at the turn of the century. The first national congress of mutual societies was held in 1883, one year prior to the Waldeck-Rousseau law that legalized workers' trade unions. Although the constituent assembly of the Confédération Générale du Travail (CGT) did not occur until 1902, this was also the founding year of the Fédération Nationale de la Mutualité Française (FNMF). Yet these coincident milestones did not mark any particular affinity. In fact, the French left, including the CGT's parliamentary allies, the Section Française Internationale Ouvrière (SFIO) viewed the mutual movement with mistrust. This, despite the often close working relationship between the Radical-Socialists, which supplied many FNMF leaders, and the SFIO. For working-class leaders, mutualists were tainted by their long cooperation with the bourgeois state and its pronounced reformist agenda.[15] But, in fact, the social protections that the movement provided to the union's rank and file permitted the CGT to ignore the service component of its leadership. Whereas this component emerged as crucial to the program of workers' unions elsewhere in Europe, the CGT expended little energy on the social welfare of its members, preferring instead to stress its commitment to revolutionary syndicalism and a wholesale challenge to the French state and capitalist economy. In addition to the ideological underpinnings of the labor-mutual movement divide, political jealousy took its toll. In 1906 the CGT claimed a membership of only 206,000 compared to the mutual movement's over three million. Hence, given the fact that many trade unionists also belonged to mutual societies, prewar leaders of the newly formed CGT inevitably regarded the larger and elder workers' association as a potential threat. This perception underwent a radical transformation during and immediately after the First World War.

Like the CGT, the FNMF was a loyal member of the wartime *union sacrée*. But in contrast to the union, the mutual movement underwent a major transformation as it assumed responsibility for the conflict's displaced and disabled. Mutual societies provided aid for refugees from German occupied areas, the organization of hospital visits, as well as the sending of care packages to prisoners of war and their families.[16] After the war, thousands of maimed and disabled veterans who never

[15] Michel Dreyfus, "Mouvement ouvrier et mutualité: l'exception française? 1852–1967," Mémoire pour l'habilitation à diriger des recherches présenté sous la direction du professeur Antoine Prost, Université de Paris I, January 1997, pp. 15–18.

[16] Jean Bennet, *La Mutualité pendant la guerre de 1914–1918* (Etampes: Société d'Imprimerie et de Publicité, 1964), pp. 16–23.

regained their prewar productive capacities, looked to a combination of state pensions and mutual aid to sustain them and their families. While most mutual societies made extraordinary efforts to accommodate their war wounded, others sought to reduce or eliminate their benefits entirely, forcing the ministry of labor to forbid such actions.[17] Meanwhile, official estimates counted over 400,000 mutualists dead or missing in action.[18] Eventually, state subsidies flowed to aid mutual societies because of their expanded role in resettlement and refugee assistance, as well as to help them recover from their wartime casualties.[19] However, by 1921 parliamentary consideration of compulsory social insurance cast a pall over relations between government and mutual leaders. Spurred by the recovery of Alsace-Lorraine, legislators began consideration of a German-style regime of social insurance that threatened to shun the mutual movement's century-long experience in social protection.

PARLIAMENT'S FIRST ATTEMPT AT SOCIAL INSURANCE:
THE VINCENT BILL

Motivations behind the Chamber's first social insurance bill were three-fold. First, political leaders sought to fulfill their wartime promises to the troops, who were now returning to the factory floor, for their sacrifices in the trenches. Because the war had proved much longer and deadlier than anyone had anticipated, the *union sacrée* had, quite necessarily, become more than a pact to defend the Republic against aggression. Political leaders had promised a postwar society of rights and prosperity in order to sustain popular support for the war. In fact, workers' representatives at Versailles drafted passages of the peace accords that served as the founding principles of the International Labor Organization (ILO). Based in Geneva and operating under the auspices of the League of Nations, the ILO documented the means through which labor standards and worker protections could be implemented in all member nations.[20] The authority of the ILO and the French government's sensitivity to international comparisons provided proponents of social reform with an ample supply of useful rhetoric.

Second, as we saw in the previous chapter, a workers' movement of unprecedented strength and stridency emerged immediately after the war.

---

[17] *Ibid.*, p. 12.   [18] *Ibid.*, pp. 4, 25.
[19] "La Mutualité pendant la guerre," *Bulletin de la Fédération Nationale de la Mutualité Française*, 1918?, pp. 12–15.
[20] See Treaty of Versailles, Part 13, especially Section 2, General Principles, Article 427. Also see A. Rey, *La Question des assurances sociales* (Paris: Félix Alcan, 1925), p. 9.

Taking advantage of a shortage of skilled workers and a pent up demand for industrial products that strengthened the hand of labor, the CGT organized several massive strikes in 1919. Although these actions did not achieve their hoped-for results, their magnitude convinced many among the French elite, both inside and outside government, of the threat of class warfare. These fears were amplified by the Bolshevik revolution and translated into private and public efforts to either pacify or assuage the working class. Employers' adoption of family allowances was clearly a pacification measure that the government had instigated during the war but which became a private movement during the 1920s. Social insurance, on the other hand, originated in government circles and was meant to assuage, rather than divide workers' unions. Proponents believed that by providing some security against illness, disability, and an impoverished retirement, workers would adopt a more bourgeois, that is, contented attitude toward their present condition. Moderate social reformers believed that such a transformation in the working-class outlook would, in turn, immunize it against the appeal of Bolshevism.[21]

The third, and most important factor in the timing of parliament's consideration of social insurance was the recovery of Alsace-Lorraine. Inhabitants of the territory enjoyed a compulsory system of social protections that had been founded by Bismarck in the 1880s. Government leaders became convinced that a successful reintegration of the three new French departments (Haut-Rhin, Bas-Rhin, and the Moselle) necessitated a swift standardization of laws, including those that governed social welfare. Heading this effort were a clique of exceptional political and industrial leaders, whose influence within the recovered territories, at the Conseil d'Etat, and in parliament assured a prompt proposal, if not approval, of social insurance legislation.

Questions from the inhabitants of the recovered territories about their place in postwar France became an urgent political issue immediately after the Armistice. In fact, an autonomist movement appeared as a potentially disruptive force in the recovered territories by 1919 and helped to focus French government attention on the transition from German to French rule.[22] The potential loss of welfare and retirement benefits, which had been guaranteed to them under the German Reich, loomed among

[21] Paul Frantzen, *Les Assurances sociales*, Les Cahiers du Redressement Français, no. 22 (Paris: Editions de la SAPE, 1927), pp. 9–10.

[22] On the autonomist movement, see Chantal Metzger, "Relations entre autonomistes lorrains et alsaciens de 1919 à 1932," 103e Congrès National des Sociétés Savantes, Nancy-Metz 1978, Histoire-Moderne, vol. II, pp. 155–170.

the most significant anxieties. In several meetings with workers' organizations in the months following the Armistice, the commissioner general
in Alsace-Lorraine, Alexandre Millerand, reassured the region's inhabitants. Millerand promised the populace that "the three branches of your
social insurance [medical, disability, and old-age] will be maintained in
their entirety... [France] will not only conserve the advantages enjoyed
by the workers of Alsace-Lorraine under current legislation but will bor-
row appropriate elements of this legislation in order to improve its own
laws and procure new benefits for all French workers."[23] Residents of the
former German region had much to lose. According to legislation that
dated from the 1880s and its subsequent expansion in 1900 and 1911,
workers and employers shared the costs of illness, maternity, retirement,
and disability insurance, and employers were solely responsible for the
risk of accidents. Family members were eligible for similar coverage if a
worker paid an elevated premium. Medical and maternity benefits were
especially generous. Incapacitated workers received an illness allowance
of 50 percent of their base pay. Medical expenses, including pharmaceuticals and hospital expenses, were covered at 100 percent for twenty-six
weeks. Pregnant women earned the aforementioned illness allowance
for fifty-seven days as well as a subsidy to offset birth-related expenses
and a small nursing stipend during the twelve weeks following delivery.
In the case of permanent disability, a worker was recompensed with a
stipend whose value depended on the degree of his or her handicap. A
death payment to the insured's survivors equaled twenty times his or her
daily base wage. In comparison to these benefits, retirement pensions
were relatively meager. A small allowance could be collected but not
before the age of sixty-five. The cost of these social protections was approximately 9 percent of wages of which employers paid one third and
workers contributed the remaining two thirds.[24]

Prominent industrialists of the recovered territories accepted the cost
of social insurance as the price of social peace. In fact, they played a
critical role in regional and national politics to extend social insurance
to the rest of France. These men included Pierre René Wendel, who
won a seat to the Chamber from the Moselle immediately after the war,
switched to the Senate in 1927, and served as president of the general

---

[23] Alexandre Millerand, *Le Retour de l'Alsace-Lorraine à la France* (Paris: Charpentier, 1923), pp. 70–72.

[24] Office général des assurances sociales d'Alsace et de Lorraine, *Les Assurances sociales en Alsace et
Lorraine*, second edn. (Strasbourg, 1922), tableaux statistiques; *L'Assurance maladie et les œuvres sociales
dans les industries d'Alsace et de Lorraine* (Metz: Paul Even, 1922), pp. 5–7; Communication de Paul
Schlumberger, vice-président de la société industrielle de Mulhouse, Comité National d'Etudes
Sociales et Politiques, *compte rendu*, 13 January 1930, pp. 15–18.

council (*conseil général*) of the department from 1924 to 1936. Wendel was joined by fellow industrialist from Haut Rhin, Paul Jourdain, who became president of the Chamber's influential Commission d'Assurance et de Prévoyance Sociales (CAPS) in 1919 and served as minister of labor in the Millerand and Leygues governments of 1920. Jourdain emerged as the leading architect of the first social insurance bill, which was presented to the Chamber by his successor at the ministry of labor, Daniel Vincent.[25] It was no small coincidence that the March 1921 unveiling of the first social insurance bill occurred shortly after Millerand's accession to the presidency of the republic. But Millerand, who had been among the most forthright proponents of spreading Alsace-Lorraine's social protections to the rest of France, had to endure nine long years of debate before his 1919 promise in Strasbourg could be fulfilled.

The Vincent bill, as it soon became known, was an ambitious piece of legislation that aroused spirited debate on several fronts. Little consensus existed as to which risks should be insured, the level of benefits, who should benefit, and how social insurance should be financed and administered. The bill encompassed the risks of illness, maternity, death, invalidity, and old age. All workers in commerce, industry, and agriculture, including sharecroppers and those who worked at home and earned less than 10,000 francs would be obliged to participate. Proponents indicated that the proposed law would provide employer-subsidized social protection to approximately 8.1 million workers. The bill also foresaw voluntary participation for small entrepreneurs, artisans, and smallholding peasants whose annual income did not exceed the 10,000 franc threshold. However, an age restriction of thirty years and a health litmus test were placed on voluntary participants. Although the Vincent bill would not become the law of the land, it served as the starting point for subsequent proposals. We must therefore examine its provisions in some detail in order to appreciate the revisions and amendments, which together became France's first national social insurance law in April 1928.

Benefits under the Vincent bill were generally more extensive, that is, paid sooner and for longer periods, but not as generous as the German system of Alsace-Lorraine. Illness insurance is a good example. Workers were divided into six wage categories. After the fourth day of incapacitation, the insured was entitled to a daily illness allowance (*allocation journalière maladie*) equal to one half the average wage of the category

---

[25] M. Degas, *Les Assurances sociales*, (Paris: Dunod, 1924), pp. xv–xvi.

to which he or she belonged.[26] The illness allowance could continue during six months at which time the payment was reduced by 55 percent and transformed into a monthly stipend. If after five years the condition persisted, a judgment as to the level – complete or partial – of the insured's disability determined the size of his or her disability pension (*pension d'invalidité*), which would be paid until he or she became eligible for retirement benefits. Complete disability could translate into a pension as high as 3,000 francs per month or as low as 500 francs per month depending on the worker's wage category. Cash benefits were, of course, accompanied by coverage for medical diagnoses and care, including surgery, and pharmaceuticals. In most cases, only nominal copayments were required of the insured. For medical treatment, the copayment could not exceed one third of the insured's daily allowance. For medications and other supplies, the worker could not be held responsible for more than ten percent of the total. Unlike the cash payments described above, these benefits continued uninterrupted for the entire duration of the worker's incapacitation or disability.[27]

Maternity benefits were offered to women workers but not the wives of insured men. During the six weeks prior to, and six weeks after birth, a woman earned a daily maternity allowance (*allocation de maternité*) that equaled her illness allowance as long as she ceased wage-earning work. Importantly, the maternity allowance was based on the insured's wage at the beginning of the pregnancy. Women workers applauded this provision because so many did piece work and suffered from decreased productivity during pregnancy.[28] In addition, if the new mother breastfed her infant, she could claim a monthly nursing stipend (*allocation d'allaitement*) equal to four times her daily maternity allowance for a period of one year. Like illness and disability coverage, maternity benefits included all medical and pharmaceuticals prescribed by the woman's attending midwife or doctor minus her copayment. Lastly, a pronatalist measure was incorporated into the bill in the form of a birth bonus. If the child survived the first year, the mother collected 200 francs, a reward that amounted to more than two weeks pay for many women workers. The birth bonus was doubled to 400 francs if the father was also insured.[29]

[26] *JO*, Documents parlementaires, Chambre, 22 March 1921, annexe no. 2369, Dispositions générales (Articles 1–11), pp. 1308–1309.
[27] *Ibid.*, Maladie et Invalidité (Articles 21–48), pp. 1309–1311.
[28] Jean Lebas, *L'Assurance sociale et le Parti Socialiste* (Lille: Imprimerie ouvrière, 1921), pp. 9–10.
[29] *JO*, Documents parlementaires, Chambre, 22 March 1921, annexe no. 2369, pp. 1297–1322, Maternité (Articles 49–52), Charges de famille (Articles 57–60), pp. 1311–1312.

The Vincent bill made retirement benefits available at age sixty rather than sixty-five, which was the case in Alsace-Lorraine. In order to collect a pension, the worker must have paid into the system for thirty years. A retiree's pension was based on his or her wage category, and thus ranged from 500 to 3,000 francs per month. However, these values constituted legal minimums. The Vincent bill foresaw a capitalized retirement fund whose resources, depending on the importance of compound interest, could provide substantially more to each category of retirees. In lieu of a monthly pension beginning at age sixty, and continuing until death, the insured could liquidate his or her benefits anytime after age fifty-five. Because pension benefits could not revert to the insured's spouse or children, lawmakers viewed this option as a just recompense for workers with relatively short life expectancies.[30] The sole benefit an insured's family members could collect was the death stipend, whose value varied according to the wage class of the insured. Families of low-wage workers had to make do with 150 francs for funeral expenses while survivors of the better paid could expect as much as 1,500 francs.[31] It should be noted that the cash pension constituted the sole retirement benefit. Once pensioned, the insured was no longer eligible for medical coverage.

Except for its retirement and disability provisions, the Vincent bill presented a self-funding, pay-as-you-go system. Workers and employers each paid a premium equal to 5 percent of the base wage, that is, excluding bonuses or family allowances. The exact premium depended on which of the six wage categories the worker belonged. The use of broad categories greatly simplified the calculation of premiums, but it also raised the ire of workers whose actual wages fell at the bottom of their category. As we saw above, a worker's wage category determined the value of cash benefits for illness, disability, retirement, and death.[32]

The Vincent bill proposed a system of withholding (*précompte*) whereby an appropriate fraction of the worker's annual premium would be deducted from his or her paycheck. The combined worker and employer's premium, i.e., 10 percent of wages, would then be deposited in the worker's name at the social insurance *caisse*. Voluntary participants were required to contribute the full 10 percent of wages according to the above wage classification system.[33] Approximately 60 percent of the system's revenue was to be used to pay current expenses, specifically medical, maternity, and death benefits. The remaining contributions were placed in capitalized funds whose growing value was projected as

---

[30] *Ibid.*, Vieillesse (Articles 61–72), pp. 1312–1313.   [31] *Ibid.*, Décès (Articles 53–56), pp. 1311–1312.
[32] *Ibid.*, Dispositions générales (Article 9), p. 1308.   [33] *Ibid.* (Articles 4), p. 1308.

sufficient to cover the expense of retirement and long-term disability payments.[34]

The financial demands on the state budget under the Vincent bill were limited. The government's responsibility fell into three main categories: family welfare, current retirees, and administrative costs. In order to aid and encourage the growth of large families, the state would supplement daily illness and maternity allowances and pay the aforementioned birth bonuses to new mothers. In order to launch the retirement system, the state would liquidate and supplement the funds of the existing retirement regime (the law of 1910) in order to pay disability and retirement pensions to those who were approaching age sixty. Lastly, the state would be responsible for meeting the administrative costs of the various social insurance *caisses*. In sum, the Vincent bill expected the state to contribute 156 million francs during its first year of operation. The state's responsibility would rise to 336 million in the tenth year (due to a rising tide of retirements) but would fall thereafter to 181 million after forty-four years. While the impact of the Vincent bill on the state budget was not insignificant, proponents argued that social insurance would result in a decrease of 50 million francs in the cost of state-run assistance to the poor.[35]

The Vincent bill created a decentralized administration for the new social insurance regime. In fact, the only national body foreseen in the bill was a *caisse nationale de guarantee*, which would redistribute moneys among local *caisses* as well as manage state subsidies to the system. Despite the absence of a national directorate, the Vincent bill clearly favored state agencies and worker control at the expense of mutual societies and employer prerogatives. Most important in the scheme were twenty-five, government-created, *caisses régionales*. Control of *caisses régionales* was confided to a governing board of thirty-six members, of which eighteen would be elected by workers, nine by employers, with the remaining nine appointed by the minister of labor. The regional *caisses* were charged with the oversight of local *caisses de remplacement*, whose character could take one of three forms: (1) a mutual aid society; (2) a designated social insurance fund run by an employer; (3) a designated social insurance fund administered by a workers' union. *Caisses de remplacement* were not permitted to administer disability insurance, which was reserved to *caisses régionales*, and could only take charge of retirement funds if they had at

---

[34] *Ibid.*, Du Fonctionnement des Assurances sociales (Articles 76–96), pp. 1314–1316; Frantzen, *Les Assurances sociales*, p. 34.

[35] *Ibid.*, Participation financière de l'Etat (Articles 118–122), p. 1318; Frantzen, *ibid.*, p. 35.

least 10,000 members. In order to assume responsibility for illness and medical insurance, the bill required that a *caisse de remplacement* group at least 250 adherents of whom at least 40 percent were between forty-four and sixty-six years of age.[36] Employers faced special restrictions under the law. They could constitute a *caisse de remplacement*, either individually or in association with other employers. However, unlike *caisses* that had been created by workers' unions, which could be governed solely by the union's leadership, at least half the directing board of an employer-created *caisse* had to be occupied by workers. One consolation in the law for employers was that it did not regulate or incorporate family allowances. However, this lacuna in the law meant that all such non-wage benefits, including retirement plans, lacked legal sanction. Thus, in order to gain promised state subsidies for administrative expenses, some employers would have to recast long-established retirement plans under the auspices of a social insurance *caisse*.[37] Mutual societies fared little better than employers. The law's size and age restrictions on *caisses de remplacement* were highly unfavorable to mutual societies. Most would be ineligible to offer retirement benefits under the new law because they fell well short of the 10,000 member threshold. Moreover, many others would be forced to modify their admissions policies that excluded new members over the age of forty. Of course, this is just what authors of the Vincent bill had in mind. The mutual movement was to become a highly regulated appendage of the regional *caisses* where state influence was concentrated.

MUTUALISM AND THE BATTLE OVER REVISION OF THE VINCENT BILL

Reaction to the Vincent bill exposed the heterogeneity of the mutual movement. The Fédération Mutualiste du Travail (FMT), which represented many industrial workers, immediately clamored for the bill's approval. This call was reenforced by resolutions passed at mutual society meetings notably in the Paris suburbs where many working-class mutualists lived.[38] Meanwhile, the FNMF, whose national circumscription bound it to more traditional mutualist doctrine, withheld an official

---

[36] *Ibid.*, Caisses de Remplacement (Article 98), p. 1316; Lebas, *L'Assurance sociale*, p. 14.

[37] *Ibid.*, Institutions Patronales de retraite (Article 106), p. 1317; Frantzen, *Les Assurances sociales*, p. 29; Lebas, *ibid.*, p. 14.

[38] Puteaux, Suresnes, Asnières, Colombes, and Courbevoie. Dominique Simon, "Les Assurances sociales et les mutualistes," *Revue d'Histoire Moderne et Contemporaine*, 34 (October–December 1987), 587–615. See especially p. 591.

declaration until after the bill had been reviewed – and inevitably amended – by Chamber committees. Indeed, the opportunities for revision before the bill went to the Chamber floor were rife. The sheer scope of the Vincent bill necessitated its consideration by no less than six committees: CAPS, finance, legislation, agriculture, labor, and commerce and industry. FNMF leaders were distressed by several of the bill's principles. They had always found the concept of compulsory social protection difficult to accept. In the case of the Vincent bill, this quarrel was further compounded by the bill's provision for automatic payroll deductions (*précompte*). Many mutualists also rejected the legislation's inherently class-based approach whereby only workers who earned under a certain annual income were obliged to participate (and therefore benefited from employer matches of their contributions). Some FNMF leaders viewed the separation of workers from each other and workers from employers as divisive. These mutualists prided themselves on the participation of well-paid workers as well as employers in their societies. Indeed, as we have already seen, many mutual aid societies relied on the honorary participation of employers to make ends meet. According to a leading FNMF spokesperson, the diversity of mutualist membership "represented the solidarity of the mutualist association in the professional realm, unifying workers, bosses, foremen, customers, and suppliers . . . for the well being and social peace of the neighborhood to which it belongs."[39] FNMF leaders were equally disturbed by the categorization of eligible workers' wages according to which both premiums and cash benefits were determined. Despite the logic of the Vincent bill, which sought equity between premiums and benefits, some mutualists found it difficult to abide the payment of dissimilar cash benefits to workers with the same illness or disability. The Vincent bill also foresaw an administrative structure for social insurance that would have been highly unfavorable to the FNMF. This was especially true in the case of pension benefits.

The bill required much higher membership levels for the management of pension funds than many mutual societies could attain. Proponents of the Vincent bill projected approximately 8.1 million obligatory participants in the new social insurance regime. Even if all these workers joined a mutual society *caisses de remplacement* – as opposed to *caisses* run by either workers' unions or employers – the resulting influx of members would still fall well short of the necessary adherents to allow existing mutual societies to supervise their own pension funds. *Caisses régionales* would

39 Porte, *Les Assurances sociales*, pp. 8–9.

manage retirement benefits for these societies, permitting the smaller associations to offer only illness, maternity, and death coverage. These regulations, mutual leaders believed, would engender a process of amalgamation, transforming the very nature of mutual aid. Although they understood the advantages of large numbers for the distribution of risks, mutual leaders were firm believers in small-scale associations. These, they argued, allowed closer supervision of the membership, resulting in better service and a strong disincentive to fraudulent medical claims. Also, a small organization tended to exhibit a camaraderie among its adherents, resulting in moral and psychological support for the sick or injured. A social insurance association of 10,000 members could never replicate such a sense of caring and fellowship. Nor could such an association hope to gather all its members in one place at one time. Indeed, mutual societies commonly compelled their members to participate in quarterly assemblies where the above-mentioned camaraderie (and supervision) could be effected. Reciting the mantra of "small is better" and the importance of traditional mutual practices to the nation, FNMF leaders lobbied the CAPS long and hard throughout 1921 and 1922. Most importantly they sought a substantial relaxation of the Vincent bill's regulations on *caisse* size and a wholesale revision of its administrative structure that would allow the mutual movement to play a much more important role in the provision of social insurance.[40]

The primary target of this lobbying was a medical doctor and deputy from Alpes-Maritime, Edouard Grinda, whom members of the CAPS had charged with drafting their final report. The Grinda report, which ultimately numbered over 300 pages, was unveiled in January 1923. Grinda left the system of worker payroll deduction and employer contributions essentially untouched, but he substantially revised the list of compulsory participants and their benefits. Moreover, to the great satisfaction of mutual leaders, Grinda recast the administration and control of social insurance foreseen in the Vincent bill.[41]

Grinda proclaimed that the revised bill represented a "social insurance [system], which is in essence, a grand mutual society."[42] As evidence of this, he pointed to revisions that abolished government-created *caisses*

---

[40] *Ibid.*, pp. 11–19.

[41] Grinda's efforts on behalf of the mutual movement during these formative years of social insurance would eventually earn him the Médaille d'Or de la Mutualité. See Bennet, *Biographies de personnalités mutualistes*, pp. 207–209.

[42] Edouard Grinda, *Rapport fait au nom de la Commission d'Assurance et de Prévoyance Sociales chargée d'examiner le projet de loi sur les assurances sociales*, Annexe au procès-verbal de la séance du 31 janvier, no. 5505 (Paris: Imprimerie de la Chambre, 1923), p. 39.

régionales, which stood at the center of the Vincent bill. In their place Grinda created a much more supple federation of local *caisses*, which he called *unions régionales*. Unlike the dominant role that Vincent had cut out for the *caisse régionale*, Grinda cast the *unions* as supportive bodies and reserved critical administrative decisions to local *caisses*. Direction of *unions* would be confided to delegates from adherent *caisses* of whom at least half must represent workers. There would be no appointees by the minister of labor as under the Vincent bill. These provisions greatly decreased the influence of the state. Both the *unions régionales* and their constituent local *caisses* faced only light oversight. Workers would be allowed to select a *caisse*, be it managed by a mutual society, a workers' union, an employers' association, or an individual firm. However, Grinda maintained the Vincent bill's membership requirement of 10,000 for the administration of retirement and death benefits. And, although Grinda deleted the Vincent bill's dictate that 40 percent of a mutual society's membership be between the ages of forty-four and sixty-six, the new bill raised to 1,000 the minimum size of any social insurance *caisse*. Nevertheless, Grinda explicitly cast mutual societies in a central role of the new regime by stipulating that absent a contrary declaration by the insured, mutual societies enjoyed a "legal presumption of affiliation" whereby current members would automatically remain adherents of their mutual society for social insurance. Lastly, Grinda diminished the controversial power of the *caisse de guarantee* to equalize wealth among local *caisses*. Under the Vincent bill, its state-dominated board could essentially tax rich local *caisses* in order to help poorer ones. Mutual leaders had vehemently objected to this provision, arguing that it punished good management while rewarding poorly-run *caisses*. Grinda maintained a *caisse de guarantee* but limited its powers to take from the rich and give to the poor. Furthermore, the report permitted rich *caisses* to decrease employer and worker contributions below the law's 5-percent-of-wages level if benefits could be maintained at legal values.[43] Through its flexibility, the Grinda report thus granted the mutual movement the potential for self-preservation and even substantial growth. This latter prospect, of course, would depend on the efficacy with which the mutualists competed with workers' unions and employers for the allegiance of social insurees. The FNMF would also have to prove itself an effective lobby in order to preserve the movement's privileges under the Chamber bill when the Senate took up consideration of the Grinda report.

[43] *Ibid.*, pp. 41–42.

Unfortunately, the FNMF became embroiled in factional strife at this critical juncture.

DISSENT AND TRANSFORMATION AT THE FNMF

The unveiling of the Grinda report caught the FNMF at an inopportune moment that constrained its ability to take advantage of a highly fluid political situation. In May 1921, the organization's board had been forced to seek the resignation of its founding president, Léopold Mabilleau, because of charges that he had embezzled or at least misappropriated Fédération funds. Mabilleau's departure marked the beginning of a difficult period for the FNMF. His leadership depended on a careful mix of ideological steadfastness and political expediency. He recognized the traditional importance of small independent mutual societies, but he also worked incessantly to bring about unions among these societies. This, Mabilleau had argued, would give the mutual movement a stronger voice in national affairs, spawn new societies, and permit existing mutual societies to improve their benefits by spreading risk. On the question of compulsory social insurance, Mabilleau had desperately sought to slow the government's momentum. In a 1920 banquet speech at the Congrès de la Mutualité, Mabilleau addressed Minister of Labor Paul Jourdain. "Give us a few years, five years, and during that time we will organize ourselves and we will attract to our ranks all those who are free and worthy in this nation. No doubt, there will be some leftovers. We'll have to enroll those through obligation."[44] While Mabilleau's position hardly represented an embrace of state intervention, his willingness to compromise with parliamentary leaders on the question of obligation earned him the enmity of traditionalists within the mutual movement, including the incoming president of the Musée Social, Georges Risler.[45] Shortly after Mabilleau's resignation, Risler evicted the FNMF from its offices in the Musée Social, which it had occupied since its founding in 1902. The FNMF relocated to a nearby building, also in Paris' seventh arrondissement. But the short physical distance belied a wide ideological divide between the FNMF and the traditional approaches to social protection that reigned at the Musée Social under the leadership of Risler during the 1920s.[46] Yet the loss of Mabilleau and its expulsion from the era's

[44] Bennet, *Biographies de personnalités mutualistes*, p. 303.
[45] As vice president of the Alliance Nationale, Risler was also a prominent pronatalist and supporter of employers' family allowance movement. See Gibaud, *Mutualité, assurances*, p. 152.
[46] This is not to say that Risler's views dominated the broader work of the Musée Social. However, his disgust for social insurance, which he termed a "legal monstrosity," was so vehement and

great meeting hall of social reformers did not mark the end of difficulties for the FNMF.

In fact, it launched an interregnum dominated by factional strife under a relatively weak president. Realists who favored collaboration with parliament in the creation of national social insurance fought traditionalists who sought to preserve the movement's conventional approach to social protection that privileged liberty and self-help over state intervention and obligation. Mabilleau's successor at the helm of the FNMF, Léon Robelin, lacked the same stature as Mabilleau and thus could not call the factions to heel. Nonetheless, Robelin persevered against traditionalists who were led by the president of Fédération Mutualiste de Normandie, Henri Vermont. Vermont led a conservative wing that had coalesced under Deputy Hippolyte Maze in the 1880s. Maze had fought against state intervention into accident insurance. During a bitter fight that involved the mutual movement, parliamentary leaders, and private insurance companies, Maze had declared any system of compulsory social insurance "unacceptable either in law or in fact." All social protection that went beyond state and private charity, Maze insisted, should be left to the exclusive prerogative of the mutual movement.[47] Passage of the accident insurance law of 9 April 1898, which required employers to insure their workers against job-related mishaps, marked a bitter defeat for traditionalists. But they refused to disperse. Henri Vermont had stood alongside Maze throughout his fight against state-mandated accident insurance.[48] After Maze's death in 1891, Vermont assumed Maze's mantle with verve. But his devotion to conservative Catholicism placed him somewhat outside the centrist republicanism of the 1920s political elite. This marginal status no doubt contributed to the fury of his attack on social insurance in which he made use of the era's most slanderous terms. Vermont called social insurance "German" and insisted that its realization in France would reduce mutual aid societies to nothing more than bureaucratic ancillaries of the state. He also demanded that if

uncompromising that it diminished the role of the Musée Social during this critical period of deliberations. See Françoise Blum, "Le Musée social au carrefour?" *Vie Sociale* 3–4 1999 (May–June–July–August 1999), 339–348; Georges Risler, "Les Assurances sociales en Alsace et en Lorraine: conférence faite au Conservatoire National des Arts et Métiers, le 10 février 1929," *Le Musée Social* 5 (May 1929), 200–228. Also see Michel Dreyfus, "L. Mabilleau et le mouvement mutualiste français et international de 1895 à 1921," in C. Chambelland (ed.), *Le Musée social en son temps*, (Paris: Presses de l'Ecole Normale Supérieure, 1998), pp. 103–118.

[47] Hyppolyte Maze, *La Lutte contre la misère* (Paris: La Cerf, 1883), p. 14. Also see Gibaud, *Mutualité, Assurances*, chs. 1 and 2.

[48] Henri Vermont "Reflexions sur le projet de loi contre les accidents du travail," *Extrait du Bulletin de la Société Industrielle de Rouen* 1 (1896), pp. 2–7.

legislators approved a social insurance law that it be immediately subjected to a referendum.[49]

Despite Vermont's attacks, Robelin attempted to carry Mabilleau's political realism forward. Through his membership on a special commission – the Conseil Supérieur des Assurances Sociales – that included government and parliamentary representatives, Robelin lobbied for Grinda's mutual-friendly revision of the Vincent social insurance proposal. Upon the unveiling of the Grinda bill in January 1923, Robelin claimed success and immediately set out to rally the FNMF behind the revision in preparation for the FNMF's 1923 national congress in Lyon. Although struck by typhoid fever on the eve of the gathering, Robelin continued to press for a declaration that would unite the mutual movement behind social insurance.[50] His triumph was significant but not complete. Delegates agreed on a carefully worded declaration that supported social insurance yet avoided mentioning the Grinda report by name, hoping for even more thorough revisions on the Chamber floor or in the Senate. The assembled delegates endorsed "the indispensable role in social progress of an obligatory regime of social insurance which generalizes the services that voluntary mutualism has provided up to this day."[51] Enthusiasm for this declaration was dampened somewhat by the Congress' preceding vote on the class distinction inherent in the Grinda bill. By a margin of only 6 votes (127 to 121) the delegates approved of the bill's delineation of compulsory participants according to their annual base wage. However, in a demonstration that political realists had gained the upper hand within the FNMF, many who opposed this aspect of the bill, voted with the majority in order to assure that the significant changes wrought by Grinda to the Vincent bill's administrative structure would not go unappreciated by the FNMF. Shortly after the conference, Robelin, still incapacitated by typhoid, could no longer carry on as FNMF president. His absence marked the beginning of a two-year transition during which political realists battled traditionalists for leadership of the Fédération. This battle was greatly influenced by a change in the government ministry charged with oversight of mutual societies.

---

[49] See the letter by Vermont addressed to the Conseil Supérieur des Sociétés de Secours Mutuels, *Bulletin des Sociétés des Secours Mutuels* (September 1921), 133–136; Vermont, "La loi des assurances sociales," *La Réforme Sociale* (January 1922), 10–34, especially p. 29. Also see Yannick Marec, "L'Apôtre de la mutualité: Henri Vermont, 1836–1928," *L'Economie Sociale* (January 1987), 3–39; Bennet, *Biographies de personnalités mutualistes,* p. 444.

[50] Bennet, *ibid.,* pp. 377–378.

[51] "Compte rendu du 13e Congrès National de la Mutualité" *Mutualiste Français* (June 1923), p. 140. Also see Degas, *Les Assurances sociales,* p. 12.

We saw earlier that the mutual movement had been brought under government regulation during the Second Empire, a supervision that had generally been conducted by the labor ministry. Bolstered by widespread support among FNMF leaders, including Robelin, the government shifted oversight to the ministry of public health and social assistance (hygiène, de l'assistance et de la prévoyance sociales) upon its creation in 1920.[52] Attachment to the new ministry worked to the advantage of FNMF realists. Because the ministry focused more specifically on medicine and public health than the labor ministry, mutual leaders were able to build a constituency within the government on behalf of their movement. This task was greatly facilitated by public health's first minister, Senator Paul Strauss, and the director of mutual society affairs, Deputy Gaston Roussel. Both men were longtime advocates of increased public health measures, state assistance to the needy, and strong supporters of a robust and independent mutual movement.[53] With the passing from power of Robelin in late 1923, Roussel quickly aligned himself with realists within the FNMF by pressing for the appointment of Deputy Raoul Péret to the Fédération's presidency. Péret's credentials as a mutual advocate were unassailable. He had long championed the movement's causes in the Chamber, serving as the leader of that body's mutual aid caucus (*groupe mutualiste*); he also held the presidency of the Fédération des Sociétés de Retraite de France.[54] What upset traditionalists about Péret's candidature was the brazen political character that it would bring to the FNMF presidency. Péret was hardly a low-profile back-bencher. Indeed, his activism had won him the Chamber presidency during the twelfth legislature (1919–1924). Previously the FNMF had prided itself on an apolitical leadership. To be sure, the president was expected to have important contacts within political circles, but these contacts were to be confined to mutual matters. Outwardly partisan behavior by a FNMF president was deemed inappropriate to the mutual movement's special role in French society. Despite these objections, however, a compromise offered a thin veil for the defeat of traditionalists like Vermont who, inexplicably, did not attend FNMF deliberations on Péret's candidature. Péret was elected to a newly created post, the office of general

52 "La Direction de la mutualité et le ministère de l'hygiène sociale, *Bulletin des Sociétés des Secours Mutuels*, March 1921, pp. 34–36; "Conseil supérieur des sociétés des secours mutuels, Rapport de Léon Robelin, concernant le projet de loi sur les assurances sociales," *Bulletin des Sociétés des Secours Mutuels* (July 1921), 103–110.

53 Bennet, *Biographies de personnalités mutualistes*, pp. 401–404.

54 "Assemblée Générale de la Fédération Nationale de la Mutualité," *Bulletin Officiel de la Fédération Nationale de la Mutualité Française*, 29 (December 1925), 4–29, especially pp. 4–7.

president (*président-général*). Simultaneously, the federal assembly selected an FNMF insider, Georges Petit, to serve as the "technical president" of the Fédération. Distinct responsibilities were assigned to each of the new copresidents. Péret would direct the FNMF's political relations, especially its dealings with the government and parliament. Meanwhile, delegates entrusted day-to-day management of the organization to Georges Petit.[55]

Petit had risen through the ranks to head one of the Fédération's largest groupings, the Union Départementale Mutualiste du Nord and therefore satisfied a number of conservative-leaning FNMF delegates. He accepted his "technical presidency" with great aplomb, thereby increasing the freedom of maneuver and effectiveness of Péret. This did not mean that Petit remained entirely off stage, but rather that he worked in a highly collaborative manner with Péret whose political experience and connections made him an ideal leader for the FNMF during legislative deliberations over social insurance.[56] In fact, despite his decidedly less glamorous role in the FNMF, evidence suggests that Petit was a realist and foresaw the mutual movement's future as clearly as anyone, including Péret. Shortly after his election to the copresidency in late 1925, Petit remarked that "the FNMF had arrived at the last page . . . of [its] first chapter . . . the second chapter will, without doubt, see the mutual movement achieve its full potential. And why the new approach? . . . [Because] we old timers of the mutual movement have presided over the emergence of a new spirit that marks a new evolution in mutual doctrine. The mutual movement would like to occupy an essential, indeed unique, place in the implementation of the social insurance legislation."[57] Later, in an address to Minister of Labor André Fallières, Petit openly challenged the parliament to give the mutual movement a chance to demonstrate its expertise and commitment to social insurance: "Mr. Minister, I must say, we've had enough. If you want social insurance, vote on it. Mr. Daniel Vincent said 'the car has been placed on the tracks.' We're good engineers and we will take responsibility for driving that train to a happy destination."[58] Petit also spoke of the need for mutual societies to improve and expand their infrastructure for the provision of medical care. He appealed for looser

---

55 Bennet, *Biographies de personnalités mutualistes,* p. 341.
56 For examples, see "Une Grande conférence de M. Georges Petit sur les assurances sociales" and "Lettre de M. Georges Petit à M. le Sénateur Chauveau," *Bulletin Officiel de la Fédération Nationale de la Mutualité Française* 31 (May–August 1926), 2–5.
57 See the text of speech by Petit at FNMF banquet of 18 October 1925 in *ibid.*, 29 (December 1925), 30–34, especially p. 31.
58 *Ibid.,* 32 (September–December 1926), 44.

government regulations that would permit mutual society unions to use their monetary reserves to build clinics, pharmacies, and hospitals. As we will see in chapter four, Petit's demand indicated a keen understanding of the changes to medical care delivery that national social insurance would engender.

The Petit–Péret presidency positioned the FNMF better than even the most optimistic realists had hoped. The copresidency transformed the FNMF from a largely non-political association of mutual societies into an avowedly partisan participant in parliamentary deliberations over social insurance. This fact became undeniable when, less than a year after Péret's election, he was appointed minister of finance in the Briand government. The appointment was greeted with joy at the FNMF where political clout was viewed as ammunition in a battle for survival against those who would seek a complete state takeover of social insurance, a development that would have suffocated any semblance of an independent mutual movement.[59]

GRINDA OFFERS CONCESSIONS TO PRONATALISTS AND EMPLOYERS

In addition to offering concessions to mutualists, the Grinda report included revisions aimed at mollifying rural interests, pronatalists, and employers. Under heavy pressure from the countryside, Grinda provided an entirely distinct and more supple regime for agriculture than Vincent had proposed.[60] In a bow to pronatalists, Grinda included provisions that made family welfare a central theme of social insurance. Finally, in a less than successful attempt to persuade employers, Grinda emphasized social insurance as an integral component of the scientific rationalization of work.

Addressing the growing familial and pronatalist movements, the report insisted that the "foundation of our bill is essentially pro-family. It is meant less to protect the single worker than the French family as a whole."[61] Nor was this simply rhetorical embellishment. To the strong displeasure of the CCAF, the CAPS seriously considered incorporating family allowances into the Vincent bill. Employers' successful effort to derail the Bokanowski bill, which would have mandated employers to pay family allowances, had been unanimously approved by CAPS. This,

[59] "M. Raoul Péret, Ministre des Finances," in *ibid.*, 30 (January–April 1926), 1.
[60] Agriculture's distinct regime of social insurance will be analyzed in chapter five.
[61] Grinda, *Rapport*, p. 48.

no doubt, gave the committee pause in attempting to push legislation on family allowances once again. Yet the committee was clearly sympathetic to complaints by workers' unions about employers' abuse of family allowances. The report noted that "programs which are entirely controlled by employers are sometimes driven by a spirit of self-interest that greatly limits their effect." The Grinda report contrasted this with its own proposed social insurance system, which "will be founded on mutual respect of rights and responsibilities . . . to maintain a strict equality between the insured and employers."[62] Ultimately, however, the CAPS decided to bestow confidence in French employers and left family allowances outside the bill.[63] Yet it did not leave out families. Grinda permitted workers with families to deduct 2,000 francs for each dependent child from their annual income in calculating their eligibility for social insurance. For example, a worker with an annual base wage of 18,000 francs, which was well above the 10,000 franc threshold for participation in compulsory social insurance, would be considered eligible if he or she could claim four dependent children. Needless to say, this provision constituted an increase by the backdoor of the threshold wage, which employers wished to maintain as low as possible since it increased the number of workers for whom they would have to match insurance premiums. Yet members of the CAPS, being well versed in the pro-family rhetoric that employers had used to defeat the Bokanowski bill, judged correctly that employers would not dare challenge this amendment. Pro-family legislation was simply too popular to assail openly. Grinda also opened coverage to the wives of the insured who paid an additional 75 franc premium. Although voluntary, this provision greatly expanded maternity care for French families. Despite these apparent disregards of employer wishes, the Grinda report included lengthy passages of Taylorist argumentation that the author hoped would persuade employers to support social insurance.

Indeed, a portion of the Grinda report sounds like the productivist voices of Picquenard and Oualid who contributed to industrialists' acceptance of the scientific rationalization of labor during the First World War.[64] Grinda promised more and better workers for French industry: "In our country of weak population growth and a shortage of workers, the employer has an interest in developing the worker's family, not just in quality but also in quantity . . . Social insurance . . . will have a strong impact on population growth." Grinda also argued for a notion of the

[62] *Ibid.*, p. 46.   [63] *Ibid.*, p. 50; Degas, *Les Assurances sociales*, p. 48.
[64] *Bulletin des Usines de Guerre* 49 (2 April 1917). Also see Moutet, "Patrons de progrès."

salaire vital: "In effect, the wage should not only provide for daily needs but must also permit the worker to confront inescapable and fearsome aspects of life." During the war, family allowances marked the incorporation of industrial workers into the national war effort. Now, during the 1920s, Grinda was insisting that social insurance could contribute to the rationalization of "human capital," which was imperative if French industry hoped to compete in international markets. "In every firm there are two essential factors: machines and labor. To the boss, the latter represents a capital investment that must be maintained, replaced, and amortized. This is one of the essential purposes of social insurance." Grinda continues in a stark Taylorist analysis of labor. "Illness insurance will reduce morbidity and thereby reduce work interruptions that impair profits; it will also diminish incubation and convalescence periods during which the quality of work falls dramatically . . . Disability and retirement insurance will ease replacement of the labor force with younger, stronger workers . . ."[65] Grinda's description of social insurance in such terms was, of course, aimed at the *grand patronat* who would understand, if not accept, the argument. We take up employers' reaction to Grinda's appeal in the next chapter. There we will see that not only did employers refuse to accept any beneficial aspect of compulsory social insurance, they responded with a sophisticated counterattack in an attempt to block parliamentary approval.

CONCLUSION

The Chamber approved Grinda's version of compulsory social insurance on 9 April 1924. The bill was introduced in the Senate on the same day where proponents hoped for a quick consideration and vote. However, as in the Chamber, such a complex proposal attracted the interest of several committees and lobbyists. Over four years would pass before French legislators could finally approve social insurance legislation. Even then the law would prompt such intense wrangling over its application that an additional two years would be required until final legislation and regulatory guidelines (*règlements d'administration publiques*) could be issued. Nevertheless, the approval of the Grinda report marked a milestone in the history of French social welfare. Although it found many critics among workers and employers alike, Grinda represented an important step in the creation of national social welfare. Its inclusion of all major risks and

[65] Grinda, *Rapport*, p. 45.

compulsory nature represented an unprecedented victory of center and center-left reformers over conservatives who favored a continuation of traditional voluntarist social protection.

Equally important is the outcome of the battle between traditionalists and realists that transformed the mutual movement into an enthusiastic backer of a state-mandated system. The accession of Raoul Péret and Georges Petit as FNMF copresidents marked a decisive victory for the realists who believed that support for a "mutualized" social insurance system presented an effective strategy at the dawn of a new era of social welfare. Through collaboration with mutual-friendly legislators, the FNMF could effectively influence parliament's reaction to the German model of social insurance that was now unavoidably within the confines of the Hexagon. Moreover, social insurance legislation that placed mutual societies at its center offered the FNMF an effective response to the transformation of work and social relations inherent in industrialization. Péret and Petit conceded fundamental aspects of mutual doctrine in exchange for the possibility of a greatly expanded membership among the working class. Although this change in strategy was not achieved without a messy public skirmish, when the last vote had been counted in parliament's first major battle over obligatory social insurance, the FNMF could be counted among the winners.

The Chamber's approval of the Grinda report instigated a flurry of maneuvers by employers. The *grand patronat* realized that their only hope of stopping social insurance lay in the creation of an employer-controlled regime of social protection that offered similar benefits. This, they believed, would dissipate parliamentary support for social insurance, leaving them in control of a cheaper and more malleable system of worker welfare. Not surprisingly, employers found their already well-developed family allowance *caisses* to be the ideal institutions around which to build a comprehensive system of worker welfare. In some cases, employers sought to bring mutual societies into the service of their *caisses*. Despite these occasional alliances, however, the critical battle for social insurance in the 1920s passed from mutual leaders to workers' unions which alone confronted employers' formidable family allowance movement. It is to this struggle between employers and workers for control of the nation's fledgling social welfare system that we now turn.

3

Battle for control of social welfare: workers versus employers

Employer control of family allowances and parliament's consideration of social insurance prompted rancorous debates within the working class. Union leaders failed to stop the family allowance movement because at virtually every turn they were confounded by divisions among their own rank and file. Workers with large families supported employers' payment of allowances. Indeed, they sometimes called on their syndicate chiefs to exert pressure on their employer to affiliate with a *caisse de compensation*. This division in the working class was exacerbated in 1919 with the creation of a new union based on social Catholic ideals, the Confédération Française des Travailleurs Chrétiens (CFTC). The 1920 Congress at Tours, where the French left split into rivaling socialist and communist parties further fragmented the working class on the question of social welfare. Two workers' unions emerged: the old CGT that remained allied with the socialists and the newly founded, pro-Soviet Confédération Générale du Travail Unitaire (CGTU). Although the CGT and CGTU leaderships fought together against employer-controlled family allowances, they attacked each other bitterly over the question of social insurance. The CGT sided with mutual leaders in support of social insurance. But leaders of the new CGTU, alongside communist deputies, denounced the Chamber-approved measure as a capitalist deception.

Employers exhibited more unity than their union adversaries did, but they too were wracked by a serious split. The rift emanated from the recovered territories of Alsace-Lorraine where German-style social insurance enjoyed the widespread support of industrialists. Employers of Alsace-Lorraine also sought to guard their autonomous practices in family assistance, an endeavor that proved increasingly difficult in the face of France's growing family allowance movement. However, on the question of social insurance, they advocated the extension of a compulsory system, which closely resembled their region's own, to the rest of France.

WORKERS, WAGES, AND FAMILY ALLOWANCES

The CGT emerged from the First World War with a greatly expanded membership and determined to gain substantial concessions from employers. The strikes of 1919 and 1920, however, were met with an equally determined *patronat*, including the newly organized GIMM, as well as a right-wing majority in the Chamber of Deputies. As a result, most labor strikes mounted in the two years following the Armistice failed to achieve significant gains. Bitter acrimony over defeat led to large-scale worker abandonment of the CGT. From a peak of approximately two million members at the beginning of 1920, CGT membership fell to only 600,000 by the end of the year due to the creation of the CGTU. These circumstances, in conjunction with the Bolshevik revolution, alienated many moderate workers and aided Jules Zirnheld in creating the CFTC. The new centrist union went on to achieve a membership of 150,000 by decade's end.

Now divided into three federations, French workers faced an increasingly sophisticated industrial *patronat* that was determined to hold down wages following wartime increases. Their wage policy, based on the *salaire vital*, prompted one contemporary observer of the Paris metals industry to comment that the institution of family allowances provided fresh evidence that Ricardo's natural price of labor theory had been right after all. According to Ricardo's theory, wages tended toward a natural price at which workers and their families could live and reproduce, nothing more, nothing less.[1] The resurrection of Ricardo was not unwarranted if one examines the remuneration trends that family allowances produced in the metals sector during the 1920s, which are illustrated in figure 5.

Under CCRP rules and similarly constructed family allowance schedules nationwide, small families fared badly because increases for first and second children lagged well behind those for later siblings. As we see in figure 5, during the immediate postwar years, the difference between childless workers' wages and the wages of their coworkers with dependent children was roughly constant, reflecting the absence of progressivity in the wartime allowance schedule. Beginning with the enactment of a progressive schedule in the mid-twenties, however, wages of workers with three or more dependent children rose much more quickly than those of their less prolific comrades. In fact, most workers (including ineligible women, childless men, and parents with only one child) saw their

---

[1] David Ricardo, *The Principles of Political Economy and Taxation*, first published in 1810 (London: Dent, 1987), p. 52.

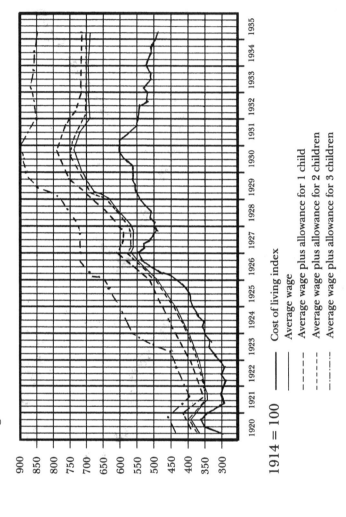

Cost of living index

900
850
800
750
700
650
600
550
500
450
400
350
300

1914 = 100

1920 1921 1922 1923 1924 1925 1926 1927 1928 1929 1930 1931 1932 1933 1934 1935

—— Cost of living index

—— Average wage

- - - Average wage plus allowance for 1 child

- - - Average wage plus allowance for 2 children

-·-·- Average wage plus allowance for 3 children

Figure 5 Cost of living and wages according to family size in the Paris metals industry, Jean Duporcq, *Les Œuvres sociales dans la métallurgie française* (Paris: Université de Paris, 1936), p. 48; *Bulletin de la Statistique Générale de la France* (July–September 1928), pp. 412–413.

real wages stagnate from the third quarter of 1925 through the first quarter of 1928. Workers with two children did not fare much better, although they did remain above the bare cost of living during the financial crisis of 1924 to 1926. During that time the French franc lost 80 percent of its value on foreign markets, leading to a surge in the cost of living due to more expensive imported products. Stable economic conditions returned to France in 1928 but were disrupted again by the worldwide economic crisis that arrived in France after 1930. The Great Depression, of course, meant deflation. Those workers who were lucky enough to remain employed, enjoyed a substantial differential between earnings and the cost of living, even though their real wages trickled downward in the early 1930s.[2]

In the light of such trends one must ask what strategies French unions pursued to counteract the corrosive effect of family allowances on wages. Unfortunately, union leaders could do very little. In late 1922, the official charged with formulating CGT policy toward family allowances, Georges Buisson, commented that to "protest against family allowances would prove, under current conditions, totally childish."[3] What Buisson sought instead was the incorporation of family allowances into the Grinda social insurance bill, which was then under consideration by the CAPS in the Chamber. This, Buisson asserted, would remove control of family welfare from employers, who brandished it as a weapon against labor, and place it properly among the "protections provided by social insurance that the collective should organize."[4] As we saw in the previous chapter, this strategy failed; Grinda refused to go beyond scolding employers for their self-serving use of family allowances and declined to include them in his revision of the Vincent bill.

The authority of the CGT and CGTU leaderships to demand the inclusion of family allowances in the Grinda bill suffered from a vocal minority of rank-and-file members with large families. What is more, these family men tended to be older, more experienced workers and therefore likely to wield influential positions in local syndicates. Thus, despite publication by *l'Humanité* of a GIMM memo written by Richemond enjoining all GIMM members to refuse general wage increases and replace them with family allowances, many local syndicates remained supportive of family allowances.[5] In direct contradiction to their national leaderships,

---

[2] CCRP Commission de gestion, *procès-verbaux*, 22 October 1920; GIMM Annuaires 1923–1936, AN 39 AS 873; Bonvoisin's annual reports "Rapport moral," Ie–XIXe Congrès National des Allocations Familiales, *comptes rendu*, 1920–1939.
[3] *Le Peuple*, 24 December 1922.   [4] *Ibid.*
[5] *L'Humanité*, 3 May 1923; *La Vie Ouvrière*, 4 May 1923.

pro-allowance *cégétistes* and *unitaires* demanded that all employers join a *caisse de compensation*. In fact, a CGT national secretary could proclaim that "two million workers benefit from the advantages accorded by employer *caisses*. It would be impossible to tell these workers that they must abstain from receiving these special allowances reserved for fathers. I am for the spread of the system because . . . there are incredible differences in the pay of workers with children according to whether they work for a firm affiliated with a *caisse de compensation*."[6] Sympathy for workers whose employers did not pay family allowances underlines the multiple divisions that the family allowance movement engendered in workers' unions. Not only did parents square off against their childless peers within factories already paying allowances, but also workers in firms that were not affiliated with a *caisse* demanded union action *in favor* of family allowances.

Official publications of the CGT adopted a defeatist attitude on family allowances.[7] *La Voix du Peuple* published a lengthy article meant to educate workers on the corrosive effect of family allowances on wages and solidarity. But the exposé exhibited a marked departure from the periodical's usually vociferous attacks on employer initiatives. Its condemnation of family allowances consisted of noting that "some of our comrades have concluded that we must fight against the extension of family allowances."[8] This half-hearted reproach was followed by an even more surprising admission: "our organizations do not have any sufficient means at their disposal to fight against the application or spread of family allowances. Union efforts can really only act on this matter in the course of collective bargaining, which up to this time has not included the issue; one cannot look for change in the near future."[9] CGT leaders recognized that they must respect workers with large families and should not "diminish their trying circumstances."[10] Their inability to rally union membership against employer allowances left the union with little choice but to warn local syndicates and offer an alternative vision of family welfare. A resolution at the Congress of 1923 remained the CGT's official position until the Popular Front in 1936. The declaration demanded collective control of family welfare and included a warning that the current system of *caisses* provided personal information to employers that might hamper workers' ultimate emancipation.[11] Although this may have

---

[6] *Le Peuple*, 29 December 1922.
[7] Audouin, *Les Caisses de compensation*, pp. 92–93.   [8] *La Voix du Peuple*, January 1923, p. 31.
[9] *Ibid.*   [10] *Ibid.*, p. 32.
[11] CGT Congrès Confédéral de Paris, *compte rendu*, "Rapports moral et financier," 17–20 September 1929, pp. 239–240.

restrained some local CGT syndicates from active support of employer-controlled *caisses*, its aims were impractical in the face of employers' formidable family allowance movement whose course by 1923 appeared immune to parliamentary interference.

The frustration of the CGT and CGTU leaderships rose in 1924 as France entered a financial crisis. In May, capital flight soared as a result of the *cartel des gauches'* campaign platform of exchange controls. A *cartel* victory combined with underlying concerns about Germany's ability to continue reparations payments cast serious doubt on the government's capacity to meet its obligations. By early summer, the French currency entered a tailspin on international markets, losing 80 percent of its value before Prime Minister Raymond Poincaré, heading a new government of national union, succeeded in stabilizing the situation. Although much of the populace praised Poincaré for his actions, the devaluation represented a serious blow to workers' standard of living.[12] Devaluation meant increased costs for imported products, further exacerbating inflationary trends built into the economy since the war. The CGTU and the CGT accused employers of profiting from the crisis at workers' expense. Industrialists, they charged, enjoyed increased export earnings because of a cheap franc while simultaneously saving on labor costs by refusing all but the most meager wage increases.[13] Instead of granting increases that would maintain the real value of wages for all workers, GIMM pressured the CCRP in 1924 and 1926 to raise family allowances.[14] In response, CGT leaders demanded "remuneration in relation to real purchasing power for all workers" instead of "pseudo-philanthropic overtures that are not distinguishable from the humiliation of charity."[15] Employers flatly refused. GIMM leaders feared the franc crisis would destabilize the economy and revitalize worker demands that wages be pegged to the cost of living.[16] The financial crisis of 1924–1926 further bolstered employers' commitment to family allowances. Allowances provided an ideal instrument for minimizing wage increases while maintaining social peace. Unions of the left were unsuccessful in fashioning an effective response to this strategy. Allowances divided workers according to family circumstances and drove a wedge between rank-and-file members and union leaders.

---

[12] Kemp, *The French Economy*, pp. 81–82.
[13] *L'Humanité*, 29 March 1924; *Le Peuple*, 24 March 1924.
[14] GIMM Conseil d'administration, *procès-verbaux*, 17 March 1926, AN 39 AS 850.
[15] *Le Peuple*, 24 March 1924.
[16] GIMM Conseil d'administration, *procès-verbaux*, 5 November 1925 and 30 July 1926, AN 39 AS 850.

In contrast to the difficulty of leftist unions, the CFTC achieved a unified stance on family allowances. Ideologically, the new union was predisposed toward pro-family policies, never quarreling with the fundamental principle that workers with children should be paid more, even if it came at the cost of general wage increases.[17] That said, it should not be assumed that the CFTC represented the workers' incarnation of nineteenth-century social Catholicism and was thus entirely pliable in the hands of allowance-paying employers. Rather, the CFTC represented the convergence of diverse tendencies toward centrist syndicalism brought together by a fear of Bolshevism. This diversity complicated the CFTC's response to the family allowance movement. Some founding members wanted a Church-centered clerical union, similar to Albert de Mun's nineteenth-century Cercle Catholique d'Ouvriers, which had welcomed employer participation. This corporatist faction within the union embraced family allowances as a munificent act and saw little wrong with the system as currently structured. Other CFTC founders rejected collaboration with employers, preferring a Catholic union that was open exclusively to wage earners, yet actively anti-Marxist. Still others called for a union with no explicit confessional affiliation at all, preferring to remain neutral on the religious question.[18]

These diverse camps of the CFTC settled on a policy of qualified support for family allowances, but they demanded that all employers be compelled to join a *caisse de compensation*. CFTC Secretary-General Gaston Tessier had been among the most vocal proponents of the Bokanowski bill in 1920–1921. Instead of rejecting employers' family allowance *caisses*, Tessier offered ample praise but he also called for substantial reforms. He noted that a large number of employers would always remain outside the family allowance movement in the absence of a legal mandate.[19] In 1924, the CFTC further insisted that the administration of *caisses* be "carried out jointly by mixed governing boards, elected by employers' and workers' organizations according to the principle of proportional representation."[20] This demand represented a significant hardening of the CFTC's position. However, similar to the CGT and CGTU, the CFTC lacked leverage to pressure employers to bring about desired reforms. During the 1920s employers and their *caisses* could effectively

---

[17] *La Journée Industrielle*, 13–14 March and 27 November 1921.
[18] Michel Launay, *La CFTC: origines et développement, 1919–1940* (Paris: La Sorbonne, 1986), pp. 21–24.
[19] Conseil Supérieur du Travail, *compte rendu et annexes*, 16 November 1921.
[20] Ve Congrès National de la CFTC, *compte rendu*, June 1924, Circulaire mensuelle, no. 45, p. 314.

ignore workers' unions. Such a response was made possible not only by divisions within workers' unions between *pères de familles* and their single comrades but also between men and women, a distinction that took on increasing importance with the scientific rationalization of work.

During the war, the ministry of armament had encouraged industrialists to rationalize production for the sake of national salvation.[21] The promise of greater productivity through scientific rationalization appealed not only to employers but also to workers, who saw in it the potential for increased wages. After the Armistice, industrialists continued their rationalizing efforts, which included the creation of new job classifications that greatly increased the division of tasks within their plants.[22] In response, the CGT and CGTU metals syndicates adopted resolutions, which demanded that the rationalization plans take working conditions into consideration.[23] Indeed, workers compared the new Taylorized job classifications with the *salaire vital*. That said, union leaders were not strictly opposed to wage bonuses, but they noted that family allowances were not proper bonuses. As one CGTU leader put it, family allowances exposed employers' "double attitude" toward the division of labor. On the one hand, worker productivity was enshrined as the determining factor in wages; on the other, a substantial wage supplement was awarded purely according to family status.[24]

Employers soon found that women workers, who had flooded the factories during wartime, bolstered their family allowance wage strategy and rationalization schemes.[25] Rationalization included the creation of new low-paying jobs as a result of task subdivisions. Women were often assigned these new positions, causing men to view them as detrimental to overall wage levels and working conditions. At a 1927 CGTU conference, metal worker Alice Brisset described the views of some of her male comrades who believed that "wages must permit a worker to have his wife at home with children . . . consequently we must eliminate women workers from the factories. That would permit us to decrease the supply of labor and demand better wages . . ."[26] Brisset attributed these sentiments to employers' rationalization schemes under which women were paid less to assume slightly modified male jobs.[27] She succeeded in obtaining a

---

[21] *Bulletin des Usines de Guerre* 49 (2 April 1917).
[22] Humphreys, *Taylorism in France*, p. 12; Moutet, "Patrons de progrès ou patrons de combat?"
[23] *L'Humanité*, 17 November 1926.   [24] *Ibid.*, 28 February 1924.
[25] See Downs, *Manufacturing Inequality*, p. 7.
[26] Fédération Unitaire des Ouvriers et Ouvrières sur Métaux (CGTU), IVe Congrès National, *rapports et compte rendu*, 1927, p. 260.
[27] *Ibid.*, p. 261.

resolution from the assembled delegates which condemned all arguments that presupposed that the elimination of women workers would resolve the problem of wages, as well as a demand in favor of "equal pay for equal work."[28] Nevertheless, disagreements between rank-and-file men and their women coworkers continued to hamper worker solidarity at the factory level.[29]

These disagreements included issues of childcare, the method of payment of family allowances, and their relative importance for women. At a general assembly of Citroën workers in December 1926, Brisset noted that far too many infants died from childhood diseases. She thus called for the company to reopen their nurseries and nursing facilities that had been available during the war. But Brisset's appeal was ignored by the overwhelmingly male audience of Citroën workers who appeared little interested in the working conditions of their female colleagues. The method by which family allowances were paid also proved divisive to relations between men and women. CGT leader Martin Labe opposed the practice by some *caisses* of delivering allowance checks directly to workers' wives, asking: "Can we accept the infliction of this gratuitous insult to fathers who are breadwinners?"[30] By voicing these sentiments, Labe distanced himself from feminists in the Communist party who preferred that allowances be sent to the mother whether she was the eligible worker or childcare giver. Communist activist Marthe Bigot charged employers who failed to pay allowances to the mother with contributing to "the economic inferiority of the woman, placing her absolutely under the domination of her husband."[31] Thus, employers gained an odd ally in their policy of making allowance checks payable to the household's primary childcare giver. The difference between male and female wages and their relation to family allowances caused yet another division between women and men. CGTU metal worker from the Seine, Marguerite Routier, noted that family allowances were equal for women and men but that men were not as sensitive to the demands of maternity and childcare. When allowances were docked for strike-related absences,

[28] *Ibid.*, p. 269.
[29] Even Brisset's presence at the conference was exceptional. Women remained almost entirely absent from the leadership of CGTU and CGT metal workers' syndicates. Fédération Unitaire des Ouvriers et Ouvrières sur Métaux (CGTU), IIIe Congrès National, *rapports et compte rendu*, 1925, pp. 205–206. Also see Fédération des Ouvriers en Métaux (CGT), XIIe Congrès Fédéral, *compte rendu*, September 1935, p. 347.
[30] Fédération des Ouvriers des Métaux (CGT), VIIe Congrès Fédéral, *compte rendu*, August 1925, p. 287.
[31] *L'Ouvrière* 22 (5 August 1922).

women were thus asked to make greater sacrifices than their male coworkers because allowances made up a larger proportion of their take-home pay.[32]

Discrimination according to gender reinforced employers' wage strategy based on the *salaire vital*. As long as equal pay for equal work for women remained an unfulfilled demand, the prospect of dismantling the system of employer-controlled family allowances remained unlikely. As worker attitudes suggested, distinction on the basis of gender was tied to that of dependency and social norms. The postwar resurgence of the domestic ideal dictated that women remain at home to care for children and, if seeking employment, accept lower wages than men. The acceptance of this social paradigm by union men contributed to the impotence of leftist unions. No matter how theoretically committed union leaders were to equal pay for equal work, rank-and-file men and local syndicate bosses remained ambivalent about wage equity and women workers in general. Thus, men's acceptance that women should be paid less regardless of their performance made wage discrimination by employers against childless workers easier to justify. In the latter case employers did not need to create elaborate job classification systems. They needed only to point to the needs of dependent children. Implicit in employers' strategy was the castigation of childless workers for their social irresponsibility, which, during an era of growing pronatalism, held significant social assent.

SOCIAL INSURANCE: PROPONENTS AND OPPONENTS

Given employers' record on family allowances, CGT leaders were initially wary of any employer involvement in social insurance. But both the Vincent proposal of 1921 and Grinda's revision in 1923, achieved such a level of benefits and worker control that the CGT supported the legislation with certain modifications. Likewise, the CFTC approved of the legislation and sought to use its influence with social Catholic employers to build support. Alone among workers unions the CGTU rejected both of the Chamber's social insurance bills, labeling them as appeasement measures by which the working class must not tricked.

The CGT's early position on social insurance ruled out employer involvement altogether. Instead, the union called for a heavy tax on production in conjunction with small worker contributions to fund

---

[32] Fédération Unitaire des Ouvriers et Ouvrières sur Métaux (CGTU), IIIe Congrès National, *rapports et compte rendu*, 1925, pp. 205–207.

benefits.[33] The Vincent bill, however, prompted cautious approval from the socialists and their CGT allies. They remarked that the "proposed reform is not socialist in nature; it demands a large contribution from the insured, which in fairness, should be born by the state as the embodiment of the collective." Nevertheless the socialists embraced the law, noting its "immediate and important advantages" and gave its parliamentary representatives a mandate to accept the bill as a solid beginning for social insurance legislation. Socialists wanted several substantial amendments, including the addition of unemployment coverage. They insisted that social protections that relied on worker and employer contributions were meaningless without a contingency for involuntary unemployment. On this point, their opponents had little reply. For if a worker became un-employed due to circumstances beyond his or her control, medical and other benefits were withdrawn, precisely at the moment when the risk of destitution became most threatening. Socialists also demanded that retirement benefits include medical coverage. This modification also ap-pealed to many social reformers since a retired worker's pension could easily be drained by medical expenses, forcing him or her to choose between pharmaceuticals and food. Lastly, the CGT sought the dele-tion of contributions for workers who fell into the lowest of the six wage categories, namely those who earned less than 1,200 francs per year.[34] Despite significant legislative support, CGT leaders had little prospect of achieving these changes in Grinda's revision because of the opposi-tion that the Vincent bill had engendered among the *grand patronat*. In fact, CGT leaders feared that Grinda might delete from the Vincent bill such fundamental measures as obligation, paycheck withholding, and the simultaneous application of illness, disability, and retirement insur-ance. For several months leading up to completion of the Grinda report, employers had been pushing for major changes to these aspects of the Vincent bill. Grinda unveiled his work in late January 1923, just as CGT delegates were gathering in Paris for their annual meeting. Prompted to quickly summarize the Grinda bill to the convoked delegates, a pleas-antly surprised CGT official announced: "I don't see myself as a fan of this parliament nor a defender of its committee ... but it must be said, the bill [Grinda] constitutes an important development that can be accepted as the basis for social insurance in our country."[35] A few

[33] Degas, *Les Assurances sociales*, pp. 19–20.   [34] Lebas, *L'Assurance sociale*, pp. 16–18.
[35] "Rapporteur de la question au Congrès de la CGT," Perrot, cited by A. Rey, *La Question des assurances sociales* (Paris: Alcan, 1925), pp. 384–385. Rey was head of propaganda for the CGT during the 1920s.

days later, the socialist party added its voice of support to the Grinda bill, noting that "although the bill does not give full satisfaction . . . it nonetheless constitutes a partial realization of workers' demands." As we saw in the previous chapter, the major revisions that Grinda undertook concerned administrative control of social insurance *caisses*. These changes, which favored the propagation of autonomous mutual societies, were accepted by the CGT without discussion. Socialists continued to demand more representation on *caisse* governing boards, but workers' unions felt comfortable with the central role that legislators had cast the mutual movement.[36]

The CFTC's reception of the Chamber social insurance bills owes much to the union's particular strength in the densely Catholic departments of the recovered territories. Indeed, the extension of Alsace-Lorraine's social insurance regime to the rest of France constituted one of the founding demands of the new Catholic trade union. CFTC leaders approved the Vincent bill at the CFTC's second national assembly in May 1921. Afterwards, CFTC Secretary-General Gaston Tessier left on a lengthy study tour of Alsace. He visited local social insurance *caisses* in Mulhouse and Strasbourg, the central *office des assurances* in Strasbourg, as well as sanatoria and spas in the Vosges mountains. Subsequently, the CFTC leadership lobbied the government, parliament, and employers in favor of the Grinda bill. In his appeals to public officials, Tessier noted that Catholic thought had repeatedly been the inspiration for measures to improve workers' lives. Albert de Mun had proposed social insurance legislation in 1886 and 1892. These initiatives were followed by others, most notably by Abbé Lemire in 1900 and Gailhard-Bancel in 1905. Tessier also appealed to employers' paternalism by recalling the Encyclical *Graves de Communi*. In it, Léon XIII asserted that "One of the glories of charity is that it is not just a transitory compassion for people in distress, but above all the support for a network of permanent institutions . . . to obtain over time that they [workers] insure themselves, at least in part, their future." Entreaties by the CFTC also pointed to Vatican support for individual *prévoyance* and savings. Thus, CFTC leaders viewed the mutualist bent of the Grinda bill as a natural complement to France's existing regime of voluntary social protection.[37]

In contrast to the CGT and CFTC, communists condemned the social insurance proposals of the early 1920s as a trick. Writing in *L'Humanité*,

---

[36] XXe Congrès National du Parti Socialiste, Paris, *compte rendu*, 3–6 February 1923, pp. 20–21.
[37] Gaston Tessier, *En face des assurances sociales* (Paris: Edition Spes, 1929), pp. 9–14.

Félix Paoli insisted that the legislation "will only be a law of appeasement, refusing, as always, the social justice for which we have fought and
will not see until there is a total transformation of the economy." Paoli
was especially incensed at Grinda's concessions to mutual societies and
compulsory worker contributions to them. He mocked the *salaire vital*
as an insufficient leftover, part of which the bourgeoisie now wants to
reclaim in order to pay for a "derisory realization" of social welfare.[38]
Criticism by CGTU syndicates was even more sweeping. The Fédération
Unitaire du Textile, for example, noted that the law denied benefits to
foreign workers, left the unemployed uncovered, and failed to foresee
fluctuations in the real value of pensions and allowances.[39] In addition
to amendments which could alleviate these concerns, the CGTU demanded radical change in the bill's financial system and function. They
suggested a nationalization of all insurance services, the profits from
which could be used to pay for social insurance. *Unitaires* were especially
leery of the bill's creation of capitalized funds, which "will place enor-
mous sums in the hands of the State. This system would give predominance to the bourgeoisie and capitalists . . . we fear that this accumulated
capital . . . would not be used for its intended purpose, but rather for war
and the reinforcement of the bourgeoisie's reign."[40] To avoid such a
scenario, communists insisted that workers' unions manage the financial resources of social insurance. Yet despite the apparent monopoly
over control of social insurance which this would entail, the *unitaires* conceded that "mutualist influence over insurance does not bother us as long
as participants can freely choose their grouping." In fact, the CGTU's
sole concern regarding mutual societies was Grinda's presumption of
association that favored the maintenance of mutual membership.[41] This
marked a remarkably soft attitude toward the mutual movement when
juxtaposed to the revolutionary demands regarding the state and employers. At first blush, communist reaction to Grinda appeared paradoxical.
On the one hand the CGTU set preconditions, such as the nationalization of the private insurance industry that, in their own words, "will only
be obtained after the proletariat achieves power through revolution."[42]

---

[38] *L'Humanité*, 11 June 1923.
[39] IIIe Congrès de la Fédération Unitaire du Textile, *compte rendu*, Paris, 28–30 November 1926,
p. 56.
[40] IIIe Congrès de la Fédération Unitaire du Textile, *compte rendu*, Paris, 28–30 November 1926,
p. 59.
[41] See chapter 2.
[42] IIIe Congrès de la Fédération Unitaire du Textile, *compte rendu*, Paris, 28–30 November 1926,
p. 60.

But on the other hand, the *unitaires* signaled their willingness to abide mutual societies, whose ties to private capital were well known. One can only conclude that despite their harsh rhetoric, communist opinion on the Grinda report remained sufficiently diverse between syndicates and national leadership that eventual approval of social insurance legislation based on a mutual model could not be ruled out. The *grand patronat*, on the other hand, engaged in a variety of maneuvers to prevent realization of national social insurance.

EMPLOYERS, WELFARE, AND SOCIAL INSURANCE

Employer opposition to the social insurance bills under parliamentary consideration during the 1920s was twofold. First, they sought to instill a fear of the unknown among legislators and the public about the ramifications of such sweeping legislation. Second, employers pursued a strategy of preemption. That is, they expanded their already extensive family allowance *caisses* into global welfare providers. Employers hoped that this second initiative would weaken legislative and popular support for compulsory social insurance. However, employers were not as unified as such a sophisticated strategy might suggest. Important rifts in their ranks appeared in the recovered territories where industrialists hoped to preserve not only the social insurance regime bequeathed to them by the Reich but also a German-style system of family welfare.

Shortly after the introduction of the Vincent bill, a train of critical articles began to appear in influential journals, especially the *Revue Politique et Parlementaire* and *L'Economiste Français*. Some made outlandish claims that flew in the face of economic principles. For example, one questioned Vincent's method of calculating the economic cost of the program. Instead of accepting the bill's predicted charge to the state budget, which totaled between 156 million and 336 million francs annually, the author insisted that one must also consider the totality of employer and worker premiums as lost to national production. This argument suggested a frightening scenario: a reduction in gross national product of approximately 4.5 billion francs. But the author conveniently overlooked the investment of workers and employers' insurance contributions as well as the insured's spending of their cash and in-kind benefits, both of which would contribute to national production.[43] Another, more sophisticated critique appeared in February 1923, this time of the Grinda revision.

---

[43] F. Achard, "Le projet de loi sur les assurances sociales," *Revue Politique et Parlementaire* (May 1922), 259–275, especially, pp. 262–264.

The author was René Hubert, a professor at the University of Lille and an adviser to the UIMM. According to André Rey, head of propaganda for the CGT, Hubert's attack proved to be one of the most effective. Instead of attempting fatuous claims, Hubert skillfully cast doubt on the suppositions contained in the bill. Having built a strong case that virtually none of the cost estimates were absolutely certain, Hubert could convincingly characterize passage of the law as "the greatest leap into the unknown" ever contemplated by a French legislature.[44] Cogent criticism also continued to be accompanied by less convincing indictments. As the outlines of the law became clear, the right-leaning press became shrill in its denunciations. One magazine characterized the 1928 legislation as "crazy . . . monstrous . . . a law for which one has to be ashamed."[45] Of course, representatives of the country's most powerful employer associations also entered the fray. These included Alfred Lambert-Ribot of the Comité des Forges and René Duchemin, president of the Confédération Générale de la Production Française (CGPF).

Speaking at a roundtable discussion sponsored by the Comité d'Etudes Sociales et Politiques in Paris, Lambert-Ribot outlined the position of the *grand patronat*. He began by predicting dire ramifications for French producers in both domestic and foreign markets. The reaction of industrialists such as Citroën and Renault, Lambert-Ribot confided, would be to pass on the cost of their employer contributions to the consumer. These costs would vary from employer to employer, depending on how much workers' unions demanded in compensatory wage hikes for their own social insurance paycheck deductions as well as the proportion of social-insurance eligible workers among their personnel. Yet price increases would not be confined uniquely to sectors affected by the law. All producers, even railroads and mining, where workers already enjoyed more extensive social welfare benefits, would raise prices because workers in these sectors would face a higher cost of living and would therefore demand compensatory wage increases. Similarly, Lambert-Ribot argued, French products would become more expensive in foreign markets, leading to export losses and pressures to further devalue the franc. Lambert-Ribot rejected the argument that since employers in other nations also bore the cost of social insurance, French producers would not be hurt. He noted that labor cost comparisons across

---

[44] *Revue Politique et Parlementaire* (10 February and 10 April 1923) cited by Rey, *La Question des Assurances sociales*, p. 215.

[45] "La Loi folle: De nouvelles protestations contre les assurances sociales," *La France Active* 102 (July–August 1929), pp. 49–56.

international frontiers were a much trickier endeavor than looking at social welfare taxes. Lambert-Ribot foresaw several negative consequences that would follow a social-insurance induced inflationary spiral. First, workers would suffer a decrease in real wages because their wage demands generally lagged behind price increases. Second, producers would not only be disadvantaged in both their foreign markets but also at home. Without prompt tariff protection, which would itself contribute to inflation, producers would cut their profit margins to meet the lower prices of foreign competitors. These profits would otherwise be invested and thereby contribute to economic growth and job creation. Lambert-Ribot placed the reduction in annual domestic investment at 1.2 billion francs out of a total of 15 billion francs. He recognized the social good that would result from the building of hospitals, clinics, and sanatoria, to which some of these funds would be devoted. But their loss to commerce and industry, he insisted, represented the most unacceptable effect of social insurance legislation. Ultimately, Lambert-Ribot predicted a long-term catastrophe for France's economy which could last as long as a decade.[46] The president of the CGPF added a wider concern to Lambert-Ribot's warnings. Duchemin believed that the imposition of social insurance would hit hardest in the agricultural sector where salaries tended to be lower and the volatility of prices much greater. These workers would nonetheless be subjected to the same increases in the cost of living emanating from the urban centers. Difficulties in agriculture, he warned, would "exacerbate desertion of the countryside and worsen the agricultural crisis." Indeed, he believed a vicious cycle would take hold where the increased cost of food (due to social insurance premiums) would abet the inevitable price increases in manufactures, resulting in a "truly perilous threat to the workings of the national economy."[47]

Employers suggested several changes to the legislation in order to prevent such a calamity. They believed that "when you want to make a reform like this, you have to first of all decide how much you can afford."[48] This approach led directly to employers' demand that social insurance be instituted in stages. In this way the full burden of each

---

[46] Alfred Lambert-Ribot, Comité National d'Etudes Sociales et Politiques, *procès-verbaux*, 10 February 1930, pp. 9–16.

[47] R.-P. Duchemin, letter addressed to the Conseil d'Etat, "La Confédération Générale de la Production Française et les Assurances Sociales," reprinted in *Les Assurances Sociales* 4 (April 1930), pp. 25–28.

[48] Lambert-Ribot, Comité National d'Etudes Sociales et Politiques, *procès-verbaux*, 10 February 1930, p. 16.

insurance, i.e. illness, disability, retirement, could be ascertained before committing additional resources. The UIMM charged that it "would be impractical and dangerous to want . . . all at once, to create a French insurance system that simultaneously covered, illness, maternity, death, disability, and retirement."[49] In other words, employers rejected the unity of insurance, a principle that the CGT and CFTC viewed as fundamental. Workers' unions were heartened by Grinda's support for the principle of unity: "Can one really insure a worker against short-term illness without foreseeing, at the same time, protective measures if the illness persists . . . It is impossible to create insurance against illness that is not complemented by disability protections nor disability insurance without retirement pensions."[50] Employers, however rejected this logic, maintaining that the country simply could not predict and therefore could not afford the risk of creating a unified system all at once. They believed that a serial application of social protections was imperative "for the working class to grow accustomed to the function of social insurance [and] for the state to overcome the challenge of training the necessary administrative personnel . . ."[51] Employers particularly condemned Grinda's commitment to retirement pensions. To guarantee a specific payment to retirees, Lambert-Ribot asserted, when so much depends on the performance of capitalized funds, "is to be obliged at some time or another to augment these funds with additional resources."[52] Employers thus raised a host of serious questions about the financial and economic ramifications of obligatory social insurance. But their deliberations behind closed doors reflected a very different fear, namely their loss of control over worker welfare.

As a creature of the *grand patronat*, the CCAF threw its weight into the battle against social insurance. Leaders of the family allowance movement had primary and secondary goals in this endeavor. In the first instance, they hoped that by voluntarily extending some version of the benefits foreseen in the Grinda bill, they could convince enough legislators that state-mandated social insurance was superfluous and therefore unnecessary. Employers viewed this as a best case scenario. It held out the promise of not only a major parliamentary victory but also of a fundamental shift in control of social welfare. In a sense, the *grand*

[49] Degas, *Les Assurances sociales*, pp. 26–27.   [50] Grinda, *Rapport*, p. 36.

[51] Degas, *Les Assurances sociales*, pp. 26–27.

[52] Lambert-Ribot, Comité National d'Etudes Sociales et Politiques, *procès-verbaux*, 10 February 1930, p. 19. Also see Jean Siegler, "Le Projet de loi sur les assurances sociales et les institutions d'initiative privée," *Revue Politique et Parlementaire* (September 1924), 399–409.

patronat sought to create a sophisticated regime of *patronage* that would obviate state intervention, bolster employer control over workers, all the while appearing as a natural system of interdependence between management and labor.[53] The cost of social protections would be shared between employer and employee, but only by being employed, a status over which the *patronat* exercised proportionally greater influence, would workers have access to low-cost welfare protections. That said, employers would not enjoy complete freedom under such a system. Only through their ability and willingness to provide a modicum of medical, retirement, and disability benefits could political pressure for state intervention be held at bay. But the creation of employer-centered social welfare, whatever its burdens on employers, nevertheless appeared as the best possible response to an increasingly urban, industrial world where class struggle posed a constant threat to economic and political stability.

If national social insurance could not be stopped altogether, employers hoped at least to achieve a secondary goal: a predominant position in the new regime. Parliamentary deliberations indicated that the new law would permit social insurance *caisses* to be created and administered by a mutual society, a workers' union, or an employers' association. This last option presented the family allowance movement, in conjunction with extant employer-run retirement *caisses*, with the opportunity to retain control over worker welfare. Through achievement of this secondary goal employers would retain some influence over labor militancy and worker turnover. Moreover, they would have more control over the vast funds that were slated for deposit into the new social insurance *caisses*. This was especially true in the case of capitalized retirement and disability funds, which were expected to amass over three billion francs annually.[54] It was with these goals in mind then that employers set about expanding social services available to their workers. For only through building real programs that engendered a significant measure of worker loyalty could employers hope to control the future of social welfare.

Approval of the Grinda bill in April 1924, which retained the employer-loathed principles of obligation and the unity of insurance, confirmed that employers faced an uphill battle. Although many dismissed the Chamber's passage of the bill as a function of election-eve campaigning, CCAF Director Bonvoisin commenced one of his most sensitive lobbying campaigns. He hoped to convince the industrialists

---

53 On my use of the term *patronage* here, see Noiriel, "Du 'patronage' au 'paternalisme'."
54 *JO*, Etienne Antonelli and Edouard Grinda, *Rapport présenté au nom de la Commission d'Assurance et de prévoyance sociales*, Documents parlementaires, Chambre, 1930, annexe no. 3187, p. 541.

and commercial entrepreneurs who governed the single largest family allowances *caisse*, the CCRP, of the need to quickly and massively expand their operations. Throughout the summer and fall of 1924, Bonvoisin attended several CCRP board meetings in order to advocate the creation of social insurance benefits for workers at *caisse* affiliated firms. UIMM president and head of the CCRP, Richemond, supported Bonvoisin's entreaties as a basis for strategic action. He insisted to his colleagues that the price of state intervention as well as the loss of employer independence in the realm of social welfare made the issue of critical importance. Richemond summarized the strategy in these terms. "We have only two defenses: the first consists of demonstrating that the spread of [family allowance] *caisses* is such that one can legitimately claim that virtually all employers will become members . . . the second consists of showing what we can do in the social realm, including services that the State would be incapable of realizing, thus the necessity of developing ancillary social services."[55] Richemond subsequently held three meetings with several of the most influential members of the *caisse*, in order to draft a medical insurance plan. This inner core of the governing board included representatives from Renault, Delage, Peugeot, and Thomson-Houston. Virtually all were in favor of the idea although some, such as Renault's representative, were reticent because of the ongoing currency crisis. For his part, Bonvoisin implored the Parisian employers to act, noting that "several provincial *caisses* are awaiting our decision in order to conform their approach to ours."[56]

In order to obtain a clear mandate, Richemond decided to take the social insurance proposal directly to the CCRP's 1,440 members at an extraordinary general meeting in November 1925. His proposal consisted of two illness-insurance plans. The first would be a wholly employer-run program for workers who lacked any coverage. The second was aimed at mutualists among the CCRP member firms' personnel. If these workers chose to maintain their mutual society membership – instead of opting for the employer plan – the CCRP would double their society's illness allowances. Richemond warned his colleagues of the need to pre-empt state action on social insurance: "We must commit ourselves to medical insurance in order to show that we are not enemies of so-called social progress before the moment when we are commanded to accept overwhelming costs. Instead, we prefer to plan prudent, progressive, and measured actions. If we do not commit ourselves to this course, the social

---

[55] CCRP Commission de gestion, *procès-verbaux*, 17 October 1924.   [56] *Ibid.*, 22 June 1925.

insurance law will be approved without us, that is to say, against us."[57] Richemond's proposal gained overwhelming support. Within weeks, the CCRP had negotiated an agreement with the Syndicat des Médecins de la Seine to provide medical care, including surgery and pharmaceuticals for eligible workers. The CCRP's illness allowance began on the ninth day of incapacitation and could continue for three months. Workers could choose their own doctors from among the Seine doctors' association.[58] The CCRP supplemented these services with itinerant practical nurses who were in the direct employ of the *caisse*. In 1926, the CCRP hired 38 *dames visiteuses* (female home-visitors), who could verify a worker's eligibility for family allowances and offer advice on childcare, help with hospital admissions, clinic visits, and make referrals to *caisse* medical retreats outside Paris. Workers' union leaders sought to stop the home-visitor program but ultimately failed to dissuade workers from allowing *dames visiteuses* into their homes. By 1931, the CCRP had expanded the size of its home-visitor corps to 120 and was conducting 150,000 visits annually.[59] As Bonvoisin had predicted, action by Parisian employers paved the way for similar initiatives by family allowance *caisses* throughout France.

Bonvoisin pursued the wholesale expansion of family allowance *caisses* into global welfare providers. At CCAF annual conferences, he lauded supplementary social insurance and other services as the logical progression of the family allowance movement.[60] In fact, the CCAF eventually added "assurances sociales" to the title of its monthly journal. By 1927, twenty-nine large *caisses* in addition to the CCRP offered illness insurance at no cost to workers.[61] The Lyon *caisse* also covered the risk of disability and the textile manufacturers' *caisse* in Roubaix-Tourcoing extended a retirement program. Two-thirds of these *caisses* mingled their insurance programs directly with their family allowance administrations, asking employers to pay a single premium to cover all

---

[57] CCRP Assemblée générale extraordinaire, *procès-verbaux*, 27 November 1925.
[58] CCRP Commission de gestion, *procès-verbaux*, 11 January 1926.
[59] *Cahiers du Bolchevisme* 6 (August 1928), 742–748, cited by Downs, *Manufacturing Inequality*, note, p. 248.
[60] Downs, *ibid.*, p. 29; Pinte, *Les Allocations familiales*, p. 88. For the CCAF resolutions encouraging members to pay medical benefits and provide social insurance, see VIe Congrès National des Allocations Familiales, *compte rendu*, 1926, pp. 119–120.
[61] These included *caisses* in Angoulême, Amentières, Auxerre, Beauvais, Blois, Bourges, Brest, Chalon-sur-Saône, Cholet, Elbeuf, Fourmies, Grenoble, Lille-Région, Lille-Métallurgie, Lyon, Marseille, Nantes, Reims, Roanne, Roubaix, La Rochelle, Saint-Etienne, Saint-Julien, Saint-Quentin, Tarare, Thizy, Tours, Troyes, and Vienne. See VIIe Congrès National des Allocations Familiales, *compte rendu*, "Les extensions sociales des caisses de compensation," 1927, pp. 19–20.

benefits. However, despite Bonvoisin's best efforts, the medical benefits extended voluntarily by employers through family allowances *caisses* remained meager. In most cases, men collected only five francs and women less than four francs daily beginning after the seventh to eleventh day of incapacitation, depending on the *caisse*. These rates were low even for workers in the provinces where average daily male and female wages were 31.34 and 18.30 francs respectively. Men and women who worked in the Parisian metals factories earned on average much more.[62] Thus, a 5 franc daily illness allowance could not allow workers to maintain their standard of living during an extended or even a brief period of illness. Most importantly, the Grinda bill promised an illness allowance that was significantly higher. Employers' reimbursement for medical expenses was also low. Most *caisses* provided only 5 francs towards the cost of a doctor's visit while compensation for surgical costs ranged greatly with some *caisses* paying as much as 300 francs and others contributing only 50 francs. Like the CCRP medical insurance program, eligibility for benefits expired after ninety days.

The CCAF also encouraged employers to aid workers with their mutual fees or to provide medical allowances on top of what these workers received from their mutual societies. These programs too, however, were of questionable efficacy because mutual membership remained relatively sparse among the industrial proletariat of large urban centers where family allowances were most common. A 1927 survey indicated that only 5 to 10 percent of family allowance *caisse* beneficiaries were mutual members in Paris, Roubaix, Lyon, Saint-Etienne, and Troyes. Although this same survey noted that the proportion of mutualists among family allowance beneficiaries in less populated regions ranged as high as 75 percent, these were not the sites of large *caisses*, which were most capable of extending medical insurance. Nationwide mutual membership among family allowance *caisse* beneficiaries amounted to only 11 percent.[63]

Employers also entered into direct alliances with mutual societies to provide insurance services. In January 1927 Desiré Ley, director of the massive textile manufacturers' *caisse* of Roubaix-Tourcoing, signed an agreement with the Union Mutualiste du Nord. In exchange for large

---

[62] Aimé Bruxelles, *Nature juridique et caractères des cotisations d'assurances sociales dans la législation française* (Lyon: Bosc Frères, 1932), p. 154; *Bulletin de la Statistique Générale de la France* (July–September 1928), 412–413.

[63] VIIe Congrès National des Allocations Familiales, *compte rendu*, "Les extensions sociales des caisses de compensation," 1927, pp. 17–33.

employer subsidies, the mutual societies of the Union agreed to provide illness insurance and retirement pensions to the Roubaix-Tourcoing textile workers. Ley foresaw the central role that mutual societies would play under the new system and hoped to buy influence in advance of the law's passage. Textile manufacturers' financial support of the Union Mutualiste du Nord permitted employers to exercise influence over the Union and thereby their workers. Employers sent workers' names to the Union in order to assure their membership. Then, in order to complete their monopoly over worker welfare, Ley wrote to Minister of Labor Louis Loucheur to propose an experiment. Employers of the Roubaix-Tourcoing consortium would pay the entire cost of illness, disability, maternity, and retirement benefits for its 100,000 workers. Workers would thus face no social insurance premiums as under the proposed social insurance legislation. Textile manufacturers, however, stipulated that their costs could not increase over the course of the trial, which was to last several years. In rejecting the deal, Loucheur noted that employers did not intend to capitalize their retirement funds, but rather to administer it on a pay-as-you-go basis. During the initial year, when employer costs became fixed, expenses would be unusually low, indeed, below the 5 percent of wages that employers would have been required to pay under social insurance legislation. Later, as retirements rose, employers could have simply lowered pension benefits, protected by their agreement with the government that employer costs could not rise.[64] The Roubaix-Tourcoing Union Mutualiste du Nord alliance and textile employers' subsequent bid to exempt themselves from the social insurance law was perhaps the most glaring attempt to obviate state intervention. Less flagrant alliances were negotiated between the family allowance *caisse* in Lyon and the Union Générale de la Mutualité du Rhône as well as between the CCRP and the Fédération mutualiste de la Seine.[65]

Although the most promising employer efforts to derail social insurance were pursued by family allowance *caisses*, individual firms who possessed the wherewithal were also active. The Michelin company provides an illustrative case of such employer tactics. Michelin had long been one of the largest family allowance *services particuliers*, that is, a firm that paid allowances and maternity benefits on its own without

---

[64] *JO*, Annales, Chambre, Documents Parlementaires, 1930, annexe no. 3187, pp. 540–544, cited by Hatzfeld, *Du Paupérisme à la sécurité sociale*, pp. 167–169.
[65] *La Documentation Catholique* (4 May 1929), 1128, cited by Dominique Simon, "Les Assurances sociales et les mutualistes," *Revue d'Histoire Moderne et Contemporaine* 34 (October–December 1987): 587–615, especially pp. 596–597.

participating in a *caisse*. Although they chose not to join a *caisse*, the Michelin brothers were strong supporters of the family allowance movement and employer prerogatives in social welfare. Well before their adoption of family allowances during the Great War, Michelin had implemented an array of social services for its workers, including illness insurance, medical retreats, company housing, and organized sports leagues. Michelin contrasted its approach to illness benefits to that of the mutual movement. Instead of insuring workers against relatively small incidents of incapacitation, which, as we have already seen, was the best that most mutual societies could achieve, Michelin insured its workers against major and repeated bouts of illness. The company offered a free medical diagnosis for all workers but generally left half the cost of all subsequent visits to the insured. Nor did the company provide an illness allowance except in cases of long-term incapacitation. However, Michelin proved much more generous when it came to serious medical conditions, such as surgery and long-term recoveries. The company insured family members under the same rules, claiming that its approach to medical welfare was "the most useful" and "the opposite" of mutual societies.[66] Although Michelin criticized mutual societies, it also rejected the model of social insurance presented by the recovered territories. The company declared the impetus for parliament's social insurance bill as "the 'governmental' solution, created by the Germans and still in use in Alsace. It is extremely costly and provides deplorable results. Con artists who declare themselves sick when they are not are legion; doctors who live off the law without really treating sick people have become a large population."[67] M. Gillet, Michelin's director of social services, attacked social insurance legislation, saying "the principles are good, but then there are men."[68] Gillet predicted that fraud and mismanagement would plague the new system. What was needed, he insisted, was not a vast new bureaucracy but "more clinics, dispensaries, maternal care, hospitals, spas, and sanatoria."[69] Of course, it was just such facilities that Michelin owned in large numbers. Thus, the company sought to steer legislators toward an employer-controlled system, albeit compulsory, but which Michelin had already excelled at creating.

In March 1928, legislative approval of social insurance appeared imminent. The CCRP leadership thus advocated the immediate

---

[66] *Œuvres Sociales de Michelin et Cie* (Clermont-Ferrand, 1927), pp. 3–5.   [67] *Ibid.*, p. 5.
[68] M. Gillet, Comité National d'Etudes Sociales et Politiques, *procès-verbaux*, 13 January 1930, p. 22.
[69] *Ibid.*, p. 27.

disassociation of its social insurance initiative from the payment of family allowances. *Caisse* leaders saw the joint administration of social insurance, which would be subject to bureaucratic oversight, and family allowances, which would remain outside state control, as a needless exposure of employer administration to government snooping. Richemond explained the threat to his fellow employers: "As you know, family allowances are not to be included in social insurance. Some would like them to be included some day, but we have no interest in associating two things that are not linked at the present time."[70] In lieu of a CCRP retirement program under the roof of a family allowance *caisse*, Richemond noted that, "the UIMM, like the CCAF, have encouraged employers to create mutual aid societies, by themselves if they are big enough, or between several firms for small and medium-sized companies."[71] The CCRP's decision to separate its family allowance component from illness and retirement insurance programs symbolized an admission by employers that the battle to stop parliamentary approval of national social insurance had been lost.

In their failed attempt to prevent state intervention on social insurance, the *grand patronat* used the same tactic that had been successful in stopping the 1921 Bokanowski bill that would have required employers to pay family allowances. Employers pointed to their voluntary actions and promised further progress soon. In this second apparition, however, their argument lacked plausibility. At the time of the Bokanowski bill, over fifty *caisses de compensation* were paying more than 30 million francs in family allowances to several hundred thousand workers annually. By contrast, in 1927, the thirty *caisses* which offered social insurance benefits were spending barely 2.6 million francs that benefited 251,000 workers per year. Indeed, even for those who offered illness insurance, costs were quite low, varying from 0.09 to 0.18 percent of wages.[72] Such premiums paled in comparison to the employer contributions that would be required under a social insurance law.

Although employers failed to achieve their primary goal of derailing social insurance legislation, the family allowance movement continued to develop several programs through which they hoped to maintain control over worker welfare and induce worker loyalty. Several family allowance *caisses* built vacation centers, organized sports leagues and other

---

[70] CCRP Commission de gestion, *procès-verbaux*, 19 March 1928.   [71] *Ibid.*
[72] VIIe Congrès National des Allocations Familiales, *compte rendu*, "Les Extensions sociales des caisses de compensation," 1927, p. 30.

leisure-time activities for their employees.[73] Others offered homemaking classes for workers' wives through which employers hoped to rationalize domestic chores and thereby make workers more productive in the factory.[74] All of these actions were celebrated in a new CCAF magazine, *La Revue de la Famille*, which extolled the virtues of family life while disseminating employers' social policy propaganda.[75] Through these initiatives, the family allowance movement hoped to bolster employer collaboration in worker welfare in order to counteract class-based appeals from workers' unions. But even as employers continued to build and diversify their family allowance *caisses* in hopes of maintaining as much control as possible over worker welfare a rift appeared within their own ranks.

EMPLOYERS AND SOCIAL WELFARE IN ALSACE-LORRAINE

Employers from the recovered territories backed social insurance legislation for three reasons. First, they viewed their system, costly though it was, as a *fait accompli* that could not be undone without serious, perhaps irremediable labor unrest. The importance that Paris attached to integrating the new departments persuaded employers of the region that either France would adopt comparable protections or they would be stripped of theirs. Concern for their own system thus drove their advocacy of a national system. Second, employers in the recovered territories believed that social insurance and their German-style family welfare contributed to relatively quiescent labor relations. Third, regional employers wanted to rid themselves of a competitive disadvantage relative to producers elsewhere in France whose labor costs did not include social insurance contributions. During the early deliberations and lobbying over the Vincent and Grinda bills, metals and mining industrialists of Alsace-Lorraine remained conspicuously silent.[76] Later, as the strategy of France's *grand patronat* to derail social insurance became apparent, employers from the recovered territories sought to reassure their colleagues. The vice

---

[73] GIMM Conseil d'administration, "Projet d'organisation d'un Centre Social de Jeunes," 21 November 1927, AN 39 AS 387. Michelin and Renault also created sports and other leisure-time activities for their workers. See Patrick Fridenson, *Histoire des usines Renault, vol. 1: Naissance de la grande entreprise, 1898–1939* (Paris: Seuil, 1972), pp. 250–251.

[74] René Hubert, "Revue de la presse," *Bulletin Mensuel des Allocations Familiales (et des Assurances Sociales)* 19 (July 1929), 138.

[75] *La Revue de la Famille* became closely tied with the Vichy regime. See Francine Muel-Dreyfus, *Vichy et l'éternel féminin: contribution à une sociologie politique de l'ordre des corps* (Paris: Editions du Seuil, 1996), p. 99.

[76] Degas, *Les Assurances sociales*, p. 28.

president of the Société Industrielle de Mulhouse, conceded that "the application of a system of laws analogous [to those in recovered territories] requires a deep analysis of the country's economic and financial health and demands people . . . to renounce some of their individualism . . ." He noted that the social insurance legislation then taking form would make use of the "marvelously developed system of mutual societies, which will insure an efficient working of the new law . . . France possesses the necessary conditions for its realization."[77] The secretary-general of the Syndicat Industriel Alsacien echoed this message. He argued that despite its inevitable inefficiencies, social insurance legislation was needed "simply to guarantee that an important portion of society, which does not possess sufficient means, can gain access to a doctor."[78] The industrialists of the recovered territories emerged as proponents not only of social insurance but also of family welfare practices that varied widely from that propagated by the CCAF. Pressure on employers of the recovered territories to conform with the national family allowance movement further illustrates the link between allowances and a broader employer strategy to control worker welfare.

After the Armistice employers in the recovered territories sought to retain the family welfare practices that, like its social insurance system, dated from the period of German rule. But unlike social insurance, family welfare benefited from very little legal codification. Thus, when Alexandre Millerand promised inhabitants of the region that their social legislation would be preserved under French law, he could only mean the region's insurance system. The German-style family and child supplements (*Familienzulage* and *Kinderzulage*), which had developed in the decades before the Great War, came under substantial pressure during the 1920s. However similar in appearance to French family allowances, German practices exhibited a critically different set of beneficiaries and mode of distribution.

First, benefits were calculated as a percentage of wages and negotiated at the collective bargaining table. This practice constrained employers' use of family allowances as a wage strategy. As we have seen, the ability of French employers to hold down wages using allowances relied on the separation of remuneration components, i.e. the *salaire vital*. Such a strategy was impossible under the German system where family and

---

[77] M. Schlumberger, Comité National d'Etudes Sociales et Politiques, *procès-verbaux*, 13 January 1930, pp. 21–22.
[78] M. Thomas, Comité National d'Etudes Sociales et Politiques, *procès-verbaux*, 13 January 1930, pp. 34–36.

child supplements were held proportional to wages. Second, family supplements (*Familienzulage*) were paid to all married couples regardless of whether they had children. Resentment may still have been harbored by single workers who received smaller paychecks for the same work. Nevertheless, a much larger segment of the work force received family welfare, avoiding the conflict between *pères de famille* and married but childless workers that existed elsewhere in France. Third, workers were not eligible for child supplements (*Kinderzulage*) until their children reached school age. The absence of cash assistance at birth indicates a relative absence of pronatalist motives in German family welfare. In contrast to France, which experienced a relatively early slowdown of population growth, Germany's demographic transition was more typical of industrialized countries of the period. That said, a falling birthrate did arouse some pronatalist manifestations in Germany, but their virulence never approached those found in France, at least not before the accession of the Nazi regime in 1933.[79] Before then, efforts to shore up population growth were focused more broadly on improving public health and decreasing mortality rates.[80] The *Familienzulage* was paid to childless married men in order to reinforce women's dependency in the absence of childbearing. The *Kinderzulage* also encouraged family formation, but like the *Familienzulage*, it was not narrowly focused on increasing fertility rates. Payable after the child's fifth birthday, its primary purpose was to offset the high cost of education in the Reich.[81]

A construction of gender that defined women first as mothers and questioned the appropriateness of women working outside the home, especially in the industrial sector, was prevalent in Germany. In fact, women workers who became pregnant were often laid off.[82] But the absence of a perceived depopulation crisis meant that neither German political leaders, feminists, nor employers were as concerned with reproduction as their French counterparts. In general, employers of Alsace-Lorraine viewed family welfare alongside social insurance more as guarantors of the social peace than a wage strategy. Over time, however, the region's customary practices in family and child

---

[79] Fascist Italy exhibited a pronatalist movement comparable to France's in the 1920s. On Nazi pronatalism, see Claudia Koonz, *Mothers in the Fatherland: Women, the Family, and Nazi Politics* (New York: St. Martin's Press, 1987).

[80] Mitchell, *Divided Path*, pp. 33–36, 44–64.

[81] Jean-François Montes and Brigitte Schmitt, *Les Organismes d'allocations familiales dans le département du Haut-Rhin, 1918–1950* (Paris: Caisse Nationale des Allocations Familiales, 1995), pp. 11–16.

[82] Sandrine Kott, *L'Etat social allemand: représentations et pratiques* (Paris: Belin, 1995), pp. 234–248.

supplements gave way to the influence of the larger French family allowance movement.

Led by the region's important coal and steel industrialists, a hybrid of French and German family welfare emerged in the 1920s. The child supplement (*Kinderzulage*) was abandoned in favor of a French-style family allowance payable after birth. But the family supplement (*Familienzulage*), whereby married men were paid an allowance for their wives, remained common. Employers also continued to negotiate allowances at the collective bargaining table. Most employers paid allowances directly to their workers without the intermediary of a *caisse de compensation*. Those that did come together to create a *caisse* did so along strictly professional lines. The relative absence of employer collaboration stands in stark contrast to elsewhere in France where employers enthusiastically colluded in the development of family allowances.

The link between family welfare practices and social insurance is exemplified by employer reaction to a narrow 1922 law that compelled only public works firms to join a family allowance *caisse de compensation*.[83] After the law's passage, the Syndicat des Entrepreneurs de Bâtiment et Travaux Publics met in Metz to decide whether to create their own *caisse* or to encourage members to affiliate with *caisses* in Paris and Nancy. Construction employers chose to create their own *caisse* because "the others did not have the same burden of social insurance as our members and would likely be incapable of understanding our interests."[84] The reluctance of construction entrepreneurs to join *caisses* outside the region reflected employers' growing opposition to French-style family welfare. They were keenly aware of additional labor costs that stemmed from the social insurance system of Alsace-Lorraine and thus rejected state intervention on family allowances. Employers viewed *caisse* affiliation as an unnecessary aggravation of their disadvantage relative to competitors elsewhere in France. After all, they argued, many firms were already paying allowances voluntarily, if not through a *caisse*.

Nevertheless, pressures on employers in the recovered territories to conform with national family welfare practices continued to mount.

---

[83] This law was prompted by large construction firms that already paid allowances and wished to force higher overhead costs onto small firms which were underbidding them on projects. See Bureau International du Travail, *Etudes et Documents*, Série D, "Salaires et durée du travail," no. 13, "Les Allocations familiales," pp. 58–62; Christian Chenut, *Les Allocations familiales dans les marchés de travaux publics* (Paris: Recueil Sirey, 1931); *Information Ouvrière et Sociale*, 31 July 1921.

[84] Syndicat des Entrepreneurs de Bâtiment et Travaux Publics de la Moselle, *procès-verbaux*, 31 January 1928.

These included the provision of extra social services by employer family allowance *caisses*. Director of Labor Picquenard wrote to employers in the Moselle: "I must insist that your *caisses* immediately create social services for the protection of children and maternity or at least participate in works of this nature."[85] Picquenard's entreaties were met with obstinacy by Moselan leaders. They argued that member firms, as participants in the region's social insurance regime, already provided the social services in question. The steel and mining *caisse* director rebuffed Picquenard's requests, declaring "all firms affiliated with the *caisse* already provide medical insurance and other services for their personnel and their families." The director of the Moselle's *caisse* added "[we] cannot envisage the creation of extra-legal social services given the special circumstances of the department where preexisting social welfare provisions are already so numerous."[86]

This correspondence between the ministry of labor and the employers in Alsace-Lorraine reveals two very different conceptions of social welfare and *caisses de compensation*. Under the influence of the national family allowance movement, Parisian officials viewed the *caisse de compensation* as a central institution of social welfare. Yet industrialists in Alsace-Lorraine held a rather different view. They too were interested in controlling their work forces and holding down labor costs, but *caisses de compensation* were hardly central to this endeavor. The system of social protections inherited from the Reich rendered *caisse* social services largely redundant. Furthermore, the continuance of German practices whereby allowances were negotiated as a percentage of wages made *caisses de compensation* less useful to the region's employers. High birthrates in the region and the convention of paying married male workers a stipend for their wives further reduced the need for equalizing costs among employers.[87] In the face of pressure from Paris, Moselan employers succeeded at rallying departmental officials, including the prefect, to their cause.[88] The focus of these efforts was the prevention of *caisses* from other regions from operating in the Moselle. Employers feared that outside *caisses* that did not pay stipends for wives and whose other members were not subject

---

[85] Memo, Picquenard to Guermont, 20 August 1936, AN F22 1550.

[86] Caisse d'Allocations Familiales de la Moselle (hereafter CAFM), Commission de gestion, *procès-verbaux*, 15 February 1935.

[87] Commission départementale des allocations familiales de la Moselle, *procès-verbaux*, 6 July 1933, ADM 6 X 12.

[88] CAFM, Assemblée constitutive, *procès-verbaux*, 21 December 1929, Assemblée générale ordinaire, *procès-verbaux*, 16 April 1932; Services particuliers, AN F22 1572–1573; Caisse de Compensation des Mines et Usines de la Moselle, AN F22 1550.

to Alsace-Lorraine's social insurance regime, would upset regional labor policies and the social peace. Moreover, they feared that if parliament failed to approve national social insurance, it would not be long before their own system came into question.

Despite the failure of employers to stop legislative progress on social insurance, the 1920s were a robust period for the family allowance movement. At decade's end, there were 258 *caisses*, encompassing over 25,000 employers and 4.17 million wage earners. In addition, some large employers were paying family allowances through their own payrolls, forgoing the potential advantages of a *caisse* in order to enjoy complete freedom of action.[89] The financial crisis of 1924–1926 witnessed renewed union demands for automatic wage adjustments, again testing the principle of the *salaire vital* and family allowances. When the crisis was over, the family allowance movement emerged reinvigorated and allowances were raised in place of general wage increases. The postwar decade also witnessed the family allowance movement break out of traditionally industrial regions to reach all corners of the national territory. Further, employers' hold on family welfare tightened as *caisses de compensation* expanded into social insurance, leisure-time, and other social activities.

Meanwhile, workers' unions failed to slow the family allowance movement or even to convince workers about its negative effects on wages and working-class solidarity. Not only were workers with large families reticent to protest against family allowances but also those who aspired to have children demanded their union to exert pressure *in favor* of employer affiliation with a *caisse de compensation*. These calls were amplified from an institutional base with the creation of the CFTC in 1919 whose leaders called for a state mandate on employers to pay family allowances. Wage discrimination against women also constrained union leaders' ability to fight family allowances. New Taylorist divisions of labor resulted in an array of wage differentials in industrial production under which women were commonly paid less for similar work and simultaneously viewed as a threat to the job security and wage levels of men. Employer strategies to "manufacture inequality" between men and women corresponded with their adherence to a wage strategy based on the *salaire vital*

---

[89] Xe Congrès National des Allocations Familiales, "Rapport Moral," *compte rendu*, 1930, p. 125. Michelin was perhaps the most notable of these solo allowance-paying employers.

and family allowances.[90] Wage discrimination against women and single workers were both based on evaluations of workers' social value. Actual work performance was therefore displaced as the paramount criterion for remuneration by an employer strategy to minimize labor costs and preempt social legislation. In so doing, employers reaped the benefits of the pronatalist movement, finding widespread support for ostensible efforts to rectify France's demographic crisis.

Given the success of employers to divide workers through control of family welfare, it is not surprising that the *grand patronat* rallied their *caisses de compensation* into battle against social insurance. This effort resulted in a network of super *caisses* with more influence than ever on worker behavior on the job, at home, and on vacation. While these new programs exhibited a sophisticated attack on labor militancy, employers were unwilling to provide a level of protection against the risks of illness, disability, and old age that could dissuade parliamentary approval of social insurance. Employers' strategy also suffered from their inability to arrive at an effective alliance with mutual societies. This failure stemmed primarily from the sparse mutual membership among workers at the factories of France's large urban centers. Finally, employers were also hampered by a dispute with their colleagues in the recovered territories. Industrialists and commercial entrepreneurs there saw Parisian employers and government officials' strategy of expanding *caisse* services as detrimental to the German-style social protections that were critical to the successful integration of Alsace-Lorraine into the Republic. These concerns became increasingly well founded after 1928 when the French state embarked on an unprecedented wave of reforms in family welfare and social insurance.

[90] Manufacturing inequality here refers to Downs' book-length study cited earlier, *Manufacturing Inequality*.

4

Parliament acts

Between 1928 and 1932 France witnessed an unprecedented wave of social reform legislation. On 5 April 1928 the nation finally saw passage of a unified social insurance law that covered the risks of illness, disability, maternity, and old age. This law also provided stop-gap payment of insurance premiums during short spells of unemployment but fell short of covering this risk entirely. However, no sooner had the first social insurance law been approved than a bitter struggle over corrective legislation broke out, a battle which would not be settled until passage of a second law on 30 April 1930. During these two years, the *grand patronat* switched tactics. Confronted with their inability to stop social insurance, employers now lobbied for a loosely regulated mutual society-based system under which they could still exert considerable control over worker welfare. Meanwhile, legislators were also considering what action could be taken to aid families more directly. On 11 March 1932 they approved legislation that required all employers to join a *caisse de compensation* for the payment of family allowances.[1]

The willingness of legislators to act so forcefully on social reform was influenced by a convergence of political and economic considerations that flowed from the franc crisis of the mid 1920s. By 1926 Poincaré's stabilization policies had gained the assent, if not the active participation, of the SFIO and the CGT.[2] Collaboration in favor of franc stabilization created a legislative environment that favored further common action and coincided with a short-lived but strong period of economic growth. By 1928, with monetary stability reestablished, legislators found themselves with an embarrassingly large budget surplus. After 44 billion francs

---

[1] In addition to social insurance and family allowance legislation, parliament also approved large spending bills for urban renewal and housing on 15 March and 13 July, 1928 respectively.

[2] The Chamber vote on monetary reform was 448 in favor, 18 against, and 133 abstentions, most of which were cast by SFIO and URD deputies. See K. Mouré, *La Politique du franc Poincaré, 1926–1928* (Paris: Albin Michel, 1998); Jacques Rueff, *Souvenirs d'un gouverneur de la Banque de France: histoire de la stabilisation du franc, 1926–1928* (Paris: Génin, 1954).

in expenditures nearly four billion francs remained in government coffers, constituting the largest surplus in monetary terms and in relation to gross national product since 1870.[3] Hence, a favorable assessment of public expenditures joined with deliberations over social insurance and family welfare to bring legislators of diverse persuasions together on an activist agenda.

We begin with social insurance, examining the circumstances that surrounded parliamentary action between 1926 and 1930. During these final years of consideration, opponents made a series of dire predictions that they hoped would dissuade legislators from final approval despite vibrant economic growth. We also witness a stupendously successful lobbying campaign by Raoul Péret and Georges Petit on behalf of the FNMF. They obtained significant concessions for mutual societies in both the 1928 and 1930 legislation. During the early years of social insurance implementation, calls for major and minor changes continued. Without doubt, the most interesting revisionist efforts emerged from the conflict between doctors' associations (*syndicats medicaux*) and the newly empowered mutual societies. Discord arose because these institutions held opposing incentives in the provision of medical services. Mutual society insurance *caisses* sought to contain the cost of diagnosis and treatment while doctors wanted to strengthen the practice of liberal medicine.

Next, we turn to parliamentary action on family welfare. However, it is important to remember that the law of 11 March 1932 which required employers to pay family allowances, did *not* constitute the initial entrance of the state. As we saw earlier, the notion of the *salaire vital*, upon which the interwar family allowance movement was built, originated with state-sponsored family welfare and industrial mobilization during the Great War. The movement's primary appeal to employers after the war lay in the macroeconomic conditions and the volatile social climate of the 1920s: inflation, devaluation, industrial rationalization, communist organizing, and growing fears of depopulation. As usual, employers guarded against state intervention, but this did not mean that state officials were merely bystanders to the development of family allowances in the 1920s. A cast of employers, legislators, pronatalists, feminists, and civil servants were actively laying the groundwork for the large-scale state intervention that occurred in 1932. Employer fears of recession after financial crises in the United States and central Europe between 1929 and 1931 led to a

3 J.-M. Jeanneney and E. Barbier-Jeanneney, *Les Economies occidentales aux XIXe–XXe siècles* (Paris: Presses de la FNSP, 1985), vol. I, p. 222, cited by Michel Margairaz, "Contexte économique, choix financiers et acteurs politiques," *Vie Sociale* 3–4 (May–June–July–August 1999), 261–268.

slowdown in family allowance *caisse* growth. Stagnation in the spread of *caisses* coincided with the waxing power of a clique of Radical legislators and civil administrators who were closely associated with social insurance and its implementation. These personalities, headed by Radical Minister of Labor Adolphe Landry, also enjoyed strong ties to the family allowance movement, pronatalist groups, and feminist organizations. Under Landry's leadership, the *grand patronat* collaborated in drafting legislation that required all employers to pay family allowances. But implementation of state-mandated allowances proved more difficult than originally thought, especially in the commercial sector where thousands of small employers sought to evade the law.

Finally, no examination of interwar social policy would be complete without a sounding of feminists. Their conceptions of gender and a woman's proper role in French society made a unique impact on the debate over social reform. The nature of French feminism and the influence of women's organizations on social insurance and family welfare are taken up at chapter's end.

THE 1928 AND 1930 SOCIAL INSURANCE LAWS

Senate committee work and hearings on the Grinda social insurance bill, which was approved by the Chamber in April 1924, delayed the full Senate's consideration of social insurance until April 1928. Seven Senate commissions were eventually called upon to render their judgments on the bill. However, the Senate Commission de l'Hygiène, de l'Assistance, de l'Assurance et de la Prévoyance Sociales (CHAAPS) undertook the most comprehensive examination. Like in the Chamber's analogous Commission de l'Assistance et de Prévoyance Sociales (CAPS), the task fell to a medical doctor, the senator from Côte-d'Or, Claude Chauveau. Ignoring calls from his Chamber colleagues and workers' unions for a prompt committee approval and floor vote on the law, Chauveau instead chose to return to the drawing board. He launched a series of lengthy hearings during which he heard the views of workers' unions, mutual leaders, employers, doctors, and agricultural associations. Chauveau followed these sessions with study trips to Alsace, Germany, and Great Britain. In October 1925, Chauveau formed a special committee of deputies, senators, and government officials that undertook a wholesale revision of the Grinda text.[4] Chauveau justified his revision by pointing

---

[4] Claude Chauveau, *Loi sur les assurances sociales: commentaire juridique, financier, et administratif* (Paris: Librarie Générale de Droit et Jurisprudence, 1928), pp. 63, 69–71.

to changes in the economic landscape since Grinda wrote his bill in 1923. Although the franc crisis had altered French financial realities, Chauveau also made fundamental modifications to Grinda's administrative organization and added unemployment coverage, neither of which could be warranted by the new environment.

In the course of his investigations, Chauveau became convinced that neglect of the involuntarily unemployed would render futile the whole endeavor of social insurance. Senator Albert Peyronnet played a critical role in his adoption of this view. He convinced Chauveau that because virtually all benefits were contingent on employment, the risk of unemployment had to be addressed. Indeed, according to Grinda's bill, eligibility for illness, disability, and maternity payments, depended on a worker – and his or her employer in the case of obligatory participants – having paid premiums for at least five days during the three months prior to incapacitation. Thus, to leave unemployed workers without means to pay their premiums was the same as leaving them uncovered. This argument found considerable support in the CHAAPS and Chauveau's bill included a daily unemployment stipend that amounted to 40 percent of average wages with increases of a half franc for each dependent.[5] Although workers' unions applauded this provision, the stipend was deleted in the final legislation of 1930. Legislators did, however, let stand state-subsidies to help the involuntarily unemployed pay their insurance premiums. Although trimmed from its original scope, parliament formally recognized involuntary unemployment as a risk against which society should provide individual relief.

In order to pay for the addition of unemployment insurance without increasing premiums, Chauveau cut back on other insurance benefits and demanded that departmental and communal governments pay a portion of unemployment benefits. Instead of a flat copayment (*ticket moderateur*) for medical services foreseen by earlier bills, Chauveau made the insured responsible for 10 to 15 percent of doctor's visits and 10 percent for pharmaceuticals. Chauveau maintained a daily illness stipend of 50 percent of the base wage, but he delayed eligibility for this benefit from the third day to the fifth day of incapacitation. He also made permanent disability benefits harder to obtain. Only maternity and death benefits were expanded in the Senate. Under Chauveau's bill, wives of the insured gained access to nursing stipends (*allocations d'allaitement*) which previously had been reserved for eligible women workers. Chauveau

---

[5] *Ibid.*, Articles 21–25, pp. 476–517; Etienne Antonelli, *Guide pratique des assurances sociales* (Paris: Payot, 1928), pp. 27–29.

also put a 1000 franc floor on the death benefit, which previously could have ranged as low as 175 francs for the lowest paid workers. Finally, in a move that pleased many workers but promised to complicate implementation, the Senate version abolished the categorization of wages for the calculation of premiums and cash payments. Instead, premiums and cash payments, such as illness stipends, were to be figured according to the worker's actual base wage. In order to compensate for inflation since the approval of Grinda, the Senate version raised the maximum annual wage for compulsory participation from 10,000 to 15,000 francs and a higher threshold of 18,000 francs was created for the Paris region.[6] Chauveau's changes in benefits attracted little opposition from workers' unions, which conceded the cutbacks in order to gain unemployment coverage and an upward adjustment in base wage eligibility.

Chauveau projected revenues at 5.275 billion francs, which equaled 10.6 percent of participants' total wages. Table 4.1 outlines how this levy was apportioned, the cost of each risk, and the bill's beneficiaries. Like the previous Chamber versions, Chauveau differentiated between the risks of illness, maternity, and death, whose expenses were to be met with actual premiums, and disability and retirement pensions, which would be dependent on capitalized funds. Indeed, aside from the addition of unemployment insurance, there were few surprises in the Senate bill's premiums or benefits. However, Chauveau proved more radical in his modifications to Grinda's system of administrative control by taking another large step toward the mutual movement.

We saw earlier that lobbying by mutual leaders had succeeded in bringing about favorable revisions to the Vincent bill. These amendments, which were revealed in the Grinda bill, abolished the powerful state-managed *caisses régionales* and confided more administrative autonomy to local *caisses*, many of which would presumably be mutual societies. But Grinda had maintained many of Vincent's high membership requirements for the management of retirement and death benefits. Hence, many small- and medium-sized mutual societies would have been subservient to Grinda's larger *unions régionales*.[7] Chauveau made two mutual-friendly changes to this system. First, he replaced the *union régionale* with a single departmental *caisse*. The departmental *caisse* would furnish the necessary diffusion of risks for *caisses primaires* that many mutual leaders hoped to create. Second, and most importantly, Chauveau referred to the Charte de la Mutualité of 1898 for the formula to govern the

---

[6] Chauveau, *Loi sur les assurances sociales*, Articles 4–20, pp. 95–96, 271–463.   [7] See chapter 2.

Table 4.1. *Revenue, outlays, and beneficiaries of Chauveau Bill*

Apportionment of revenue	
Workers' premiums	5 percent
Employers' premium	5
Employer contribution for uninsured	0.1
Government subsidies (state, departmental, communal)	0.5
Total	10.6 percent
Apportionment of outlays	
Illness	2.82
Maternity	0.35
Death	0.30
Disability	2.10
Retirement	3.20
Unemployment	0.10
Misc. benefits for wives of insured	0.04
Supplemental payments for dependent children	0.10
Supplemental payments for low income workers	0.04
Administrative expenses	0.50
Expense for transition from 1910 Retirement Law	1.05
Total	10.60 percent
Beneficiaries	
Insured	
Men	5,009,000
Women	3,002,000
Unwaged wives of insured men	1,300,000
Dependent children of insured	5,000,000
Total	14,311,000

Source: Projections compiled from André Bernard, "Schema du mécanisme financier des assurances sociales d'après le projet de la Commission sénatoriale," in Frantzen, *Les Assurances Sociales,* p. 49.

function and size of social insurance *caisses primaires*. However, he did not elaborate, preferring to leave this matter to later legislation and regulatory guidelines. Nevertheless, mutual leaders greeted this reference with great hope. In the event that favorable regulations were adopted, existing mutual societies would immediately be eligible to administer the full range of social insurance services, albeit some of them under the wing of a departmental *caisse*. And the departmental *caisse* represented even less of a threat than Grinda's lightly regulated *unions régionales*. In fact, its board could be constituted without any state representatives at all. It would be governed by eighteen members with six seats each for mutual society leaders, agricultural mutual *caisses*, and workers' unions. Nor did Chauveau require the presence of state officials on the governing boards of *caisses primaires.* They too would be governed by at least eighteen members, composed of at least one half workers, one third employers, with two spots set aside for medical professionals. However, *caisses primaires* founded by workers unions' could exclude employers entirely. Oversight *(contrôle)* – but not administrative control – of the entire system was confided to an Office National des Assurances Sociales whose leadership consisted of a newly created Conseil Supérieur des Assurances Sociales. This body, presided by the minister of labor, had advised Chauveau during his revisions and included representatives of employers, workers' unions, mutual societies, and doctors associations. Departmental Offices des Assurances Sociales were slated to assist the office nationale. Beneficiaries also dominated their nine-member governing boards: five workers, two employers, one medical representative, and one official from the ministry of labor.[8] In sum, the Chauveau bill maintained the administrative control of social insurance that had been guaranteed to workers' unions in the Grinda bill and guaranteed social insurance a warm reception from the mutual movement.[9]

Debate on the Chauveau bill opened in the Senate on 9 June 1927. A series of minor amendments were accepted and several major ones rejected. The final vote counted 269 in favor and 2 against. Changes wrought by the Senate to social insurance caused an uproar among some deputies who considered the more populous Chamber a more appropriate body to legislate on the matter. Yet the lengthening delay, which now surpassed six years since the Vincent bill had been introduced in March 1921, and the upcoming legislative elections, led deputies to seek a quick vote on Chauveau's creation. On 14 March, the Chamber passed the Senate's version of social insurance by a vote of 477 to 4. Legislative recess delayed the date of legal promulgation until 5 April 1928.[10] Critics of the legislation immediately attributed the law to election eve campaigning, which no doubt played a large role. For no sooner had the vote been taken than legislators and government officials alike announced the need for corrective legislation. Wrangling also began on the regulatory directives that would accompany whatever final legislation

---

[8] Chauveau, *Loi sur les assurances sociales,* Articles 26–36, pp. 96, 560–744; Antonelli, *Guide pratique,* pp. 102–106.

[9] Antonelli, *ibid.,* pp. 112–117.

[10] It is worth noting that many of the Third Republic's most important social reform laws were approved in April. These include the Mutual Charter (1 April 1898), Accident insurance (9 April 1898), Retirement for workers and peasants (30 April 1910), and both the 1928 and 1930 Social insurance laws (5 April and 30 April respectively). Legislatures often ended in April and deputies did not want to campaign empty handed.

emerged. Indeed, the Chauveau bill itself, even if it had emerged as a definitive text, left much to administrative decree.

Passage of a social insurance law prompted the same diverse reactions among workers' unions that had been evident throughout the 1920s. The CGT and their socialist allies expressed support and vowed to safeguard their legislative victory during implementation. Meeting in September 1929, the CGT metals syndicate noted that powerful opponents remained committed to "thwarting the realization and application of this social reform for which the syndicate has unceasingly worked..."[11] Socialist party leaders voiced similar concerns. They insisted "first of all upon the explicit principle that this law, so impatiently awaited by the proletariat, must be implemented in February 1930." In addition to delay, socialist leaders feared employer initiatives that would dilute worker control of social insurance *caisses*.[12] In their fight against those who wanted to delay and amend the new law, socialists found only spite from the communists who rejected the law and made plans to subvert it. They continued to call social insurance "an illusion that would distract workers from their true struggle by appearing to offer an amelioration in their condition through simple class collaboration." The PCF hoped to disrupt application of the law; CGTU leaders were instructed to "organize an internal opposition to the law in each *caisse*" and "when the first paycheck deductions are implemented, instigate workers to fight for an increase in wages."[13] The continued split in strategy between the two largest trade unions hampered the ability of workers to exert influence over the contentious parliamentary debates regarding the final legislation of 1930.

Mutual leaders, on the other hand, clearly gained the upper hand and even came to enjoy the support of the *grand patronat*. Having failed to stop social insurance legislation altogether, employers now believed that stronger prerogatives for mutual societies would come at the expense of state control and workers' unions. Indeed, CCAF Director Bonvoisin announced that the family allowance movement wanted to preserve "the independence of insurees" from state control through a further "mutualization" of the 1928 law.[14] If the 1928 law were further mutualized

[11] IXe Congrès Fédéral, Fédération des Ouvriers en Métaux (CGT), *compte rendu*, 15–16 September 1929, p. 32.

[12] XXVIe Congrès National, SFIO, 9–12 June 1929, *compte rendu*, pp. 414–415.

[13] VIe Congrès National du Parti Communiste Français, 31 March–7 April 1929, *Manifeste, Thèses et Résolutions*, pp. 32–33.

[14] *Bulletin Mensuel des Allocations Familiales et des Assurances Sociales* (October 1929), 177 and (November 1929), 196, cited by Simon, "Les Assurances sociales et les mutualistes," p. 599.

employers could continue to exert pressure on worker welfare in at least three ways. They could sponsor their own mutual societies and thereby benefit directly from light state oversight. Also, as we saw earlier, many employers had already allied themselves with mutual societies in order to maintain influence over worker welfare.[15] Many of these alliances remained in place and offered employers a potentially pivotal role in mutual society social insurance. Finally, the corporatist outlook of mutual leaders meant that honorary membership, which was often held by employers, would remain an open venue for influencing mutual-society led social insurance *caisses*. However, all of these avenues of employer control over social welfare administration could only be effective if mutual societies were sufficiently unbridled from state mandates.

Deliberations of the mutual aid society that was associated with automobile manufacturer Renault indicated the hopes of employers in securing control of social insurance administration. Shortly after approval of the Chauveau bill by the Chamber, the president of Renault's mutual society for Paris-area workers announced to the governing board that "a mutual society composed of at least 10,000 members six months before application of the law will be able to create a *caisse primaire*, which means it will be able to control its own funds instead of these moneys going to a state-run *caisse*."[16] With barely 3,000 members in 1928, Renault's mutual society leaders launched a campaign among workers in the hope of achieving the requisite membership. But by April 1929, with hopes of creating its own *caisse primaire* waning, board members learned that "the factory management has asked our president to plan for... the affiliation of our society to the Fédération Mutualiste de la Seine as well as the Union des Sociétés de Secours Mutuels d'Usine et Similaires de la Région Parisienne."[17] The latter was a consortium of employer-created mutual societies, which, by banding together, could meet the law's minimum membership requirements for a *caisse primaire*. Also, as preexisting mutual societies, they were eligible to invoke the law's assumption of affiliation and thereby automatically retain members who did not formally renounce their association in favor of another social insurance *caisse*.[18] As employers such as Renault positioned themselves for implementation of the law, they became increasingly enthusiastic supporters of FNMF

---

[15] See chapter 3.
[16] Remarks of President Mille, Conseil d'Administration, Société de Secours Mutuels des Usines Renault, *procès-verbaux*, 6 July 1928.
[17] Conseil d'Administration, Société de Secours Mutuels des Usines Renault, *procès-verbaux*, 18 April 1929.
[18] *Ibid.*, 19 July 1929.

copresidents Péret and Petit who were fighting for the preeminence of mutual societies under the new law. While the *grand patronat* could never hope to match the organizational and numeric strength of the mutual movement in the provision of social insurance outside industrial centers, increased mutualization of the 1928 law meant that more power would reside in private rather than state hands.

The propaganda and reorganization plans at Renault's mutual society paralleled a national effort by the FNMF to increase the size of its constituent member societies, through both recruitment and amalgamation. Gaston Roussel, director at the ministry of hygiène, de l'assistance et de la prévoyance sociales, had long lobbied Péret to consolidate the mutual movement. Roussel argued that the size of many mutual societies, even if organized into regional unions, would constrain their ability to create capitalized funds for retirement and disability under the new social insurance legislation. Roussel believed that the solution to this problem lay in the creation of federations of existing unions and larger societies, which could then benefit from collaborative administration and larger funds. Indeed, Roussel lauded the FNMF for the growth in mutual membership, which between 1923 and 1927 grew by over 2 million to 5.9 million and during which time the number of mutual societies actually declined.[19] Péret and Petit appeared to follow Roussel's counsel. After passage of the first social insurance law in 1928, they beseeched presidents of the FNMF's constituent societies to recruit "the 2,000 members that are necessary for an autonomous departmental *caisse* or, where it is possible, an interdepartmental *caisse* . . . if you do that, but only if you do it, will the French mutual movement be saved."[20]

While the FNMF positioned itself for implementation of the new law, the Tardieu government, aided by Radical-Socialists, pushed hard for a final text. These efforts led to a series of extraordinary day and night Chamber sessions in late April 1930. On 26 April 1930, by a vote of 550 to 20, the Chamber approved a definitive text of social insurance.[21] By all accounts, the final legislation, which became known as the law of 30 April 1930, awarded mutual leaders with near total victory and promised a

---

[19] Speech by Gaston Roussel, *Bulletin Officiel de la FNMF* 34 (June 1927), 31–35.
[20] "Instructions relatives à la participation de la Mutualité à l'application de la loi du 5 avril 1928 sur les assurances sociales," *Bulletin Officiel de la FNMF* 35 (March–December 1928).
[21] The Senate voted 255 to 17 to approve the legislation. See *JO*, Annales du Sénat, débats parlementaires, 22 March 1930, p. 449; Annales de la Chambre, débats parlementaires, 23 April 1930, p. 1941; Annales du Sénat et de la Chambre, débats parlementaires, 26 April 1930, pp. 1460 and 2083.

privileged place for their organizations under the new regime.[22] Indeed, the emerging system could be called "compulsory mutualism." The primary administrative institutions, the *caisses primaires* of the new regime, were to be created according to the general guidelines provided in the 1898 Charte de la Mutualité. Presumption of affiliation was maintained and mutual societies would be permitted to manage social insurance funds for the good of their organizations. In order to qualify as a *caisse primaire* for the administration of all risks, mutual societies would still have to meet a 10,000 member minimum. This requirement, however, could be satisfied by preexisting federations and through regional unions. Alongside the freedom afforded to mutual societies, the state maintained powerful oversight powers through its Offices des Assurances Sociales and the Conseil Supérieur des Assurances Sociales, both of which were presided over by the minister of labor but also included substantial representation from the FNMF. Within months of the law's implementation, some mutual leaders, again backed by employers, would move to challenge the state's role even here. But in the spring of 1930, mutual leaders were content to celebrate their victory and thank government officials for their support. Labor Minister Pierre Laval received a warm telegram from the FNMF that expressed gratitude for "your influential sympathy for the mutual movement through which these very important improvements [in the law] were obtained."[23] Laval responded in kind. At the FNMF national congress in June 1930, he confided that "the mutual movement will safeguard the financial health of social insurance. This law is your law. Its future depends on you. It will be what you make of it. It will be your work."[24] With mutual leaders on board, all now appeared clear for a successful launch of France's long-debated social insurance system on 1 July 1930.

IMPLEMENTATION OF SOCIAL INSURANCE

Social reform legislators and members of the Tardieu government, such as Adolphe Landry and Pierre Laval, had reckoned that their concessions to the FNMF would assure a smooth implementation of social insurance. But this was not to be. Employers, mutual leaders, and doctors repeatedly violated the spirit if not the letter of the law.

[22] XVe Congrès National de la Mutualité Française, *compte rendu sommaire*, *Bulletin Officiel de la FNMF* 43 (May–June 1930), 4–7.
[23] *Le Matin*, 26 April 1930.
[24] *Les Assurances sociales* (July 1930), 28. Also see *Bulletin Officiel de la FNMF* 43 (May–June 1930) 23.

In his speeches on social insurance, Comité des Forges board member Alfred Lambert-Ribot took delight in citing former Prime Minister Camille Chautemps. According to Lambert-Ribot, Chautemps once said that: "Great social reforms are only durable and stable when they are realized with the general consensus of all citizens."[25] The *grand patronat* was no doubt pleased by the freedom afforded to mutual societies in the final legislation of 1930. Yet they also remained painfully aware that they had lost the war against obligation. In preparation for implementation, the president of the Confédération Générale de la Production Française (CGPF), René Duchemin, advised members to meet the letter of law but no more. Employer contributions and worker wage deductions should be scrupulously conducted, however, he strongly advised employers to refuse compensatory wage increases.[26] Indeed, the vast majority of employers faithfully applied the law. A 1930 survey of 13,376 firms by labor ministry inspectors revealed that nearly all were conducting their social insurance wage deductions correctly. Differences in wage policies, however, were perceptible according to the nature and size of firms. 44 percent conformed to CGPF directives, offering no compensatory wage increases. But fully 38 percent granted a wage increase of some sort in order to avoid work stoppages and labor conflict. This list included the metals employers of Saint Quentin and textile manufacturers in Armentières. Finally, labor inspectors found that in 18 percent of the firms surveyed employers assumed the total cost of their workers' social insurance premiums. This list was primarily made up of small and medium-sized operations whose owners either did not possess the administrative capability to ensure accurate wage deductions and/or who preferred to preserve a familial environment between themselves and their workers.[27] These statistics offered comfort to state officials. At various junctures during deliberations over the law, voices associated with the *patronat* had hinted at widespread non-compliance.[28] Yet while the vast majority of employers faithfully abided by the law, some took advantage of the legislation to concoct new wage strategies.

Implementation of social insurance resulted in the hatching of yet another initiative by the Roubaix-Tourcoing consortium of textile manufacturers to control workers. Employers duly carried out the wage

[25] Lambert-Ribot, Comité National d'Etudes Sociales et Politiques, *procès-verbaux*, 10 February 1930, p. 19.

[26] *Les Assurances sociales*, April 1930, pp. 25–26.

[27] Rapport de l'Inspecteur Divisionnaire, 4 August 1930, AN F22 211–213.

[28] See a series of articles that appeared in the run up to the law's implementation in *L'Economiste Français* (7 December 1929), 705–707 (15 March 1930), 321–333 (25 April 1930), 513–515.

deductions and made their own social insurance contributions according to the law. However, the low remuneration of many textile workers led workers' unions to call for negotiations over compensatory wage increases. The consortium ignored these calls and instead instituted what it called a regularity prime (*prime de fidélité*). Under this policy, only employees with perfect work attendance records were granted a reimbursement equal to their social insurance wage deductions at the end of the year. Any sort of incapacitating illness, disability, maternity or participation in work stoppages and strikes promptly excluded a worker from this benefit. As was so often the case with the tactics of Desiré Ley, director of the consortium, the policy had the reverse effect of its intention. Ley had calculated that the regularity prime would pre-empt worker demands and accompanying strikes for compensatory wage increases. Instead, the policy itself prompted an extraordinary rapprochement between the CGT, CGTU, and CFTC. Strikes erupted in the beginning of July 1930 in Lille and quickly spread to surrounding textile as well as metals plants. By the first week of August, nearly 80,000 consortium workers had walked out in protest of the consortium's regularity prime. In all, 150,000 stopped work throughout the Nord. In mid-August, Labor Minister Pierre Laval intervened in an attempt to end the strike but made little headway until workers' unions had reached the breaking point later that month. The accord that finally prompted a return to work left the regularity prime firmly in place but stripped it of the interdiction against a worker's participation in strikes.[29] Although this outcome appeared as a near total victory for Ley, the consortium emerged fragmented. During the strike 75 of the consortium's approximately 500 firms had left the association in order to negotiate compensatory wage increases devoid of the regularity prime. Nevertheless, as the crisis came to a close Ley was reelected to another five-year term as director of the consortium, indicating that a significant number of consortium members believed they had at least forced workers into a draw.[30] Indeed, employers emerged victorious much more often than workers in the battle over compensatory wage hikes. Workers launched 565 strikes between July and September 1930, the vast majority of which (344) owed their origins to social insurance wage policies. Of the total strikes, only 58 were successful, 199 failed, 245 ended in compromise, and the outcome of 59 was not known when

---

[29] Some press reports referred to the payment as a *prime d'assiduité*. The final accord renamed the benefit *prime de présence*. See AN F22 212–213 and *Le Matin*, 1, 4–6, 8–15, 17–31 August 1930 and 1–5, 10, 13 September 1930.

[30] *L'Information Sociale*, 4 September 1930.

the labor ministry drew up its report.[31] Workers quickly lost enthusiasm in the battle for compensatory wage increases. Strikes launched for that reason fell from 306 in July to 38 in August and to zero in September. Meanwhile, social insurance proponents and foes continued to joust in parliament over revisions to the new law. The most serious battles involved disgruntled mutual leaders, employers, and doctors, all of whom mounted serious challenges to the law's basic principles.

ATTEMPTS TO REVISE SOCIAL INSURANCE, 1930–1936

By the end of 1931 the mutual movement had demonstrated its pre-eminence under social insurance. Mutual societies controlled more than 80 percent of distributional *caisses*, that is, those that provided medical, maternity, and death benefits. They could also claim fully 85 percent of *caisses* that handled capitalized funds for retirement and disability pensions. In sum, mutual societies served approximately 60 percent of the approximately 8.5 million social insurees in one fashion or another. Labor union and employer *caisses* split the remainder.[32] Despite their predominance, FNMF leaders complained of the stifling bureaucracy that had been created by the new law and lobbied for a lightening of government regulations. In November 1930, deputies Maurice Dormann and Jean Montigny introduced legislation that would have abolished obligatory paycheck deductions and set mutual societies almost completely free from state oversight. Specifically, the deputies called on their colleagues to amend article 2 of the 1928 law so as to read: "The employer is released from conducting wage deductions . . . for obligatory participants who are members of mutual aid societies and thereby enjoy benefits at least equal to or superior to the present law."[33] The bill would have also permitted mutual societies to commingle revenues from social insurance participants, i.e. worker premiums and employer contributions, with their general funds from non-social insuree mutual members. In other words, social insurance premiums would become, in effect, a large subsidy to mutual societies, which, in return would provide services to social insurees, but neither special accounting nor state oversight would be required.[34] Finally, the Dormann-Montigny legislation would have repealed language in the 1930 social insurance law that constrained mutual societies from owning medical diagnostic and treatment centers.

---

[31] *L'Economiste Français* (16 May 1931), 615–616.   [32] *La France Economique* (1931), 626.
[33] *JO*, Annales de la Chambre des Députés, documents parlementaires, Chambre, Annexe no. 3961, 4 November 1930, p. 40.
[34] Georges Buisson, *Les Assurances sociales en danger* (Paris: Edition de la CGT, 1932), p. 36.

While FNMF leaders did not support the abolition of automatic wage deductions and compulsory participation, they viewed the Dormann-Montigny bill as a beneficial development that could result in a lightening of state regulation.[35] Social insurance had proven far more bureaucratically burdensome than many had expected and they thus saw the bill as a vehicle for relief.

Employers also supported the Dormann-Montigny bill. Once again, they saw a further mutualization of social insurance and lighter state oversight as providing increased maneuver room for their own initiatives.[36] CGT leaders were quick to identify the tactics of employers that would become even more rampant if the Dormann-Montigny bill were approved. They pointed to the case of a mutual society with close ties to the Société des Forges et Aciéries du Nord et de l'Est, the Caisse Interprofessionnelle du Bassin de la Sambre. According to the CGT, workers at the Forges and Aciéries were required to belong to this *caisse* and were effectively discouraged from protesting against its services. If a worker did protest and sought to transfer social insurance coverage, the *caisse* promptly informed the management of the Forges who asked the worker to sign a declaration that disavowed any complaints against the *caisse*. A refusal to sign, according to the local CGT syndicate, meant a certain layoff for "lack of work."[37] Thus, CGT leaders reasoned that if the *patronat* was already compelling worker membership in their "false mutual societies" and the Dormann-Montigny bill passed, such behavior would surely increase since it would discharge employers of dealing with a truly independent entity chosen by the insured.[38] Indeed, the CGT regarded mutual leaders' qualified support for the revisionist legislation as a betrayal of their earlier commitments to loyally implement the law. So contentious did the bill prove that legislators delayed action and the bill had to be reintroduced in a new legislature that was seated in June 1932. But by this time the Dormann-Montigny bill had been joined by a host of even more radical proposals.[39] The broader attack on social insurance

---

[35] Remarks by Léon Heller, Etats Généraux de la Mutualité, *compte rendu*, *Bulletin Officiel de la FNMF* 49 (May–June 1931), 6–7. Also see the remarks by Gaston Roussel, Assemblée Générale de la Fédération Nationale de la Mutualité Française, *procès-verbaux*, *Bulletin Officiel de la FNMF* 54 (March 1932 numéro spécial), 17.

[36] Simon, "Les Assurances sociales et les mutualistes," p. 607.

[37] Letter, C. Jenot, Secrétaire de l'Union Louvroil des Syndicats Confédérés de Maubeuge et Environs, to Préfet du Nord, 19 August 1932, reprinted in Buisson, *Les Assurances sociales en danger*, pp. 31–32.

[38] Buisson, *ibid.*, p. 32.

[39] "Extrait du procès-verbal de la réunion du Conseil d'Administration du 1 avril 1932," *Bulletin Officiel de la FNMF* 55 (March–April 1932), 7. See a summary of these revisionist proposals in Buisson, *ibid.*, pp. 43–48.

as well as the modified Dormann-Montigny bill, however, suffered a widespread loss of appeal when doctors mounted an exposé of mutual society practices under existing law.[40]

Professional medical associations (*syndicats medicaux*) had long played an influential role in deliberations over insurance that covered therapeutic procedures and health.[41] As early as 1858 Napoleon III had supported a resolution of the Association Générale des Médecins de France that prohibited medical professionals from divulging confidential information to private insurance companies. This imperative gained greater salience with passage of the 1898 law on accident insurance. At that time it was feared that insurance companies would use workers' personal medical files to discriminate against employers who were required to purchase accident insurance.[42] Given the sweeping nature of the 1928 and 1930 laws, which went well beyond the 1898 law's limited coverage for job-related accidents, doctors foresaw tremendous dangers for the practice of liberal medicine, this time emanating from mutual societies. The journal of the Confédération des Syndicats Médicaux Français, *Le Médecin de France*, announced that, "No doctor, no matter what his circumstances or level of achievement, in practice or in teaching, can pretend that he is somehow protected from the upheaval that the implementation of social insurance will bring to the profession." Indeed, the Confédération estimated that between 60 and 70 percent of the clients of more than half its membership would be social insurees under the law of 1930.[43]

In exchange for their cooperation with social insurance, doctors had insisted on respect for what they labeled "the medical charter." It consisted of four principles: (1) Freedom of social insurees to choose their own doctor; (2) Preservation of patients' financial liability for the direct payment of services; (3) Doctors' unhindered prerogative in diagnosis and treatment; (4) Respect of medical confidentiality.[44] Each of these principles gained varying degrees of support among doctors' associations. Notably, the rejection of any third payer (*tiers payant*) responsibility for fees proved highly controversial, causing a schism in the Confédération, which was only settled by the departure of several

40 *Le Médecin de France* (1 May 1932). The FNMF's response is in the *Bulletin Officiel de la FNMF* 56 (May–June 1932), 2–3.
41 On French medicine in the nineteenth century, see Jacques Léonard, *La Médecine entre les savoirs et les pouvoirs* (Paris: Aubier Montaigne, 1981).
42 Gibaud, *Mutualité, Assurances*, pp. 122–125.   43 *Le Médecin de France* (1 January 1929), 1.
44 Paul Marcadé, *Le Médecin français et la loi sur les assurances sociales* (Bordeaux: Imprimerie-Librairie de l'Université, 1933), p. 81. Also see Gabriel Batier, "Le Projet sur les assurances sociales jugé par un médecin d'Alsace," *Revue Politique et Parlementaire*, (February 1926), 245–253.

syndicates from the Nord.[45] Yet despite this schism, the Confédération effectively threatened legislators with non-compliance by doctors if the medical charter were not incorporated into the social insurance legislation of 1930.[46] After passage of the law in April, the Confédération polled its membership in a vote whose outcome was too close to predict only days before. The assembled delegates approved of the 1930 law but reserved the right to cease cooperation if the medical charter were not upheld in practice.[47] One development, in particular, was especially feared because of its threat to the entire charter: the creation of what doctors called industrial medicine (*médecine industrielle*) or *caisse* medicine (*médecine de caisse*).

Doctors defined both of these terms – the former gave way to the latter by 1932 – as the provision of medical services by an institution, be it a clinic, hospital, sanitarium, dispensary, etc., that was under the substantial control of an insurer. Use of the term industrial medicine originated from early concerns that legislators would model the new illness insurance on the existing system for miners, whose care was strictly regulated and often conducted at employer-run clinics.[48] Nowhere did the 1928 law contemplate such a circumscribed approach to medicine. Nevertheless, doctors insisted that the 1930 legislation foresee the possibility that negotiations between *caisses* and doctors may fail, in which case a tripartite commission made up of *caisse* representatives, doctors, and state officials would arbitrate the dispute. The revised law also created a medical advisory committee, comprised of doctors, within the *caisse* administration.[49] Satisfied that these revisions would safeguard their medical authority and sufficiently bolster their negotiating position with *caisses*, doctors gave their conditional support to social insurance.

In theory, the 1930 legislation afforded the social insuree the freedom to choose his or her own doctor or other health professional.[50] The patient paid the full cost of treatment according to a fee schedule negotiated between his or her *caisse* and the applicable medical association. The insured then applied for a reimbursement of approximately 85 percent from his or her social insurance *caisse*. In practice, however, relations

---

[45] Chauveau, *Loi sur les assurances sociales*, pp. 116–117.
[46] *Le Médecin de France* (1 June 1929), pp. 291–293.   [47] *Ibid.* (1 September 1930), 673–676.
[48] Batier, "Le Projet," p. 248; Chauveau, *Loi sur les assurances sociales*, Article 6, paragraphs 1 and 2, pp. 327–329.
[49] *JO*, Lois et décrets, 1 May 1930, "Loi modifiant et complétant la loi du 5 avril 1928 sur les assurances sociales," Articles 6 and 7, pp. 4821–4822.
[50] *Caisses* commonly entered into contracts with a variety of *syndicats medicaux*, including surgeons, dentists, midwives, and pharmacists.

between *caisses* and doctors' associations quickly became strained over fees and diagnoses. In order to reach agreement on fees, social insurance *caisses* and doctors' associations resorted to schedules that included a wide range of prices. In effect, the negotiated fee schedule came to indicate merely a minimum charge rather than, as had been intended by legislators, a closely delimited maximum. The lack of clarity in fee schedules resulted in numerous disputes between medical professionals and *caisses*. Doctors insisted that they should be free to practice medicine with the sole interest of the patient in mind, irrespective of cost considerations. *Caisses*, on the other hand, accused doctors of using the presence of a third payer to raise prices, in some cases, in violation of the contracts they had signed.[51] Caught in the middle of this conflict, of course, were social insurees who commonly found themselves with doctors' bills that their *caisses* would reimburse at only 40 or 50 percent.[52] Moreover, in some cases, doctors and *caisses* could not even agree on a common medical diagnosis and treatment.

The law of 1930 set up a system of technical oversight that was meant to expose fraudulent or unnecessary medical treatments.[53] Under its guidelines doctors who practiced bad medicine were subject to warnings, fines, and, as a last resort, exclusion from the treatment of social insurees. This system of technical control, however, quickly became yet another point of friction between *caisses* and doctors. In a widely circulated book, medical doctor Paul Marcadé recounts that of the approximately 70 doctors' associations, 21 complained about *caisse* criticism of their diagnosis and treatment decisions under the oversight regime. 18 of the 21 added that *caisse* officials made criticisms in front of patients in disregard of ethical and professional behavior.[54] For their part, mutual leaders noted large and inexplicable variations in medical practices. In one case, they compared pharmaceutical prescriptions of two doctors with similar caseloads. For 700 patients, doctor X prescribed drugs at an average value of 28 francs while doctor Y treated his patients by recommending drugs valued at 13 francs per patient. *Caisse* officials had no doubt as to which was the better doctor. In their view it was surely the

[51] Romain Lavielle, *Histoire de la mutualité*, p. 117.

[52] Assemblée Générale de la Confédération des Syndicats Médicaux Français, *procès-verbaux*, 19 December 1937, reported in *Le Médecin de France* (1 March 1938), 220. Also see *Le Médecin de France* (March–April 1946), 267–269.

[53] *JO*, Loi et décrets, 1 May 1930, "Loi modifiant et complétant la loi du 5 avril 1928 sur les assurances sociales," Articles 65–68, pp. 4830–4831.

[54] Marcadé, *Le Médecin français*, pp. 73–76.

cheaper of the two.[55] As with the discord between doctors and *caisses* on fee schedules, patients risked being placed in an uncomfortable position if their case became the subject of an oversight exercise. If a disagreement arose and treatment had already begun, the *caisse* refused to reimburse the patient for his or her expenses. If disagreement arose at the diagnostic stage, the patient was left with two conflicting medical opinions but no chance of reimbursement for one of them.

Unable to rein in doctors' fees or quell doctors' protests against their prerogatives, FNMF leaders demanded changes to social insurance so that mutual societies could provide care directly to their insurees. But such an amendment would have abrogated special guarantees that had been given to doctors in the law of 1930.[56] Marcel Martin, adjunct director of the Caisse Interdépartementale des Assurances Sociales de Seine et Seine-et-Oise, suggested "the direct intervention of social insurance *caisses* in the diagnosis and even the treatment of ill social insurees" and called for the "creation or development of treatment and prevention institutions, placed at the disposition of family medicine." Martin further asserted that "certain rules which doctors hold due to tradition are incompatible with the smooth implementation of social insurance"[57] Doctors viewed such declarations and legislative lobbying to fulfill them as evidence of the mutual movement's desire to control medical care in France. If permitted, they warned, all of the sacrosanct principles of the medical charter would be sacrificed on the altar of cost effectiveness. Evidence of this potential calamity was provided by a survey conducted by the doctors' Confédération that indicated the extent to which the implementation of social insurance, especially by mutual society and employer-run *caisses*, had already resulted in numerous violations of the medical charter. The survey showed that patients' freedom of choice was encumbered by some *caisses* through their recommendation of specific doctors. These *caisses* also commonly steered their social insurees toward special pharmacies associated with the mutual society and, in direct violation of doctors' prescriptive authority, refused normal reimbursement for specialty drugs. Others limited the amount of a pharmaceutical prescription for which an individual could be reimbursed. Finally, the survey

---

[55] René Hubert, "Les Assurances sociales et l'opinion publique," *Revue Politique et Parlementaire* (October 1929), 30–42. See especially p. 33.

[56] See the comments of Léon Heller, president of the FNMF, published in *Le Matin*, 14 April 1932.

[57] Marcel Martin, speech of 1 February 1933 given at the Bourse du Travail, cited by Marcadé, *Le Médecin français*, pp. 77–78.

revealed systematic violations of medical confidentiality by two provincial *caisses*. These *caisses* required doctors to communicate their diagnoses and treatments to the *caisse* as part of the reimbursement process. Doctors warned that the sharing of medical information with insurers was a dangerous practice which would be amplified by the promulgation of *caisse* medicine. Medical professionals' loss of autonomy under *caisse* medicine, argued doctors, would make them far less able to refuse the directives of the *caisse*. Simultaneously, the temptation of employers to learn about the health of their workers would grow in inverse relation to doctors' ability to preserve its confidentiality.[58] Nonetheless, the FNMF continued to call for substantial revisions to the medical insurance portion of the 1930 law throughout the 1930s.[59] But these calls faced stiff opposition from doctors, workers' unions, and ultimately from within the mutual movement itself.

The CGT and the *cégétiste* mutual society federation, the FMT, viewed the Dormann-Montigny bill and other revisionist legislation that would further mutualize the 1930 law as much too radical. To be sure, the CGT was not pleased with the function of medical insurance and had, in fact, opposed Chauveau's institution of a reimbursement system in place of the copayment (*ticket moderateur*) system in the earlier Grinda bill. The CGT maintained that "it is necessary to move away from traditional, purely individual and curative medicine, and toward social medicine, which is preventative and defensive, an evolution that is imperative for the public health of the country."[60] Nor did the FMT, like the FNMF, refrain from criticizing the burdensome paperwork required by the 1930 law.[61] But neither the FMT nor the CGT would sign on to the remedies advocated by the FNMF, preferring instead to give the new law more time for adjustment. This included their relations with doctors' associations, which the CGT admitted were "far from perfect."[62]

FNMF efforts to revise the 1930 law were also damaged by the near simultaneous loss of Raoul Péret and Georges Petit. Implicated in the Oustric scandal of 1930, Péret resigned from the general presidency of the FNMF in June 1931. Petit left his post for personal reasons, probably

---

[58] Leaders of the Confédération des Syndicats Médicaux Français reported the most egregious violations of the medical charter by mutual society social insurance *caisses* in *Le Médecin de France*. See *Le Médecin de France* (1 January 1932), 25; (26 January 1932), 97–105; (12 February 1932), 133–143. Marcadé, *Le Médecin français*, also provides a summary, pp. 66–72.
[59] Letter, Heller, president of the FNMF to Camille Chautemps, 16 July 1937, AN F60 651.
[60] Buisson, *Les Assurances sociales en danger*, p. 38.
[61] *Le Réveil Mutualiste*, June 1932, cited by Simon, "Les Assurances sociales et les mutualistes," p. 610.
[62] Buisson, *Les Assurances sociales en danger*, p. 39.

the illness of his wife, later the same year.[63] With the departure of Péret and Petit, FNMF delegates eliminated the copresidency and selected a well-connected mutualist from the Somme, Léon Heller, as president. New in office, Heller could not mount the necessary political pressure to bring about any substantial modifications to the 1930 social insurance law. He nevertheless maintained that "the satisfaction we had during the initial months of implementation [of the law] turned out to be totally unfounded."[64] However, at the Etats Généraux de Mutualité in September 1932, which brought together mutual leaders of all stripes, including the pro-CGT FMT, Heller brokered a final declaration that reiterated the mutual movement's support for "obligation and mandatory wage withholding, which should be considered as one of the fundamental pillars of social insurance."[65] Legislative momentum to amend the 1930 legislation was further slowed by a series of solid financial statements that were released by social insurance *caisses* in 1932. Social insurees continued to flock to mutual societies so that by September 1934, over 9 million workers had elected a mutual society for their insurance coverage under the law of 1930.[66] These developments left little doubt that no matter how contentious the relations between doctors and mutual societies, the new regime had benefited (and transformed) the mutual movement like no reform since the Charte de la Mutualité of 1898. Parliament refrained from modifying the social insurance law until 1935 when a limited revision expanded participation among commercial and industrial workers and tinkered with the administrative structure. Legislators dared not to tamper with the relative power between mutual societies, doctors associations, employers, and workers that they had so painstakingly constructed.

Radical Deputy Adolphe Landry, who served as minister of labor during this critical period, had predicted the mixed reactions that social insurance would face across professional and class lines. Writing in 1929, he remarked that "the institution that we are creating will not provide complete satisfaction to all who aspire for a more just organization of our society . . . The social insurance law will nevertheless provide a precious benefit to an entire class that does not possess it."[67] Indeed, by 1936 the social insurance regime had achieved a modicum of

[63] Bennet, *Biographies de personnalités mutualistes*, p. 343.   [64] *Ibid.*, p.228.

[65] "Déclaration, Etats Généraux de la Mutualité, 17 September 1932,"*Bulletin Officiel de la FNMF* 58 (September 1932). Also see Buisson, *Les Assurances sociales en danger*, p. 49.

[66] "Allocution de M. le Président Heller," Etats Généraux de la Mutualité, *compte rendu des Travaux, Bulletin Officiel de la FNMF*, numéro spécial (September 1934), p. 5.

[67] Emile Fleury, *Commentaire pratique et critique de la loi du 5 avril 1928 sur les assurances sociales*, preface by Adolphe Landry (Paris: Recueil Sirey, 1929), p. ix.

stability which permitted it to survive the upheaval of the Popular Front. Landry also played a formative role in family allowance legislation, an endeavor whose difficulties proved far more controversial and ultimately irresolvable.

Several factors coalesced to bring about a fundamental change in attitude among legislators toward family allowances. These included the passage of the social insurance laws of 1928 and 1930, growing fears of economic depression, and heightened concern about depopulation. The eight-year-long battle over social insurance law eroded long-held ideological prohibitions against mandatory social welfare measures. Pierre Laroque, who served on the Conseil d'Etat throughout the period, insisted that the success of social insurance created a momentum for state intervention in family welfare.[68] Evidence of legislators' new attitude toward family allowances was apparent in Deputy Jean Lerolle's 1929 bill that demanded all employers to affiliate with a *caisse de compensation*. Lerolle, a social Catholic legislator from Paris' seventh arrondissement, noted that a large proportion of industrial and commercial workers already received family allowances. But their number did not match the 9 million beneficiaries who were slated to be covered under the recently approved social insurance law.[69] Clearly, a new standard had been set. Employers of the family allowance movement could no longer easily impress legislators with the magnitude of private initiative if it did not match the scope of social insurance.

The depression also abetted the willingness of legislators to intervene. Just as rising prices during the 1920s had encouraged many employers to adopt family allowances in order to stave off general wage increases, expectations of depression, in reverse logic, dampened employer enthusiasm for the movement. Since the days of the Bokanowski bill, CCAF leaders had boasted to state officials that the persistent growth in size and number of *caisses* obviated the need for state intervention. This strategy placed the burden of proof on state officials to show that a state mandate could increase the rate of family allowance *caisse* creation faster than private initiative.[70] During the 1920s, when dozens of *caisses* were created every year and the membership of existing *caisses* rose quickly, the case

[68] Author's interview with Pierre Laroque, Paris, 2 December 1995.
[69] *JO*, Proposition Lerolle, 24 January 1929, Documents Parlementaires, Chambre, 1929, annexe no. 1135, p. 97.
[70] CCRP Commission de gestion, *procès-verbaux*, 17 October 1924.

Workers (in millions)   *Caisses* created

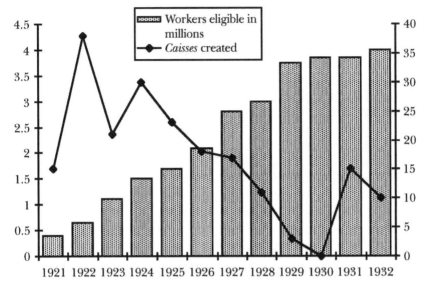

Figure 6   *Caisse* creation and workers eligible for family allowances 1921–1932.
Ie-XIVe Congrès National des Allocations Familiales, *comptes rendus*, 1921–1934. The
rebound in *caisse* creation during 1931 and 1932 does not reflect a new-found
enthusiasm for the movement but rather action by employers who found it
advantageous to create *caisses* before the 1932 family allowance law went into effect.
Most of these *caisses* existed only on paper, having little effect on workers.

for legislative action proved difficult to make. But as economic forecasts
were tinged by bank failures in central Europe and the New York stock
market crash, the family allowance movement stalled. Figure 6 illustrates
a stagnation in the number of workers who were eligible to collect allowances and a slowdown in *caisse* creation; the latter fell to zero in 1930.
This diminution underlined the practical failure of private initiative in
many legislators' eyes.

Simultaneous with the slowdown in *caisse* growth, employers' own
arguments were turned against them. Time and again during the debate over whether to include family allowances under social insurance,
CCAF leaders argued that children were a "social good" and should
not be considered an insurable risk.[71] While this point was entirely con-
sistent with the principle of the *salaire vital*, it opened the way for the

[71] Gustave Bonvoisin and Georges Maignan, *Allocations familiales et caisses de compensation* (Paris: Sirey,
1930), p. 219. Also see Marie-Magdeleine Laporte, *Les Allocations familiales dans le commerce et
l'industrie en droit français et étranger* (Paris: Dalloz, 1938), p. 35.

inevitable observation by public authorities that state action was required to widen the availability of family allowances if employers could not do it themselves. Key legislators began to justify family allowance legislation on the grounds of national solidarity and as a solution for France's demographic crisis.[72]

An array of pronatalist and social Catholic leaders also stepped up their support for compulsory family allowances for the sake of national revival. Elements within pronatalist circles had been poised to demand legislation since the early 1920s, but the continued voluntary growth of *caisses* had restrained them. However, in June 1927 a major familial group, the Fédération nationale des familles nombreuses, broke with its colleagues of the Congrès National de la Natalité (CNN) and issued an official call for obligation. Virtually all pronatalist groups followed suit within a year. Even the leading pronatalist organization with which the CCAF had fostered a special relationship, the Alliance Nationale, proclaimed its support for obligation in early 1928. Alliance Nationale leaders couched their support for obligation in terms that were congenial to employers, noting that "all employers should be required by law to affiliate with a *caisse de compensation* on the condition that all *caisses de compensation* remain private organizations."[73] They also likened the future mandate to the accident insurance legislation of 1898, thereby distinguishing it from the more intrusive social insurance law.[74]

As the magnitude of the world economic crisis became evident, pronatalists attributed the relative strength of the French economy to family allowances: "If the crisis is less serious in France than elsewhere, it is . . . due to the existence of family allowances for which 4 million workers in industry and commerce are presently eligible."[75] Requiring employers to pay family allowances, they argued, would further immunize France by resolving related problems of overproduction and unemployment. Pronatalists contended that overproduction was simply another way of saying depopulation. If there were enough consumers to purchase the quantity of available goods, overproduction could not exist. Hence, the best way to avoid recession lay in increasing the birthrate. The Alliance Nationale also maintained that unemployment was exacerbated by the employment of women but that family allowances could solve this problem. The legal obligation of allowances, pronatalists argued, would

---

[72] *JO*, "Rapport fait au nom de la Commission d'assurance et de prévoyance sociales," 11 July 1930, Documents parlementaires, Chambre, 1930, annexe no. 3827, pp. 1391–1399.
[73] Alliance Nationale Conseil d'administration, *procès-verbaux*, 13 January 1928.
[74] *Revue de l'Alliance Nationale*, 187 (February 1928), 39.   [75] *Ibid.*, 228 (July 1931), 562.

encourage more couples to have children and keep women at home to take care of them, thereby freeing up jobs for unemployed men.[76] While many social Catholics in parliament and the CFTC consistently supported state intervention on family welfare in the 1920s, their voices were magnified by the papal encyclicals *Casti Connubi* in 1930 and *Quadragesimo Anno* in 1931. *Casti Connubi* reaffirmed Church doctrine regarding the inviolability of marriage, emphasizing that procreation was its primary purpose. *Quadragesimo Anno* built upon *Casti Connubi* by addressing the circumstances in which parents, specifically mothers, raised children: "It is ... a harmful abuse and at a high cost that mothers disappear from the home due to the sheer modesty of the paternal wage, searching far from home for professional employment and neglecting their incumbent duties, especially the raising of their children."[77] Meant as a reaffirmation of Leo XIII's *Rerum Novarum*, *Quadragesimo Anno* was used by social Catholic legislators, such as Senator François Saint-Maur, to urge action on family allowances.[78] Social Catholic legislators played an important role in creating an environment in which state intervention on family allowances could succeed. For their part, CFTC leaders hoped that the prominence of their allied legislators in the debate over obligation would sway parliament to stipulate a role for workers in the administration of *caisses*. They were disappointed. Jean Lerolle's bill on obligation was, in fact, rejected because of its call for workers to participate in *caisse* management. Employer interests remained much too powerful to be overawed by social Catholic moralism. Instead, pragmatic employers found the malleable philosophy of solidarism, which had long fired the reformist instincts of the Radical center, a more useful approach to the problem of family welfare.[79]

Solidarism was born of nineteenth-century French philosophical efforts to reconcile moralistic utopianism with materialist conceptions of human nature. It thus offered an accommodation between the individualistic tendency of liberalism and the collectivist dictates of socialism. According to solidarists, a new philosophy was needed to achieve the Republic's promise of *fraternité* and balance the dominant bourgeois conception of liberty as *laissez-faire*. In 1895, Radical Léon Bourgeois,

[76] *Ibid.*, 232 (November 1931), 677–682. Also see *ibid.*, 256 (November 1933), 243–245 and Elzéar Abeille, *Le Problème des allocations familiales en face de la sous-consommation et de la dénatalité*, Rapport présenté au Chambre de commerce de Marseille, 28 April 1939.

[77] Cited by Talmy, *Histoire du mouvement familial en France*, vol. II, p. 199.

[78] *JO*, "Rapport fait au nom de la Commission d l'hygiène, de l'assistance, de l'assurance et de la prévoyance sociales," 11 June 1931, Documents parlementaires, Sénat, annexe no. 545, p. 1035.

[79] Author's interview with Pierre Laroque, Paris, 2 December 1995.

succeeded in adapting the various strands of solidarist thought into a usable political platform. In the process, however, he jettisoned much of its proletarian character. The solidarism of early twentieth-century Radicals evolved from Bourgeois' creation, offering restrained criticism of the status quo and a gradualist reform program. Wielded by centrist politicians, solidarism appealed to the middle classes who feared a violent struggle between uncompromising communists and liberals for control of the Republic. With the rejection of children as insurable risks under the social insurance law, solidarists promoted the notion that national solidarity dictated state action to generalize employer payment of family allowances.[80] Thus, it was neither social Catholics nor lawmakers of the left who authored successful legislation on family allowances but rather centrist Radicals who enjoyed close ties to the CCAF, the Alliance Nationale, and feminists.

THE LANDRY CLAN AND FAMILY ALLOWANCE LEGISLATION

The nature and timing of family allowance legislation were influenced by a clique of the Third Republic's political elite that were tied by bonds of blood, marriage, and professional loyalty. At the center of this web of personal relations stood Adolphe Landry, deputy from Corsica (1910–1932), sometime minister of labor (1931–1932), and member of the Alliance Nationale governing board from 1912 until his death in 1956. Landry's early career was dominated by his interest in demography where he eventually distinguished himself as a master, publishing some of the discipline's most important early works.[81] Initially unsuccessful in his bid for a Chamber seat in 1906 as an independent socialist, Landry associated himself with the secular republicanism of the Radicals, especially Aristide Briand. Elected to the Chamber in 1910, his legislative activities reflected his interest in population issues and social welfare. In 1913, Landry supported the first bill on state-sponsored aid to large families and its augmentation in 1923. In 1911, Landry and Alliance Nationale cofounder André Honnorat founded a pronatalist Chamber caucus that grew to include over half of all deputies by 1935.[82]

---

[80] Hayward, "Solidarity" and "The Official Social Philosophy."
[81] *Bulletin Mensuel des Allocations Familiales* 119 (November 1937), 200. My biographical discussion of Adolphe Landry is guided by Anne-Emmanuelle Demartini, "Le Clanisme politique en Corse: un cas particulier, le clan Landry," Mémoire de maîtrise d'histoire, Université de Paris IV, (1988).
[82] Groupe de la protection de la natalité et des familles nombreuses. See Tomlinson, "The Politics of 'Dénatalité'," pp. 338–342.

Landry's promotion of family allowances began in 1920, just as the movement was gaining momentum. In July of that year, large construction firms demanded that all building contractors who conducted work for the state be obligated to join a *caisse de compensation*. The president of the construction employers' association was Lucien Lassalle, founder of the construction employers' family allowance *caisse* and Adolphe Landry's brother-in-law.[83] By requiring the payment of family allowances, large construction employers hoped to limit the number of firms that were competing for the postwar reconstruction of northeastern France.[84]

Lassalle initially found no support for family allowance mandates in the legislature. He then contacted Landry who arranged for Lassalle to meet with Director of Labor Charles Picquenard.[85] Picquenard liked Lassalle's idea and he agreed to inject it as a compromise solution into the current deliberations over the Bokanowski bill.[86] In public, Picquenard justified family allowance mandates on construction employers on moral grounds; because they were engaged in civil infrastructure projects, a special responsibility to their workers applied.[87] In December 1922 Lassalle's private campaign came to fruition. Radicals Victor Jean and Raoul-Etienne Persil authored successful legislation that required all firms engaged in public works to join a family allowance *caisse de compensation*. The law positioned the ministry of labor, and thus Picquenard, as the arbiter of new *caisses*.[88]

Although the building trades represented only a small fraction of the family allowance movement, its experience with obligation served as a model for the generalization of mandatory family allowances in 1932. Indeed, those involved in the passage of the 1922 law gained considerable standing in their respective camps. Lassalle was elevated to vice president of the CCAF in 1925 and later became president of the Paris chamber of commerce. Meanwhile Picquenard became a regular guest at CCAF

---

[83] Lassalle was married to the sister of Landry's wife. Specifically, Lassalle headed two groups: the Groupe Syndical du Bâtiment and the Syndicat des Entrepreneurs de Travaux Publics. He was also founder of the Caisse d'Allocations Familiales du Bâtiment de Paris.

[84] Bureau International du Travail, *Etudes et Documents*, Série D, "Salaires et durée du travail," no. 13, "Les Allocations familiales," pp. 58–62; *Information Ouvrière et Sociale*, 31 July 1921.

[85] Interview with Aymé Bernard, Second phase, 17 December 1975, AN 37 AS 2.

[86] Commission d'Assurance et de Prévoyance Sociales, Chambre, *procès-verbaux*, 29 April 1921, 12th legislature, 1919–1924, A13, Dossier 1105, vol. 2, Archives de l'Assemblée Nationale; Conseil Supérieur du Travail, *procès-verbaux*, 16 November 1921.

[87] CCAF Assemblée générale, *procès-verbaux*, 9 June 1925, Report by M. Allusson, "Les Allocations familiales dans les marchés de travaux publics," pp. 13–38.

[88] *Ibid.*, p. 35.

conferences, reinforcing his relations with employers and his position as director of labor, a post he would hold until 1938.

The experience of the building trades became a favorite example of both state officials and those within the family allowance movement who had accepted the inevitability of state intervention. In November 1928 Minister of Labor Louis Loucheur received a delegation of *caisse* leaders which included CCAF Director Bonvoisin and CCRP President Richemond. Loucheur described the sentiments of the Poincaré government toward family allowances in stark terms and presented the assembled employers with an offer of government collaboration: "Small firms will always escape your movement, and since this has become politically untenable, generalized obligation is inevitable whether you like it or not . . . But we wish to take your efforts into account and want to see generalized obligation accomplished by private *caisses de compensation* and not by a state-managed system. The government asks you to collaborate in the drafting of our bill."[89]

The following month, Picquenard attended the customary banquet that followed the CCAF annual general assembly and announced the creation by the minister of labor of a Commission Supérieure des Allocations Familiales (CSAF). The new commission, comprised almost exclusively employers, contained no representatives of workers' unions. Indeed, Picquenard foresaw little change in *caisse* management under the new legislation. The CSAF served merely as a vehicle to facilitate employer influence over the law's technical details. But a consensus on excluding workers from *caisse* governing boards could not obscure several important differences between employers.

The most important of these concerned the treatment of firms who wished to pay family allowances directly to their workers without the intermediary of a *caisse de compensation*. In the parlance of the family allowance movement, these independent providers were known as *services particuliers*. Although they were relatively few in number, *services particuliers* accounted for a significant fraction of total allowances due to the size of their workforces.[90] Their aloofness from the *caisse* movement during the 1920s had earned them little more than indifference from the CCAF.

---

[89] CCRP Commission de gestion, *procès-verbaux*, 13 March 1929.

[90] Exact statistics on *services particuliers* are difficult to obtain since they were entirely outside the purview of state record keeping before 1933, nor did they constitute a centralized lobbying organization as did *caisse*-affiliated employers. According to spotty reporting at CCAF conferences in the 1920s, *services particuliers* numbered about two dozen and paid approximately one fifth of all family allowances in any given year. See Bonvoisin's "Rapport Moral" of the Congrès National des Allocations Familiales, *comptes rendus*, 1921–1933.

Services particuliers were generally found in heavy industry and mining. Hence, their work forces possessed a relatively high concentration of eligible beneficiaries, that is to say, family men. Their decision not to participate in *caisses* was thus greeted with quiet relief among *caisse* members, since affiliation of these firms would have raised premiums for other members. Once obligation appeared on the horizon, however, the CCAF became concerned about the creation of *services particuliers* by firms that employed relatively few eligible workers.

Caisses de compensation were based on the principle that employers should share the burden of paying allowances to workers with varying numbers of dependent children. This principle had already been eroded with the constitution of strictly professional *caisses* that limited their membership to employers of a certain industry, such as textiles, which employed relatively large numbers of ineligible workers, especially women and young men. *Services particuliers*, however, constituted an even larger threat to *caisses*. If the new legislation allowed firms with small numbers of eligible beneficiaries to constitute themselves as *services particuliers*, existing *caisses* would be flooded with mandatory affiliations from firms that employed workers with larger than average families. The government's proposal recognized the legitimacy of existing *services particuliers* but tightly circumscribed the creation of new ones, noting that "approval of *services particuliers* must be strictly exceptional and motivated by irrefutable justification and a material impossibility of affiliation with a *caisse de compensation*."[91] This language proved acceptable to the CCAF and represented a triumph for Picquenard in reconciling CCAF concerns with the acquired privileges of existing *services particuliers*. His ability to broker this accord rested on his power to personally oversee recommendations to the minister of labor concerning new *services particuliers*.[92]

Instead of creating an entirely new law, legislation on family allowances amended the Code du Travail. This strategy served two objectives. First, it gave the minister of labor (and thus Picquenard) direct responsibility for implementation and enforcement. Second, all legislation that amended the Code du Travail automatically opened jurisdiction to the Chamber's labor committee (Commission du Travail), whose members the government judged to be more sympathetic to the bill's liberal principles. The competing parliamentary committee, the CAPS, had shown

---

[91] *JO*, "Projet Poincaré, Loucheur, et Hennesy," 25 July 1929, Documents parlementaires, Chambre, 1929, annexe no. 2171, pp. 1235–1237.

[92] Recommendations for action written by Picquenard accompanied all applications by existing and new *services particuliers* which were sent to the minister of labor. See AN F22 1560–1580.

itself to be too interventionist for the likes of employers, having approved the Bokanowski bill eight years earlier. The CAPS had also presided over deliberations on social insurance, an episode that remained awkward at best for the *grand patronat*. In the end only minor changes were made to the government's proposal and the Chamber approved legislation to require the payment of family allowances on 30 March 1931.[93]

In contrast to social insurance legislation, the Senate quickly approved the Chamber bill. A small group of senators argued that French employers should not be burdened with additional social costs during the current economic crisis. They reminded their colleagues that the cost of family allowances, estimated at 2.7 percent of wages, would fall on top of social insurance premiums. They also demanded that all major employers' associations be consulted before the law could be implemented in their sector.[94] The eventual success of the legislation rested on the government's promise to implement family allowance mandates slowly, by sector and by department.[95] In the end, the opposition counted very few voices and the obligation of employers to join a *caisse de compensation* for the payment of family allowances was signed into law by President Doumer on 11 March 1932.

IMPLEMENTATION OF THE LAW ON FAMILY ALLOWANCES

The *grand patronat* reacted favorably to the new law. CCRP President Richemond celebrated the legislation, noting that "the legislation is very liberal, to an extent unhoped for by us...If ever there was an inherent danger of state intervention, we can relax now, we should be well satisfied."[96] Implementation of the new law, however, proved considerably more difficult than leaders of the family allowance movement or state officials had foreseen. The first challenge fell to employers and concerned the influx of thousands of small firms into their *caisses*. Second, the ministry of labor had to formulate an enforcement strategy that was

---

[93] Commission d'Assurance et de Prévoyance Sociales, *procès-verbaux*, 25 October and 8 November 1929, 14th legislature, 1928–1932, A10, vol. 699/1; Commission du Travail, Chambre, *procès-verbaux*, 6 and 13 November 1929, 14th, legislature, 1928–1932, A67, vol. 4601, Archives de l'Assemblée Nationale; *JO*, Documents parlementaires, Sénat, 1931, annexe no. 545, p. 1035.

[94] See especially the remarks of Senator Farjon, *JO*, Débats parlementaires, Sénat, 21 January 1932, pp. 36–37.

[95] *Ibid.*, pp. 36–42.

[96] CCRP Commission de gestion, *procès-verbaux*, 13 March 1929. This session covered several important issues related to obligation and was attended by CCAF Director Bonvoisin and Adolphe Pichon, attorney for the Comité des Forges and husband of Marguerite Pichon-Landry.

capable of covering over a million firms with only 160 inspectors.[97] The third and by far the most difficult problem lay in the various forms of resistance to the law mounted by small firms, especially in the commercial sector.

In the fall of 1933 CCRP industrialists confronted the imminent application of thousands of small, mostly commercial and artisanal enterprises that were now subject to the family allowance law.[98] The industrialists wanted to attenuate the power of new members which they deemed potentially untrustworthy members of the *caisse*. The butcher or grocer, they thought, could not be trusted to understand complex *caisse* regulations. Hence, CCRP leaders instituted rules whereby only relatively large employers of the *caisse* could pay allowances directly to their personnel. Allowances of small enterprises were to be paid by the *caisse*. Voting rights within the *caisse* were also reapportioned in order to preclude the possibility that new members could outvote long-standing GIMM members. According to Richemond, "it would be inadmissible for a few hundred little commercial operators, employing a few thousand people, to make the rules for our industrial enterprises that employ several hundred thousand workers."[99] By the end of 1934, the CCRP had succeeded in absorbing the new applicants while preserving large employers' control.[100]

Enforcement of the law, of course, fell to state officials, especially the ministry of labor, which was responsible for formulating its technical regulations. Picquenard's enforcement strategy rested on the *caisse de compensation*. Employers in affected sectors, regardless of whether they employed personnel with children, were required to join a *caisse de compensation*. By placing *caisse* affiliation at the center of his implementation strategy, Picquenard also enhanced the leverage of the ministry of labor. According to the law, all *caisses* had to apply for approval from the ministry of labor.[101] Through his power to withhold approval, Picquenard succeeded in compelling some *caisses* to provide more social services. He argued that the 1932 law amounted to the state's adoption of the system created by the family allowance movement. Thus, the allowances and social services practiced by preexisting *caisses* constituted minimum requirements for new ones. In this way, Picquenard aided employers in their bid to maintain control of worker welfare. As we saw earlier, the

97 Circulaire, Minister of Labor to Directors of *caisses de compensation*, 23 November 1934, Archives Départementales de la Moselle 6 X 14.
98 CCRP Commission de gestion, *procès-verbaux*, 13 March 1929.
99 *Ibid.*; CCRP Assemblée générale, *procès-verbaux*, 3 December 1929.
100 CCRP Commission de gestion, *procès-verbaux*, 11 October 1934.   101 *Ibid.*, 3 March 1932.

grand patronat had used its family allowance *caisses* to create employer-controlled welfare institutions that also offered social insurance. Although ultimately unsuccessful at stopping social insurance legislation, the *caisses* and employer-created mutual societies still had much to gain by preserving their prerogatives during this crucial phase of social welfare implementation. Picquenard also took advantage of the institutional structure he had erected to enforce the 1922 law that mandated the payment of family allowances in public works and construction. This structure consisted of departmental family allowance commissions whose membership included state officials and construction entrepreneurs. Picquenard simply expanded these commissions to include employers from the newly affected sectors. Picquenard charged the departmental commissions with making recommendations to the ministry of labor on the approval of new *caisses* and providing information on relevant local conditions. Again, representatives of workers' unions suffered from a near total exclusion from the departmental commissions, a practice carried over from the 1922 law.[102]

Despite the apparent institutional advantages held by the ministry of labor, enforcement of the 1932 law proved extremely difficult. Professional *caisses de compensation* became a legally sanctioned refuge for recalcitrant employers. Small commercial firms created professional *caisses* that brought together employers of personnel that had relatively few children. Consequently, firms whose workers exhibited more typical numbers of children suffered higher expenses because they were left behind in interprofessional *caisses*. While not all professional *caisses* were created expressly to minimize costs, the facility of doing so proved attractive to many employers. This undermined the 1932 law and stirred resentment among employers whose allowance costs remained high. The ministry of labor's sole weapon against professional compensation was to deny employers the right to create a professional *caisse*. But this sanction only prevented the most egregious cases. In fact, the 1932 law explicitly permitted the creation of professional *caisses* as long as the employers fell into the same professional subcategory according to the Statistique Générale de France and the *caisse* maintained a membership of at least 50 percent of all such employers in the region. Many small and medium-sized firms easily attained these criteria, resulting in a proliferation of professional *caisses* in which expenses were well

[102] Circulaire no. 1, 25 June 1932, Minister of Labor to the Prefects, Circulaires ministérielles concernant les allocations familiales, Comité Central des Allocations Familiales, 1932–1934; CCRP Commission de gestion, *procès-verbaux*, 3 March 1932.

Firms/workers eligible (thousands)   Total allowances (millions)

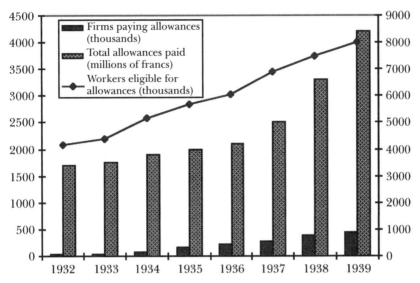

Figure 7   Growth in the institution of family allowances, 1932–1939. Figure compiled from Bonvoisin's annual reports at the Congrès National des Allocations Familiales, *comptes rendus*, 1932–1939.

below average. Some employers even maintained professional *caisses* that lacked approval from the labor ministry and stonewalled state officials who attempted to bring them into compliance. Prosecution of these employers forced Picquenard into politically unpopular battles. Legislators preferred that the labor ministry's limited number of inspectors concentrate on firms that refused to join any *caisse* instead of prosecuting employers who, after all, were paying allowances, even if the legality of their *caisses* was questionable.

Figure 7 shows a large increase in allowance payments as a result of the 1932 law, but as this number rose, so did the inequity in employer costs. Leaders of the family allowance movement complained that the spirit of the law was being violated by professional *caisses*.[103] Bonvoisin echoed this dismay at the CCAF annual conference in 1935, noting "the inherent difficulties in a laconic law, which until now, we have extolled for its virtues of discretion and suppleness and put confidence in the spirit

[103] See comments by Etienne Partiot, Vice President of the CCRP, Commission Départementale des Allocations Familiales de la Seine, *procès-verbaux*, 29 June 1933.

of solidarity and understanding among affected employers to carry out the law in harmony and in the interest of the cause."[104]

Complaints by employers of the family allowance movement about the shortcomings of the 1932 law were deeply ironic since they were primarily responsible for its drafting. They had not foreseen that many of their fellow employers would take advantage of the law's liberal approach to escape the burden of family welfare.

FEMINISTS AND SOCIAL REFORM LEGISLATION

Feminist organizations followed parliament's deliberations over social insurance and family allowances closely, lobbying legislators and voicing their views on numerous occasions. Their interest in social welfare policy reflected the dominant ethos of most French feminist groups. They exhibited what one historian has labeled "relational feminism."[105] Relational feminists did not dwell on abstract concepts of individual human rights but rather emphasized women's rights as women. Most important among these were women's childbearing and nurturing capacities. Hence, feminists were keenly interested in virtually all social welfare initiatives because of their influence on family life, maternity, and children's health.

Feminists' enthusiasm for social insurance emerged early and from the highest levels of the movement. One of France's first women lawyers and president of the largest feminist organization, the Conseil National des Femmes Françaises (CNFF), Maria Vérone, was an outspoken advocate of social insurance.[106] Vérone also served as secretary-general, and later, president of the Ligue Française des Droits des Femmes whose journal published a glowing appraisal of the Vincent bill in 1921. "Our legislators, out of concern for all kinds of misery, have presented a universal remedy, a beautiful social reform that will place France at the head of civilized nations." The CNFF was joined by the second largest feminist organization, the Union Française pour le Suffrage des Femmes (UFSF) and France's principal social Catholic women's group, the

---

[104] XVe Congrès National des Allocations Familiales, *compte rendu*, 1935, p. 95.

[105] Karen Offen, "Defining Feminism: A Comparative Historical Approach," *Signs*, Journal of Women in Culture and Society 14:1 (1988), 119–157, see especially pp. 134–39. Also see Offen, "Depopulation, Nationalism, and Feminism in Fin-de-Siècle France," *American Historical Review* 89:3 (June 1984), 648–676, especially p. 654.

[106] Anne Cova, "L'Assurance-maternité dans la loi de 1928–1930," Colloque sur l'Histoire de la Sécurité Sociale, Paris 1989, Actes du 114e Congrès National des Sociétés Savantes, pp. 68–69.

Union Féminine Civique et Sociale (UFCS).[107] Throughout the 1920s, feminist praise for the Vincent, Grinda, and Chauveau bills especially celebrated maternity benefits. In addition to covering medical care, each bill offered several weeks of compensated leave before and after birth as well as special payments for mothers who breast-fed their newborns. These provisions were a great improvement over previous laws under which women could gain only limited financial and medical assistance during maternity and postnatal care.[108] As the UFSF's weekly, *La Française*, put it in 1927, "Finally, the arrival of a baby in a modest household will no longer constitute a financial catastrophe!"[109]

During implementation of social insurance in the 1930s, however, feminists found shortcomings in the law.[110] The most problematic concerned the ministry of labor's rules that determined eligibility for social insurance. To the great detriment of women, these assumed regular employment under traditional employers, usually under a work contract. As a result, substantiating eligibility proved much more difficult for low-income women than men. While both fell under the law's income thresholds, women more often did piece work at home or worked as household help. Unlike wage earners in large industrial concerns, these women possessed no work contracts to verify their employment status and in many cases their employers preferred to avoid the social insurance levy. Social insurance *caisses* required all claims to be accompanied by a paycheck stub that substantiated the employer's contribution to the *caisse*. Thus, many low wage-earning women were denied the benefits of social insurance.[111] Indeed, a lack of clarity of what constituted a wage-earner (*salarié*) and the evidence needed to prove it plagued the 1930s social insurance regime. Women bore the pain of this juridical defect in greatly disproportionate numbers until a 1935 reform specifically forbad the exclusion of workers solely based on the absence of a work contract. Women's civil incapacity, combined with a relative lack of working-class organizations to represent them, no doubt contributed to parliament's lengthy indifference to the matter.

Feminists also sought the revision of social insurance benefits for maternity. A previous champion of this section of the law, Maria Vérone, complained that medical coverage for childbearing should not be governed by the same provisions as that for illness. Instead of reimbursement at 85 percent for medical and pharmaceutical expenses, women should

---

[107] *Le Droit des Femmes*, September 1921, p. 682.   [108] Cova, "*L'Assurance maternité*," pp. 65–66.
[109] *La Française*, 29 January 1927.   [110] *Ibid.*, 13 June 1931.
[111] *Le Droit des Femmes*, January 1936; *Vendredi*, 26 June 1936.

have to pay nothing. With more than a little sarcasm, Vérone noted that partial reimbursement was meant to prevent fraud and that, "it's not easy to fake being pregnant and it's absolutely impossible to feign a birth."[112] In their fight to improve maternity coverage feminists benefited from the ever growing concerns over depopulation. As we have already seen, pronatalists had been hard at work since before the war to encourage traditional women's roles through fiscal and civil measures as well as propaganda. This made for strange political bedfellows. For French feminists also advocated full civil rights for women, including suffrage. In contrast, social Catholics and conservatives in the pronatalist movement, such as Auguste Isaac, president of the Fédération Nationale des Associations des Familles Nombreuses, regarded the changing roles of women as a principal cause of depopulation. Despite the combined lobbying of feminists and pronatalists for increased maternity benefits, parliament failed to respond. Instead, legislators enacted a large birth bonus, but not until 1939, and as we will see in the next chapter, not under social insurance.

An examination of how French feminists responded to employer-controlled family welfare brings their relational feminism and class loyalties into even sharper relief. We have already seen that family allowances worked in conjunction with prevalent gender conceptions to reinforce men's dominance in the labor market and consign women to impecunious work.[113] Yet mainstream French feminists' regard for women's special nature led them to support employer-controlled family welfare as a way to facilitate motherhood and to gain compensation for women's domestic travails. Cecile Brunschvicg, longtime editor of *La Française* and founding member of the UFSF, called upon women to render primary allegiance to their nation: "True feminism consists of preparing women for the vicissitudes of life without losing track of the duty that nature has assigned us. Our role has no other purpose other than to know precisely how to find the right balance between our rights and our duties."[114] Moreover, like other relational feminists, Brunschvicg believed in the existence of a hypothetical choice between the feminist program and a woman's commitment to motherhood and the Republic. "France risks being unable to defend its rights *vis-à-vis* competing peoples who are much more prolific. I can say in all honesty that . . . if I had to choose between French security and the realization of the feminist program, I would sacrifice the latter without the least hesitation."[115]

[112] *L'Œuvre*, 22 January 1936.   [113] See chapter 3.
[114] *La Française*, 21 February 1931.   [115] *Ibid.*, 10 January 1931.

Brunschvicg's pledge and similar stances by other feminists bespeaks a feminist ideology of republican motherhood.[116] It placed women's role in childbearing and childcare above any other, effectively defining those functions as the most important outlet by which women could serve society and the Republic. Among its far reaching prescriptions for women and gender roles, republican motherhood exhibited the same sort of geopolitical rationale for family allowances found in earlier eras. Motherhood became a woman's "natural" patriotic duty to the state that she should perform for "the grandeur of France"[117] Nor was this essentialist view of women restricted to bourgeois feminists. It also prevailed among working-class leaders. Marguerite Prévost, secretary of the CGT Stenographers and Secretaries syndicate of the Fédération des Employés de la Seine, described the difference between women and men in the following terms. "Nature has made of man a marvelous working machine, with a powerful and inventive brain and a well muscled body . . . It has made of woman a mother, a creature truly constructed for maternity, which clings to her body and heart and from which she cannot escape despite rebellion against this premier social duty."[118] While feminists of the period urged French women to take up their "natural" role of childbearing, they simultaneously demanded improvements in the material conditions of maternity and motherhood. They believed that women's maternal duty for the nation should be repaid by the collective's increased responsibility for child welfare. These demands were congruent with the philosophy of solidarism, which entailed a reciprocal exchange of rights and duties among citizens.

In the world of male-dominated politics, feminists thus found their closest allies in the Radical party, which claimed solidarism as its birthright and advocated moderate social reforms, including employer payment of family allowances.[119] Shortly after approval of family allowance legislation, Brunschvicg praised political leaders for their action, especially their liberal approach to obligation. "We celebrate the passage of this law that will bring considerable social progress. We are certain that

---

[116] On republican motherhood, see Linda K. Kerber, *Women of the Republic: Intellect and Ideology in Revolutionary America* (Chapel Hill NC: University of North Carolina Press, 1980).

[117] Edme Piot, Senateur de la Côte-d'Or, to Emile Combes, Président du Conseil, "Une décoration pour mères de famille," *Revue Philanthropique* 13 (1903), 273–274, cited by Rachel Fuchs, "France in Comparative Perspective," in Accampo, Fuchs, and Stewart, *Gender and the Politics of Social Reform*, p. 182. Also see Françoise Thébaud, "Maternité et famille entre les deux guerres: idéologies et politique familiale," in Rita Thalman (ed.), *Femmes et fascismes* (Paris: Editions Tierce, 1986), pp. 85–98.

[118] Marguerite Prévost, *Pour l'éducation ouvrière – les jeudis de l'employé* (Bordeaux, 1923), p. 17.

[119] Jane Jenson, "Gender and Reproduction: Or, Babies and the State," *Studies in Political Economy* 20 (Summer 1986), 9–46, especially pp. 39–40.

its forthright application will permit a large number of women to stay at home from now on . . . Let us pay our respects to those visionary French industrialists, the first who, at their own risk and peril, blazed the way for others."[120] Feminists also applauded the CCRP's addition of medical insurance and other services, discerning no ulterior motives on the part of employers to stymie the realization of social insurance.[121] Bourgeois class affinity also drove feminist support for a liberal approach to family welfare. This affinity was epitomized by Adolphe Landry's sister, Marguerite Pichon-Landry, who emerged as an influential feminist leader in the 1920s and played a pivotal role in determining support for family welfare legislation. In 1905, Pichon-Landry joined the legislative council of the CNFF, working side by side with some of the most important French feminists of the day, including Madame d'Abbadie d'Arrast. In 1922, she replaced Avril de Sainte-Croix as secretary-general of the CNFF, and in 1932 she assumed the presidency of the organization, which she held until 1952. Her marriage to Adolphe Pichon, an attorney for the Comité des Forges and secretary-general at the Elysée Palace during the Poincaré presidency, further strengthened her already potent familial ties.[122] In many ways, Pichon-Landry epitomized a cadre of well-connected French feminists of the era.[123] According to one observer, she was a *"conservatrice liberale* incarnated, friend and ally of wisdom and progress and a typical product of families of her standing since the end of the Empire . . . It never would have occurred to her to fight for a reform whose application might, one day or another, overturn her family's privileged position."[124] In addition to leading the CNFF, Pichon-Landry participated in Ernest Mercier's Redressement Français, a right-of-center organization that championed technocracy in its quest to lead a national revival.[125] Serving in the Redressement's Third Section, which developed reforms on the organization of social life, Pichon-Landry collaborated with key actors in the family allowance movement, including CCAF Director Bonvoisin, Alliance Nationale Secretary-General Fernand Boverat, and CCRP Vice President Jacques Lebel.[126] Nor was Pichon-Landry alone in her pronatalist stance.

---

[120] *La Française*, 13 February 1932.   [121] *Ibid.*, 17 June 1933.
[122] Marguerite Landry and Adolphe Pichon married in 1903. See Françoise Blum and Janet Horne, "Féminisme et Musée Social, 1916–1939," *Vie Sociale* 8–9 (August–September 1988), annexe 2, 367–379, especially pp. 372–374.
[123] Christine Bard, *Les Filles de Marianne, histoire des féminismes 1914–1940* (Paris: Fayard, 1995), p. 384.
[124] Louise Weiss, *Combats pour les femmes* (Paris: Albin Michel, 1980), p. 34, cited by Bard, *ibid.*, p. 384.
[125] See Richard Kuisel, *Ernest Mercier: French Technocrat* (Berkeley: University of California Press, 1967).
[126] *Les Cahiers du Redressement Français*, Premier Congrès National de l'Organisation Métropolitaine et Coloniale, *compte rendu*, April 1927, pp. 11–13.

Madame de Witte-Schlumberger, president of the UFSF, served as a founding member of the Conseil Supérieur de la Natalité in 1921 and remained active in government sponsored efforts to raise the French birthrate throughout the 1920s.

During the CNFF's debate over the family allowance legislation of 1932, Pichon-Landry built support for their brother's employer-friendly approach to family welfare. She advocated inclusion of family allowances on the agenda of the Etats Généraux du Féminisme and her report offered glowing praise of her brother's liberal approach to obligation and explicitly evaded critical evaluation of the legislation. "Monsieur Landry correctly understands that we will never see the generalization of family allowances without making them compulsory, not that he wants to create a new state institution, attaching them, for example to social insurance. For diverse reasons, he judged it better to make use of the work already done by private initiative and restrict state intervention to a bare minimum."[127] Mainstream French feminists placed great esteem in women's reproductive and familial roles. In so doing, they aided Radical legislators as they sought support for social insurance and family allowance legislation. On social insurance, feminists argued for more extensive maternity coverage and raised issues that were especially problematic for working-class women, the nature of whose labor left them outside traditional trade unions. However, in the case of family welfare, feminist organizations adopted a much less critical role and helped to consecrate the industrial model. Feminist leaders' class affinities, familial ties, and association with the pronatalist movement explain these differing attitudes and involvement. The Landry family, with its ties to employers in the building trades and metals industry, the CNFF, as well as parliament and the government, played a pivotal role in assuring continued employer control of family welfare.

CONCLUSION

The most striking feature of the wave of social reform that swept France between 1928 and 1932 is the mistaken prognoses of the respective laws by the *grand patronat*. Employers condemned social insurance as ruinous to the economy and a precipitator of moral decline. Meanwhile, they welcomed parliament's liberal approach to family welfare as sound social reform. True, the application of social insurance encountered serious difficulties, especially its provisions for medical care and reimbursement.

[127] Etats Généraux du Féminisme, Conseil National des Femmes Françaises, *compte rendu*, 14–16 February 1929, p. 122.

But state officials, doctors, mutual aid societies, and workers' unions succeeded in working within the confines of an imperfect law. The pre-eminence that legislators had granted to mutual societies no doubt permitted some employers to usurp control of worker welfare, especially in heavy industry. Yet mutual societies and their allied employers ultimately found their match in doctors who almost single-handedly prevented passage of revisionist legislation that would have gutted the law's already loose regulatory framework. In general, the mutual model of social insurance proved sufficiently flexible to permit significant conflict within the regime without causing its collapse.

The family allowance legislation of 1932 presents an altogether different case. It also appropriated a preexisting model, this time from heavy industry, but legislators failed to properly revise this model for the diverse world of artisanal and commercial enterprises. Within a year of its implementation, a congenital flaw had become apparent as employers sought to minimize their expenses by grouping themselves together in low-cost professional *caisses de compensation*. Also, in contrast to the support which social insurance enjoyed among workers' unions, the family welfare regime suffered from an antagonistic relationship with union leaders who were entirely excluded from *caisse* administration and the labor ministry's departmental commissions. Legislators' fundamental error of adopting an industrial model of family welfare would become even more apparent when the Popular Front came to power in 1936.

5

Challenges from city and countryside, 1930–1939

The Depression and accompanying political turmoil greatly influenced the course of social reform in France. The country suffered nearly a million and a half unemployed at the height of the economic crisis. Fascist leagues proliferated and nearly toppled the Third Republic in rioting on 6 February 1934. The rightist threat and a rapprochement between France and the Soviet Union led to the reunification of the CGT and CGTU in 1935. Fence mending by union leaders paralleled creation of a Popular Front by parliamentary socialists and communists. Membership in the unified CGT increased dramatically after reunification, growing from 1 million in 1935 to 5.3 million in 1936. In the metals sector, CGT membership grew from 50,000 in February 1936 to 775,000 one year later. The CFTC also witnessed unprecedented growth, ballooning from 150,000 in 1935 to over half a million members and 1,750 syndicates by 1937.[1]

The family welfare system approached collapse during these stressful years. Artisanal and small commercial employers persisted in their subversion of the 1932 law through the creation of professional *caisses de compensation* that enrolled employers in sectors where child dependency ratios were extraordinarily low. This, of course, meant rising premiums for interprofessional *caisses* whose membership became dominated by firms where workers had above average numbers of dependent children. Conflict between employers over burden sharing would remain a burning ulcer for family welfare until 1945. A particularly strident piece of Popular Front legislation further challenged the industrial model of family welfare. Shortly after taking office, the Blum government gained approval for a binding arbitration law that forced family allowances onto the collective bargaining table, thereby striking a serious blow to employer prerogatives.

[1] GIMM intelligence report on CGT, AN 39 AS 938; GIMM intelligence report on CFTC, AN 39 AS 940.

Despite ongoing battles over family welfare, reformers pushed ahead with the extension of social insurance and family allowances to rural inhabitants. These initiatives further demonstrated the strengths and weaknesses of the mutual and industrial models of social welfare. For diverse reasons the mutual model permitted legislators to maintain the principle of obligation while adjusting social insurance to the diversity of rural France. In contrast, the Popular Front's naïve initiative to bring family allowances to agriculture, which theretofore had been exempt, exposed the extent to which employer-controlled welfare relied on class and status distinctions that were not easily delineated outside the city. Ultimately, further state intervention emerged as the only possible solution to the problems of welfare reform in the countryside.

Another challenge to the industrial model of family welfare arose out of the heightened pronatalist fervor that overtook France in the late 1930s. We have already seen the formative role that pronatalism played in the development of family welfare during the 1920s. By the late 1930s pronatalist groups and legislators dominated the highest levels of social policy making. Not surprisingly, they sought to exploit their power and found a ready-made vehicle in extant family allowance legislation, which they retrofitted in order to encourage exceptionally large families and traditional gender roles. Their *chef-d'œuvre*, the 1939 Code de la Famille, was unveiled just weeks before the outbreak of the Phony War and included a transformation in the priorities of family welfare. Although the Third Republic lacked enough time to implement the Code, its principles formed the basis of Vichy family policy.

SOCIAL INSURANCE IN THE COUNTRYSIDE

Leaders of rural France in the 1930s did not speak with one voice. Radical agrarians, such as Henri Dorgères and Fleurant Agricola, used compulsory social insurance to whip up support for their movements. Yet despite a growing popularity of rural radicalism in certain regions throughout the 1930s, most representatives of more staid organizations, especially agricultural syndicalists, accepted the extension of social insurance to agriculture as long as peasants enjoyed plentiful state subsidies and local control.[2] Indeed, moderate rural leaders thought that they had already won the battle for special treatment in 1924. They had rejected the 1921

---

[2] *L'Economiste Français*, "Les Assurances sociales: sur le projet de loi rectificatif concernant les assurés agriculteurs" (21 September 1929).

Vincent bill because of its similar treatment of city and countryside. Grinda's revision of 1924 consoled rural leaders by creating a separate and less regulated regime for peasants, rural artisans, and their workers.[3] Yet this victory proved short-lived. Senator Chauveau's bill, which became the hurriedly approved law of 5 April 1928, put agriculture back in the mix alongside commerce and industry. This prompted a storm of protest from the countryside. But instead of stoking peasant resentment against social insurance at market-day rallies, which was the practice of agrarian radicals, leaders of the Fédération Nationale de la Mutualité et de la Coopération Agricoles (FNMCA), the Assemblée des Présidents des Chambres d'Agriculture, and the Société des Agriculteurs de France lobbied parliament for modifications to the law.[4] In fact, the director of the last organization, Bernard de Lestapis, dismissed radicals, like Dorgères, "who would . . . deprive the peasant of some security in his old age . . . who would prevent him from amassing a savings for his children in whose care he will find himself one day."[5] While leaders such as Lestapis conceded the application of social insurance to agriculture, they adroitly exploited fears in governing circles of rural radicalism in order to obtain changes in the law. In a round table discussion on social insurance, the president of the Union des Syndicats du Périgord attacked the Chamber's champion of social insurance, Edouard Grinda: "My dear M. Grinda, perhaps you skipped over [social insurance in agriculture] because you're embarrassed . . . A special regime for agriculture was proposed only after some table pounding and the threat of revolution in the southwest."[6] As long as it was modified to their liking, agricultural syndicalists supported the promulgation of social insurance for reasons analogous to those of urban mutual leaders. Like realists at the FNMF, they saw the opportunity to control significant resources on behalf of their constituencies, an opportunity which, if left unattended, could prove ruinous to their organizations. However, in the case of agriculture, this circumstance flowed not only from demographic and social change but also from the fractious development of agricultural syndicalism since the late nineteenth century.

---

[3] Grinda, *Rapport*, p. 103.

[4] See a compelling account of Dorgères' incitement of peasant action in Robert O. Paxton, *French Peasant Fascism: Henry Dorgères's Greenshirts and the Crisis of French Agriculture, 1929–1939* (New York: Oxford University Press, 1997), chapter 3.

[5] M. Lestapis, Comité National d'Etudes Sociales et Politiques, *procès-verbaux*, 20 January 1930, p. 20; Henriette Martin, *Les Assurances sociales et l'agriculture* (Paris: Editions Domat-Montchrestien, 1932), p. 11.

[6] M. de Marcillac, Comité National d'Etudes Sociales et Politiques, *procès-verbaux*, 13 January 1930, p. 38.

The Waldeck-Rosseau legislation of 1884 encouraged the formation of nationally federated economic interest groups, including agricultural syndicates. Prior to 1884, the Société des Agriculteurs de France, an organization dominated by clerical and conservative rural notables, held a dominant position among agricultural associations. They were faced by a smaller, much less wealthy republican association, the Société Nationale d'Encouragement à l'Agriculture. Passage of the Waldeck-Rosseau law unleashed a flurry of organizing activity by both clerical and republican groups. The Société des Agriculteurs promptly created a federation of like-minded local *syndicats* known as the Union Centrale des Syndicats des Agriculteurs de France (UCSAF), which shared the same Paris address on the Rue d'Athènes as its conservative parent association. In 1910 republicans at the Société Nationale organized the Fédération Nationale de la Mutualité et de la Coopération Agricoles (FNMCA) with headquarters on Paris' Boulevard Saint-Germain. A fierce competition ensued for the peasantry's allegiance. The UCSAF labeled its rivals harbingers of socialism while the FNMCA characterized conservatives as enemies of the republic.[7] However, despite their important ideological differences, rival local *syndicats agricoles*, pursued similar strategies to recruit and retain members. This similarity explains their common cause to amend the 1928 social insurance law.

Each local *syndicat agricole*, whether associated with conservatives on the Rue d'Athènes or republicans on the Boulevard Saint-Germain, stood at the center of a web of agricultural services and institutions. Local cooperatives permitted peasants to cheaply purchase seed, fertilizer, and machinery as well as to effectively market their produce. Mutual insurance societies protected peasants against crop and property damage from fire, hail, freezes, and floods. Rural savings and loan institutions (*crédits mutuels agricoles*) made low interest loans to peasants and rural artisans for everything from capital improvements to seed grain. Many local *syndicats agricoles* played critical, albeit indirect roles, in all these activities. They were especially interested in keeping social insurance deposits in their communities and away from a state-affiliated bureaucracy which they mistrusted. Experience informed syndicalists'

---

7 On the creation of the UCSAF and the FNMCA, see Mark Cleary, *Peasants, Politicians and Producers* (Cambridge University Press, 1989), pp. 33–34, and Gordon Wright, *Rural Revolution in France: The Peasantry in the Twentieth Century*, (Stanford University Press, 1964), pp. 19–22, 47. On conservative and republican areas of rural France, see Pierre Barral's typology in *Les Agrariens français de Méline à Pisani* (Paris: A. Colin, 1968).

insistence that local agricultural institutions manage social insurance. Earlier, a 1922 law entrusted agricultural accident insurance to rural mutual insurance societies, instigating a robust period in their growth. Also during the 1920s rural mutual societies created regional unions in order to reinsure themselves against misfortunes that could affect large portions of their memberships.[8] Moderate rural leaders of both republican and clerical stripes pointed to this collaboration as evidence that these same mutual societies could effectively manage social insurance for their communities.[9] Syndicalists therefore favored a "mutualized" social insurance system for agriculture that contained even less state oversight than that which had been created for urban workers.

They also demanded autonomy from urban social insurance. Rural leaders believed that those who worked the land were far healthier than industrial workers. Without a separate regime, syndicalists argued, a relatively poor countryside would be forced to subsidize the cost of industrial maladies. One leader rebuked the 1928 law's equal treatment of farm and industrial workers: "Same premium, same risk! Take an agricultural worker. He has little ability to pay insurance premiums but at sixty years of age he's still vigorous. How about a glass worker. He has a much greater capacity to pay premiums, but at fifty, he's finished."[10] Statistics from German social insurance funds supported the basic contention, if not the actual facts of the charge. In 1927, annual average benefit outlays were 126 marks for mining *caisses*, 92 marks for mixed urban *caisses*, and only 36 marks for *caisses* that insured exclusively rural inhabitants.[11] Rural leaders thus rejected any sort of plan that would have peasants and agricultural workers share the burden of social insurance on an interprofessional basis. This reluctance to view social insurance as a national and interprofessional endeavor closely resembled the attitude of many small commercial entrepreneurs when confronted with the requirement to pay family allowances.

The precarious circumstances of agricultural product and labor markets further bolstered agricultural syndicalists' demand for a separate system. Although much worse times were still to come, several important farm products suffered from chronic overproduction and stiff

---

[8] For more on the development of agricultural mutuals and the protections they offered against property damage, see Chalmin, *Les Assurances mutuelles agricoles.*

[9] Martin, *Les Assurances sociales,* p. 13, Chalmin, *ibid.*, pp. 128–130.

[10] M. de Marcillac, Comité National d'Etudes Sociales et Politiques, *procès-verbaux,* 13 January 1930, p. 39.

[11] M. Lestapis, Comité National d'Etudes Sociales et Politiques, *procès-verbaux,* 20 January 1930, p. 21.

competition from low-priced imports. These difficulties were exacerbated by a shortage of agricultural laborers due to country-to-city migration. Rural leaders feared that the 1928 law's 5 percent wage deduction would accelerate the flow of workers to urban workplaces where higher wages made such a levy more acceptable. They similarly contended that the 1928 law would raise the average smallholder's taxes by 250 percent, a blow that would destroy family farming in France.[12] The magnitude of this tax hike was explained by the extraordinarily light income tax burden born by the rural sector. While representing approximately one-third of the active population, rural residents contributed only 5 percent of total income taxes.[13] Not surprisingly, legislators proved more mindful of votes than tax revenue. The sheer electoral weight of rural interests meant that neither government nor parliamentary leaders could ignore agricultural leaders' demands. Legislators agreed to subsidize premiums for many rural social insurees in order to facilitate their participation. Agricultural syndicalists insisted that no strings be attached to these funds, but the large government role in provisioning rural social welfare would presage later, more forceful government intervention in family welfare. In the political fray over social insurance, however, the demands of agricultural syndicalists appeared wholly congruent with those of urban mutual leaders who were also fighting for further freedom under the new law.

Hence, social insurance in rural France emerged as a mixed system based on the mutual model. In contrast to urban mutual society-run social insurance, it relied heavily on state subsidies. True, legislators reduced rural public assistance programs to help offset their new commitment, but the large state role relative to commerce and industry remained striking. Urban employer and worker premiums covered all but a fraction of benefits and deposits into capitalized funds.[14] Meanwhile, in agriculture the state matched 80 percent of the funds that social insurees over the age of thirty deposited into pension and disability accounts. It also provided a 50 percent subsidy to accounts that covered distributed risks, i.e. maternity, illness, and death.[15] State largess toward the rural sector allowed much lower premiums than levied in urban sectors and

[12] *Ibid.*, p. 22.
[13] Annie Moulin, *Peasantry and Society in France since 1789*, M.C. and M.F. Cleary (trans.) (Cambridge University Press, 1991), pp. 136–141. Also see Henri Digard, *Les Assurances sociales et l'agriculture* (Paris: Recueil Sirey, 1931), pp. 27–28.
[14] Digard, *ibid.*, p. 91.
[15] *JO*, Loi et décrets, 1 May 1930, Loi modifiant et complétant la loi du 5 avril 1928 sur les assurances sociales, Articles 81–82, pp. 4832–4833.

the extension of benefits to a wider swath of the population. Instead of a levy of 10 percent of wages, rural social insurees and employers split a low flat monthly fee of ten francs per participant.[16] Also, the distinction between worker and employer, which connoted so much importance in urban social insurance, became blurred under the rural regime, aiding peasant acceptance of the new law.

Legislators accomplished this in two ways. First, sharecroppers were included among the list of obligatory participants as long as they fell under a maximum annual income threshold of 15,000 francs and did not own a substantial herd of livestock. The inclusion of sharecroppers brought nearly 340,000 independent producers into the system as compulsory participants.[17] Second, the revised law for agriculture permitted a large number of peasant smallholders and rural artisans to participate voluntarily on an equal footing as agricultural wage earners and sharecroppers. That is, their premiums were no higher than obligatory participants because state subsidies covered the "employer" portion. Like sharecroppers, landowners had to fall below the law's income and livestock limitations. But the law's primary criterion for voluntary participation ignored land owning status and instead allowed the participation of all "those who live principally from product of their labor."[18] Moreover, subsequent legislation further expanded the eligibility of peasant smallholders by increasing the applicable income threshold from 15,000 to 18,000 francs per month.[19]

The flexibility of agricultural social insurance also extended to its administrative control and management. Like in commerce and industry, eligible social insurees simply joined an approved agricultural mutual society. Yet along with autonomy came less state oversight. Legislators set no minimum benefit levels for agricultural social insurees, leaving the matter to the minister of labor who proved reticent to do so. After a lengthy delay, parliament mandated minimum standards for retirement

---

[16] *Ibid.*, Article 75, p. 4832; *Règlement*, Caisse Mutuelle Agricole d'Assurances Sociales d'Eure-et-Loir, p. 2.

[17] *JO*, Loi et décrets, 1 May 1930, Loi modifiant et complétant la loi du 5 avril 1928 sur les assurances sociales, Articles 73–74, p. 4832. Initially, sharecroppers who owned any livestock were excluded, but a 30 October 1935 revision permitted the ownership of livestock whose value did not exceed 1,000 francs. See Georges Buisson, *Que disent les décrets sur les assurances sociales: entretiens sur les décrets-lois des 28 et 30 Octobre 1935 modifiant le régime des assurances sociales* (Paris: Editions de la Fédération Nationale des Mutuelles Ouvrières, 1936, p. 67; Digard, *Les Assurances sociales*, pp. 53–56.

[18] *JO*, Loi et décrets, 1 May 1930, Loi modifiant et complétant la loi du 5 avril 1928 sur les assurances sociales, Article 37, pp. 4826–4827.

[19] The law of 30 October 1935 modestly expanded eligibility for compulsory status among urban and rural workers. See Buisson, *Que disent les décrets*, p. 73; Digard, *Les Assurances sociales*, pp. 79–80.

pensions. But other benefits varied depending on region and mutual society.[20] In sum, the social insurance law of 1930 met the concerns of agricultural syndicalists. They had insisted that the 1928 law, albeit largely mutualized, could not be fairly applied to rural France where incomes were lower and work and production defied urban distinctions between employer and worker.

Surveys conducted by the Assembly of Presidents of Chambers of Agriculture in 1936 and 1937 revealed a general complacency, punctuated with complaints, about social insurance. Most striking was peasants' unwillingness to participate. Fully three-quarters of those surveyed who could participate on a voluntary basis stayed away.[21] When questioned further, these respondents indicated two related reasons for their aloofness. Peasants and rural artisans viewed capital and land as the most promising way to secure their futures. Money that they could afford to set aside, therefore, was more often dedicated to future land, livestock, or equipment purchases. Trust in land was matched by a mistrust in cash benefits, which were an inherent part of social insurance. Inflation during the Great War and the 1920s had demonstrated the potentially ephemeral value of money and the long-term value of land. The same survey also revealed peasants' faith in their local *syndicats agricoles* and their associated mutual societies which were the primary managerial instruments of rural social insurance. Yet confidence in local mutual insurance societies and mistrust in social insurance did not necessarily constitute a paradox. Peasants were more likely to purchase insurance from their mutuals against short-term risks to property, which permitted a reasonably high level of certainty that the insurance premium matched the value of the annual crop at risk. *Crédits mutuels agricoles* were also important and familiar sources of low interest loans for seed-grain and land. Thus, the role of rural mutual societies in social insurance did not necessarily translate into enthusiasm for the law. But it did go a long way toward making compulsory social insurance acceptable. In fact, a 1937 Chamber of Agriculture survey registered complaints that focused almost entirely on technical matters. Peasants complained that they should not be responsible for their workers' timely premium payments. (There was no requirement in agriculture for employers to effect wage deductions.) Others demanded that the government establish an amnesty period for those who had earlier ignored the law but now wished

---

[20] Digard, *ibid.*, pp. 63–64, 73–74; Buisson, *ibid.*, pp. 69–70.
[21] Comments of M. Harent, President from the Somme, Assemblée Permanente des Présidents des Chambres d'Agriculture, Session ordinaire, 28–29 May 1936, *compte rendu*, p. 191.

to abide by it.[22] The survey resulted in a declaration from the presidents of chambers of agriculture: "we find no serious or justified complaint against the current social insurance system in agriculture . . . proposals to reform agriculture's special social insurance system should be abandoned except for the piecemeal technical improvements forwarded by agriculture's two large mutual associations."[23]

In contrast, rural radicals called for the repeal of agricultural social insurance.[24] Although their appeals garnered significant support in some regions, social insurance did not raise peasant ire nearly as much as mandatory family allowances. The mutual model permitted legislators to build on peasants' well-developed trust in the mutual movement and to efficiently inject large state subsidies without assuming administrative control. Even if rural social insurance failed to enroll the hoped-for number of peasant smallholders, it nevertheless brought social protection to over three million rural residents.[25] What is more, unlike family allowances, the mutual model permitted a transcendence of urban notions of class. In so doing, agriculture's separate regime of social insurance achieved a milestone in the evolution of France's fledgling welfare state. As we will see later in this chapter, this achievement stands in stark contrast to the Popular Front's troubled attempt to extend the industrial model of family welfare to the countryside.

THE POPULAR FRONT AND FAMILY ALLOWANCES IN THE CITY, 1936–1938

The Popular Front ushered in labor legislation that proved impossible to reconcile with exclusive employer control of family allowance *caisses*. The left's electoral victory in May 1936 unleashed an unprecedented wave of sit-down strikes that were settled only after the new prime minister, socialist Léon Blum, summoned representatives of employers and workers to his Matignon office. The resulting accords

---

[22] Report presented by Félix Garcin, Président from the Loire, Assemblée Permanente des Présidents des Chambres d'Agriculture, Session ordinaire, *compte rendu*, 27–28 May 1937, pp. 363–370.

[23] Motion adopted by the Assemblée Permanente des Présidents des Chambres d'Agriculture, Session ordinaire, *compte rendu*, 27–28 May 1937, pp. 370–371.

[24] Henri Dorgères, *Haut les fourches* (Paris: Les Œuvres Françaises, 1935), pp. 182–188. Also see Président de la Confédération et Union de Défense Professionnelle des Syndicats et Groupements Agricoles de Tarn-et-Garonne to Président du Conseil, 8 January 1936, AN F60 645.

[25] Digard, *Les Assurances sociales*, pp. 9–10; Harent, President from the Somme, Assemblée Permanente des Présidents des Chambres d'Agriculture, Session ordinaire, 28–29 May 1936, *compte rendu*, p. 191.

granted wage hikes of 12 to 15 percent to most industrial workers. It also opened the way for parliamentary action. Legislators enacted a forty-hour week, paid vacations, and iron-clad protections of union organizing and collective bargaining.[26] Although family allowances were not mentioned in the accord, they could not have been far from the minds of the negotiators. All four employers who signed the Matignon agreement for the Confédération Générale de la Production Française (CGPF) were deeply involved in the family allowance movement. CCRP President Richemond and governing board members Lambert-Ribot and Duchemin were joined by the president of the Groupe Syndical du Bâtiment, Dalbouze. Across the table, CGT Secretary-General Léon Jouhaux had been a critic of employers' use of family allowances since the early 1920s. Each side preferred to keep allowances out of the Matignon accord for its own reasons.

Employers had created family allowances as a discretionary wage supplement that could be used to stave off general wage increases and pacify worker militancy. They hoped that allowances could again be manipulated to restore social peace. Throughout the strikes of June, the CCRP had continued allowance payments in an attempt to alleviate grievances among workers with large families. After their defeat at Matignon, employers turned to allowances for their counter-offensive. At a tense meeting of the CCRP governing board just two weeks after Matignon, CCAF Director Bonvoisin lobbied employers to immediately grant increases in family allowances for workers with more than two children. Such a move was actually made easier by the recent wage increases because most *caisses de compensation* calculated their premiums based on total wage outlays. Since June, wages had risen but not allowances, resulting in large surpluses for family allowance *caisses*. In the face of resistance by some who felt that such a move would indicate further employer weakness, Richemond and the majority of the board sided with Bonvoisin.[27] In September 1936, the CCRP granted significant allowance hikes for workers with two or more children. Table 5.1 shows CCRP allowance schedules before and after the Matignon agreement.

The CCRP was not alone among employer *caisses* in this strategy. By November 1936, fifty provincial *caisses* had also raised allowances for workers with three or more children. These moves, in fact, forced more

[26] "Convention collective Matignon," 6 June 1936, AN F22 236.
[27] CCRP Commission de gestion, *procès-verbaux*, 25 June and 22 July 1936.

Table 5.1. *CCRP family allowances before and after the Matignon accord of June 1936*

Children	Before Matignon	After Matignon	Percentage increase
1	30/month	30/month	0
2	70	80	14
3	120	200	67
4	200	400	100
each additional	80	200	150

Source: CCRP Commission de gestion, *procès-verbaux*, 15 September 1936.

reticent *caisses* to follow suit since the 1932 family allowance law dictated that rates could not vary significantly within a particular region.[28]

In virtually all cases, however, allowance increases were aimed at large families, of which there were relatively few. In the case of the CCRP, the apparently large hike in allowances actually cost employers very little, less than one quarter of 1 percent of wages for most of the *caisse*'s employers. Meanwhile, just as they had done fifteen years earlier to sway public opinion, *caisse* leaders publicized the increases with great fanfare. Under the new schedule, a family with five children received 600 francs monthly, up from 280 francs. One family of twelve children received special press attention because of their windfall gain; their monthly family allowances rose from 840 francs to 2,000 francs, a small fortune.[29] Employers raised allowances in the hope of regaining control of workers. In Bonvoisin's words, it was necessary "to show workers that gains will not always be obtained by strikes and collective bargaining."[30] Allowance hikes for large families were, quite simply, a relatively inexpensive investment that experience had shown to pay substantial returns in labor pacification.

Meanwhile, union leaders did not neglect the opportunity to force changes in family welfare under the Popular Front. However, instead of demanding large allowance increases at Matignon, they pursued binding arbitration. CGT leaders knew Picquenard had been correct four years earlier when he had remarked that the family allowance law had consecrated employer control.[31] To overcome employer prerogatives the CGT pushed the government to pass a law on compulsory arbitration (*arbitrage*

[28] *Bulletin Mensuel des Allocations Familiales* (November 1936), 183–185 (December 1936), 204–206.
[29] *Ibid.*   [30] CCRP Commission de gestion, *procès-verbaux*, 15 September 1936.
[31] XIIe Congrès National des Allocations Familiales, *compte rendu*, 1932, p. 217.

obligatoire). It simultaneously forced family allowances onto the collective bargaining table and reined in pesky CGT syndicates whose wildcat strikes were an embarrassment to national leaders. The CGT had long opposed arbitration as a method of settling labor-management disputes, preferring instead to rely on strikes to force employer concessions.[32] Now, however, under a leftist government, union-friendly arbitration legislation offered a way to restrain zealous local leaders in whose hands strikes had become a symbol of working-class disunity. The government of Léon Blum, desperate to stabilize the economy, granted national CGT leaders arbitration rules that both permitted further gains in worker remuneration and eroded employer control of family allowances.

Why didn't the left simply design a whole new family welfare system? In the prevailing social context, repeal or radical revision of the 1932 law would have been a perilous course. Pronatalist leaders were already upset that the Matignon accord did not include increases in family allowances. Leading pronatalist and Senator Georges Pernot complained that Matignon was "an accord between workers and employers reached under government supervision that dealt with everything except family allowances; they thought of everything except the most important!"[33] Blum's government also relied on Radical support in parliament. As we have already seen, Radicals were the principal architects of the family allowance law and would have strongly resisted its repeal. Thus, instead of entering what would surely have been a long battle over reforming *caisses*, labor leaders opted for an arbitration law that diminished employer control over them.

The law constituted one of the few compulsory arbitration measures ever adopted by a democratic industrial nation during peacetime, and its operation significantly altered French labor relations and remuneration practices. Although strikes were not abolished, their incidence was greatly reduced.[34] It required parties to choose arbitrators to mediate a negotiated solution. If they failed, a chief arbitrator (*surarbitre*) stepped in. Chief arbitrators were government-appointed officials whose decisions

---

[32] In 1896, Jean Jaurès led a successful effort to defeat legislation that would have compelled arbitration of labor disputes. In 1904, when socialist Deputy Alexandre Millerand authored a more labor-friendly proposal, rank-and-file labor syndicalists remained divided on the issue, resulting in its defeat. See Mitchell, *The Divided Path*, pp. 179–180, 186–190.

[33] Quoted by Vice President of the Conseil Supérieur de la Natalité and Deputy Louis Duval-Arnould, in his speech at the 19th Congrès National de la Natalité in 1937, reprinted in *Dossiers de l'Action Populaire* (25 November 1937), 2250. Also see Fernand Boverat and Étienne Partiot, "Rapport sur le relèvement des traitements et salaires ou augmentations des allocations familiales," Conseil Supérieur de la Natalité, no. 4, *procès-verbaux*, June 1936, pp. 24–29.

[34] Pierre Laroque, *Les Rapports entre patrons et ouvriers* (Paris: Fernand Aubier, 1938), p. 361.

could not be appealed. Of the 2,471 arbitration settlements between March 1938 and February 1939, arbitrators named by the parties could only settle 4 percent; in most cases then, final settlements required a chief arbitrator.[35] According to the law, if wages were adjusted upwards, chief arbitrators were required to make "proportional increases in family allowances" in relation to "wages whose modification was deemed necessary," taking into account "local, regional, and national conditions."[36] As a result of this stipulation, employers effectively lost control of allowance schedules.

Union leaders wasted little time in using the new arbitration procedures to seek upward revisions in wages and allowances. In the Paris metals industry, the CGT called for compulsory arbitration in January 1937. Since the Matignon agreements the previous summer, GIMM employers had resisted any discussion of general wage increases, preferring instead to raise family allowances. Union and GIMM appointed arbitrators failed to mediate the conflict and a chief arbitrator was appointed to resolve the dispute. Socialist Labor Minister Jean-Baptiste Lebas and Labor Director Picquenard chose William Oualid to arbitrate this important case in the Paris metals sector.[37]

Oualid's arbitration in the metals sector had far-reaching consequences for employers' family welfare regime. On wages, Oualid awarded workers an average increase of 8.5 percent, a finding that had been anticipated by employers. On family allowances, however, his decision rocked the very foundation of the CCRP. In addition to raises granted voluntarily by employers in the aftermath of Matignon, Oualid dictated augmentations across the schedule, including 100 percent hikes for families with just one or two children. Oualid's decision on family allowances is shown in figure 8.

The Oualid arbitration provoked three serious setbacks to the family allowance movement. First, at the behest of workers, a government-appointed official had entered what had theretofore been an exclusive employer domain, ignored employer entreaties to respect their prerogative, and radically altered a family allowance schedule. Second, the alterations themselves greatly increased the burden of family allowances for employers by doubling payments for first and second children, a measure

---

[35] Val Lorwin, *The French Labor Movement* (Cambridge: Harvard University Press, 1954), note, p. 78; Henry W. Ehrmann, *Organized Business in France* (Princeton University Press, 1957), p. 37.

[36] Charles Rondel, "Nature et portée de l'arbitrage obligatoire," *Le Droit Social* (February 1938), 121.

[37] As discussed in chapter 1, Oualid and Picquenard had worked closely to promote the *salaire vital* during the First World War.

Francs

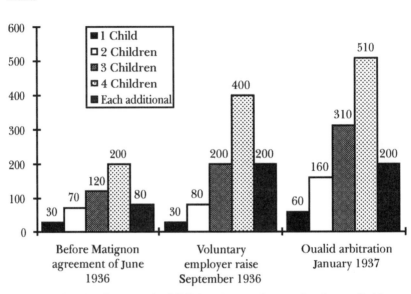

Figure 8   Family allowances for GIMM workers 1936–1937. Graph compiled from
information in "Arbitrage Oualid," AN 39 AS 976.

employers had repeatedly eschewed. Third, and most devastating, the
arbitration undermined the basis of the *caisse* itself, which had previously
paid identical allowances to all workers. Since only GIMM employers
were affected by the arbitration, the CCRP was forced to create new
divisions among its members for purposes of compensation. In all, the
higher allowances and new administrative costs totaled about 2 percent
of wages for metals employers.[38]

Oualid's arbitration proved to be only the beginning of a long train.
Indeed, it became a model for chief arbitrators throughout France, un-
leashing a torrent of intervention into *caisse* schedules. In the Marne, chief
arbitrator Charles Blondel decided that family allowances of chemical
workers should be raised by 50 percent. Grunebaum-Ballin awarded a
similar increase to dock workers in Bordeaux, as did Suquet to miners in
Meurthe-et-Moselle. Nor had the CCRP seen the last of its arbitrations.
Less than six weeks after the Oualid decision, chief arbitrator Vilette
granted another 4 percent increase in wages and family allowances, once
again, for only a portion of CCRP firms. November 1937 witnessed still

[38] CCRP Commission de gestion, *procès-verbaux*, 24 February 1937.

another arbitration in Paris, raising wages and family allowances by an additional 6 percent and further fragmenting the integrity of the CCRP.[39] Remarks by the CCAF spokesperson in May 1938 indicated serious confusion among leaders of the national family allowance lobby: "we don't even know the number of family allowance schedules imposed by arbitration since the application of the law."[40] Bonvoisin filed a formal complaint with the minister of labor over the Oualid decision, hoping to influence the outcome of future arbitrations, but he learned that little could be done.[41] For his part, Oualid regretted the arbitration law's negative effect on *caisses* but noted that chief arbitrators had little choice. "The procedures of conciliation and arbitration . . . accentuate the diversity of schedules. Their multiplication in the same *caisse* renders the practice of employer compensation, a fundamental principle of the 1932 law, impossible."[42] CCRP President Richemond outlined the difficulties faced by his *caisse* at the general meeting of June 1937. "The *caisse* no longer knows which [allowance] schedule to follow from one firm to another. Compensation is becoming impossible . . . personnel of the same firm, governed by differing collective bargaining contracts, can lay claim to different allowances."[43] This turn of events for employers cannot be attributed entirely to the Popular Front and a resurgent CGT.

Pronatalists stood alongside union leaders, encouraging chief arbitrators to raise family allowances. In March 1937, Alliance Nationale Secretary-General Fernand Boverat, wrote to all prefects announcing the Alliance Nationale's support for Oualid's and subsequent arbitrations that raised family allowances. In his letter, Boverat included extracts from the Oualid arbitration and suggested it as an exemplar for the prefects. "You will probably be called to arbitrate wage conflicts. This will provide you with an opportunity to contribute to social justice and the fight against depopulation"[44] The Conseil Supérieur de la Natalité (CSN) joined the Alliance Nationale in the quest to raise family allowances. The CSN also noted the absence of allowances in the Matignon accords

[39] "La Répercussion de la hausse des salaires sur les prix de revient," June 1937, AN 39 AS 943; *L'Usine*, 11 December 1937.

[40] Remarks of Fernand Rey, XVIIIe Congrès National des Allocations Familiales, *compte rendu*, May 1938, p. 74.

[41] CCAF Assemblée générale, "Rapport Bonvoisin," *procès-verbaux*, 4 May 1937, pp. 4–6.

[42] "Rapport relatif aux procédures de conciliation et d'arbitrage dans les différends collectifs du travail," 26 July 1937, AN F2 2023.

[43] CCRP Assemblée générale, *compte rendu*, 28 June 1937.

[44] Boverat to prefects, 3 March 1937, Archives Départementales de la Moselle, 6 X 10.

and recommended increasing allowances during arbitration, pointing to the Oualid decision as an appropriate precedent.[45]

After seventeen years of ineffectual resistance, union leaders had finally landed a major blow to the family allowance movement. The integrity of many of the country's most important *caisses* lay shattered, and families with only one or two children realized substantial raises. Pronatalists' entry into the fray between employers and unions angered the leadership of many *caisses*. While pronatalists professed no desire to destroy employer *caisses*, their support for disruptive arbitrations belied a priority of radically higher family allowances.[46] By 1938, compulsory arbitration had so fragmented family allowance *caisses* that legislators deemed state action necessary to reestablish order.[47]

STATE INTERVENTION AFTER THE POPULAR FRONT

In July 1937, and again in October 1938, Adolphe Landry proposed legislation to rescue *caisses* from the disruptive effects of compulsory arbitration.[48] Landry's bills, which were enacted by decree on 12 November 1938 rationalized family allowances but did so by further diminishing employer control. The new rules mandated the payment of allowances according to an average monthly male wage in each department that was set by the prefect. Allowances were to be calculated as a percentage of this average wage. The allowance for the first child was set at 5 percent of the average wage, 10 percent for families of two children, and 15 percent for each subsequent child. The November 1938 legislation also established a home-mother allowance (*allocation pour la mère au foyer*). All mothers who were not professionally employed and whose husbands collected family allowances were eligible. The home-mother allowance had been advocated by pronatalist and Catholic women's groups since 1929 but generally opposed by employers in the family allowance movement.

---

45 Conseil Supérieur de la Natalité, "Allocations familiales et surarbitrages," no. 4, *procès-verbaux*, June 1937, pp. 9–11; Raises in family allowances were subsequently added to the Matignon accord on 25 November 1937, AN F22 1633. This amendment, however, did not restrict arbitrators from adjusting allowances according to particular circumstances.

46 Conseil Supérieur de la Natalité, "Les Allocations familiales: l'état ou la profession," *procès-verbaux*, no. 4, June 1937, pp. 12–16.

47 Commission du Travail, Chambre, *procès-verbaux*, 30 December 1937, 16th legislature, 1936–1940, B102, Vol. 1, Archives de l'Assemblée Nationale.

48 *JO*, Documents parlementaires, Chambre, 2 July 1937, annexe no. 2756, pp. 552–555 and 4 October 1938, annexe no. 4344, pp. 5–6.

Use of an average male departmental wage to standardize allowance schedules divided employers. Some leaders of the family allowance movement feared that the confusion created by compulsory arbitration increased the likelihood of a state takeover of their *caisses*. They argued that the November 1938 decree would obviate more forceful state intervention by reestablishing order. The director of the *caisse* in Roanne spoke for supporters of the legislation. "The loss of [employer] control . . . despite its seriousness, is compensated for by the fact that arbitrators will no longer be able to interfere in matters."[49] Bonvoisin joined supporters of the 1938 decree, arguing that even higher state-regulated allowances were better than wage hikes for all. "If families continue to be disadvantaged . . . you can bet that union leaders will publicize the plight of family heads, however few they are, and demand massive wage increases for all."[50] In opposition stood leaders of France's largest *caisse*, the CCRP. They regarded Landry's proposal as but a first step in the state takeover of family welfare. CCRP President Richemond proclaimed that "the alert has been sounded . . . and at least there is no more doubt as to the intention of certain elements of the ministry [of labor] to seize control of our institutions."[51] Richemond preferred to take his chances under the anarchic regime of arbitration rather than submit to state-regulated allowances. In his view, the new system would lead to the automatic adjustment of allowances for inflation and the integration of family allowances into the social insurance system, the very developments he had fought so hard to prevent since 1920.[52]

Calculation of the average male departmental wage proved a difficult undertaking for the ministry of labor, which called for assistance from prefects and departmental family allowance commissions. Minister of Labor Paul Ramadier cautioned local officials from attempting to calculate a mathematical average wage. Instead, he urged them to consult chambers of commerce, employers' associations, *caisses de compensation*, and employment offices.[53] In the absence of a statistical average, however, the departmental wage inevitably became a political compromise between relatively well-paid industrial workers and lower paid rural artisans and commercial wage earners. In the end, average departmental

---

[49] Speech by Michel, "Examen de certaines dispositions du décret-loi du 12 Novembre 1938," XIXe Congrès National des Allocations Familiales, *compte rendu*, 1939, p. 44.
[50] CCAF Assemblée générale, *procès-verbaux*, 24 May 1938, p. 36.
[51] CCRP Commission de gestion, *procès-verbaux*, 23 March 1939.   [52] *Ibid.*, 25 January 1938.
[53] Circulaire ministérielle, Minister of Labor to the prefects, "Décret-loi du 12 novembre et fixation du salaire moyen mensuel dans le département d'un salarié du sexe masculin," 7 December 1938.

wages were usually set much lower than actual wages, thereby holding down family allowance levels. In Paris the average monthly male wage was set at 1,500 francs, which a simple survey of workers revealed was far from a mathematical average.[54]

The other major provision of the November 1938 decree was the home-mother allowance. Like family allowances, home-mother allowances had been pioneered by industrialists in Grenoble during the First World War. Workers' wives who were not employed and cared for dependent children were granted a pay supplement of 12.50 francs monthly. The Grenoble *caisse* abolished its home-mother allowance in 1919 due to the difficulty of ascertaining the employment status of workers' wives.[55] Ten years later, a Catholic women's organization, the Union Féminine Civique et Sociale (UFCS), launched a national campaign for the establishment of home-mother allowances by all *caisses de compensation*.

The UFCS cannot be considered a feminist organization even in the context of France's predominantly relational feminist movement. Unlike groups such as the Conseil National des Femmes Françaises (CNFF) or the Union Française pour le Suffrage des Femmes (UFSF), the UFCS protested neither the unequal distribution of power between the sexes nor the absence of women's civil rights. Rather, the UFCS identified itself as the feminine branch of social Catholicism and believed that a woman's all consuming goal should be the well being of her family. According to UFCS doctrine, this required self-abnegation.[56]

The UFCS began its campaign for a home-mother allowance after release of a study that documented a large proportion of French mothers working outside the home. According to the study, 8.4 million married women were professionally employed. Of these, 4 million were in agriculture, 2.4 million worked in industry and a little more than a million were commercial employees of various sorts. UFCS leaders Andrée Butillard and Eve Baudouin argued that high female employment rates threatened family life as laid down in the papal encyclicals *Casti Connubi* (1930) and *Quadragesimo Anno* (1931). In a 1931 tract Baudouin also argued that urban working mothers actually cost the family money,

---

[54] CCRP Commission de gestion, *procès-verbaux*, 11 January 1939.
[55] *Bulletin du Ministre du Travail*, nos. 3–4, March–April 1920, p. 122.
[56] Susan Pedersen, "Catholicism, Feminism, and the Politics of the Family during the Late Third Republic," in Seth Koven and Sonya Michel (eds.) *Mothers of a New World: Maternalist Politics and the Origins of Welfare States* (New York: Routledge, 1993), pp. 246–276, see especially note 6, p. 270.

since domestic chores like clothes mending and food preparation were replaced by expensive restaurant meals and unneeded new clothes. Baudouin further insisted that employed women, having their own money to spend, became infected with an unnatural independence and individualism. According to Baudouin, the working woman too often "gives into the temptation of life outside, walking the streets where luxurious shops offer their seductions . . . the woman who earns often loses her sense of economy."[57] The result, according to Baudouin, was large-scale abandonment of motherhood by French women, leading to a higher incidence of childhood illness and a dramatic drop in the birthrate.[58]

The UFCS campaign for a home-mother allowance gained support from social Catholic and pronatalist employers and legislators. In 1933 a textile employer and member of the Roubaix-Tourcoing *caisse*, Philippe Leclerc, founded a special *caisse de compensation* for the payment of home-mother allowances to workers whose wives cared for two or more children if one was less than three years old. The following year, the Conseil Supérieur de la Natalité passed a resolution in support of the home-mother allowance, calling upon all *caisses* to institute its payment alongside family allowances.[59] In 1935 social Catholic deputies Louis Duval-Arnould and Jean Lerolle introduced legislation that would have required *caisses* to pay a home-mother allowance but would have allowed them to abolish their first-child allowances.[60] As unemployment worsened in the mid-1930s, measures aimed at inducing women to give up their jobs became popular. According to one deputy, legislation was needed "to facilitate the return of the mother to the home where she has an eminent social responsibility . . . and to liberate little by little a certain number of jobs."[61]

Feminist leaders too were supportive of efforts to provide financial support to mothers who chose to stay at home with their children. But they were concerned that extremists might take advantage of popular sentiment and seek legal restrictions on women's employment.[62] Ida See

---

[57] Eve Baudouin, *La Mère au travail et le retour au foyer* (Paris: Librarie Bloud et Gay, 1931), p. 24.
[58] *Ibid.*, pp. 25–27. Also see Eve Baudouin, "Pour la mère au foyer," *Chronique Sociale de France* (15 March 1939), 199–211.
[59] Conseil Supérieur de la Natalité, Communications 1934, no. 3, Section permanente, *procès-verbaux*, 16 January 1934, pp. 16–18.
[60] *JO*, Documents parlementaires, Chambre, 28 March 1935, annexe no. 5193, p. 777.
[61] *Ibid.*, remarks of Deputy Reille-Souille, 27 April 1937, annexe no. 2276, p. 515. Also see legislation by Henri Becquart, *JO*, Documents parlementaires, Chambre, 6 June 1936, annexe no. 176, p. 222.
[62] See comments by UFSF leader Cecile Brunschvicg, *La Française*, 30 March 1935.

wondered whether employers of women would ever accept a home-mother allowance, fearing that women would instead lose their jobs. "What can be said about those bosses who set 'no children' as a condition of employment for waitresses, concierges, and building attendants!"[63] Marguerite Pichon-Landry sought to allay these concerns among her fellow feminists, arguing that her brother's legislation sufficiently protected women against discrimination while allowing "a woman to renounce further earnings in order to devote herself to her children."[64]

Workers' unions were divided over the home-mother allowance. CFTC leaders embraced it and joined the UFCS campaign shortly after its inception in 1929. They also pressured employers at the collective bargaining table throughout the 1930s to begin payment of the new allowance.[65] In contrast, CGT leaders rejected the notion that women workers created unemployment any more than their male colleagues. As we have already seen, however, rank-and-file men were more likely to view women as an obstacle to male employment. But CGT members also saw the home-mother allowance as a threat to the first-child allowance since legislators appeared disposed to compensate employers in some fashion.[66] By December 1937, a dozen *caisses* had instituted some sort of the home-mother allowance. Most employers, however, withheld their support. Earlier, at a CCAF general meeting in 1934, Bonvoisin urged employers to fight a home-mother allowance because it presented "more disadvantages than advantages, especially since it would probably translate into higher costs."[67] In 1938, in response to mounting pressure from pronatalists, the CCAF chose to support a home-mother allowance as long as it targeted mothers with children under three years old. CCAF leaders argued that only by restricting eligibility to mothers of young children could the allowance be large enough to induce women away from professional employment. They believed that 30 percent of the average male departmental wage, would impel a substantial number of women to leave (or not enter) the work force.[68] Indeed, the Commission Supérieure des Allocations Familiales, which was dominated by employers and pronatalists, approved a home-mother allowance proposal with these age and wage provisions.

---

[63] *La Française*, 23 and 30 October 1937.   [64] *Ibid.*, 3–10 December 1938.
[65] Baudouin, "Pour la mère au foyer." Also see 1930s memos from CFTC leaders to CCRP Director Georges Maignan and GIMM President Pierre Richemond, AN 39 AS 976.
[66] *Le Peuple*, 21 April 1938.   [67] CCAF Assemblée générale, *procès-verbaux*, 26 May 1934, p. 9.
[68] CCRP Director Georges Maignan's speeches at the XVIIIe and XIXe Congrès National des Allocations Familiales, *comptes rendus*, 1938, pp. 39–49, 1939, pp. 19–27. Also see P. Kula, "Salaires et budgets familiaux," *Les Nouveaux Cahiers* (15 November 1938), 4–9.

However, the 1938 decree was much too vague on the question of home-mother allowances for employers' liking. It left important issues, such as eligibility and allowance rates, to be decided by the Conseil d'Etat, which interpreted the law such that all workers who benefited from family allowances were eligible. In recompense to employers, the Conseil set the home-mother allowance at only 5 percent of the average departmental wage.[69] These regulations represented a major setback for employers. Their costs rose substantially while effectiveness of the allowance as an unemployment-fighting measure proved virtually nil. CCAF vice president and member of the CCRP governing board, Etienne Partiot, summed up the debacle, declaring that "an allowance of 40 to 45 francs monthly in exchange for abandoning a job worth 600 to 700 francs is a cruel joke on families. The moral result is deplorable; the material result is certainly nothing! Meanwhile, this derisive allowance constitutes a considerable cost [for employers]."[70] In Paris, the CCRP paid a monthly home-mother allowance of 75 francs to nearly 200,000 families, representing a 1 percent hike in employer wage costs.[71] Angry letters poured into the ministry of labor from the provinces, claiming labor cost increases of up to 10 percent. Employers further complained of their inability to ensure that recipients were, in fact, at home caring for children. Since mothers of children well into their school years (aged fourteen) were eligible, actual childcare was difficult to determine.[72] Hence, the Landry-inspired decree of 12 November 1938 rescued employers from the chaos of varying arbitration decisions but only to deliver them into a world where state officials determined allowance schedules and where a new allowance for unemployed mothers was required.

Popular Front legislation and the 1938 decree also shattered German-style family welfare in Alsace-Lorraine. Like their colleagues elsewhere in France, *caisses* leaders in the Moselle raised allowances for all children in the weeks following the Matignon accord.[73] Just as elsewhere, however, these voluntary raises did not prevent government-appointed arbitrators from granting additional increases under terms of the binding arbitration law. March 1937 witnessed the first of several arbitrations in the region. Arbitrator Charles Rist granted a 9 percent wage increase

[69] *JO*, Règlement d'administration publique, 2 April 1939, p. 4346. Also see CCRP Commission de gestion, *procès-verbaux*, 23 March 1939.
[70] *L'Elan Social*, 13 May 1939, AN 39 AS 976.
[71] Memo from Maignan to CCRP members, AN 39 AS 976.
[72] Correspondence addressed to M. Pinel, Direction du Travail, 7e Bureau, AN F22 1511.
[73] CAFM Commission de gestion, *procès-verbaux*, 7 July 1936; CAFM Commission de gestion, *procès-verbaux*, 23 April 1937.

to steel workers and a substantial hike in family allowances. Steel workers gained an additional 4 percent wage increase and another raise in family allowances in the Crussard arbitration of February 1938.[74]

Strikes and arbitrations led the region's employers to terminate many of the German practices that had previously set them apart from the national family allowance movement. Employers abandoned the negotiation of family allowances at the collective bargaining table, deeming this practice incompatible with binding arbitration.[75] They also refused to raise allowances for married workers' wives (*Familienzulage*), which were not covered by arbitrations. In response to the November 1938 decree that mandated employer payment of a home-mother allowance, most employers abandoned the *Familienzulage* altogether. The demise of the *Familienzulage* signalled the final triumph of French over German family welfare in the recovered territories. The home-mother allowance asserted the primacy of childbearing in determining family assistance and further delineated gender roles. Women were not only encouraged to bear children to gain benefits for their husbands but discouraged from working outside the home. This latter restriction was, in part, driven by the belief that women workers contributed to high unemployment rates among men. But it was also the product of a pronatalist construction of motherhood, which condemned working women as responsible for the demographic crisis and penalized men with few children. Such sentiments were less present in German family welfare that had been inherited from the Second Reich in 1918. But they were strikingly similar to contemporary Nazi family policy.[76]

In 1941, the acting president of the CCRP, Richard Cheylus, reflected on the state's role in family allowances between 1932 and 1939, recalling the good ol' days of employer liberty. "From 1932 to 1937, the family allowance system worked perfectly . . . After 1937, the situation changed. First, there were the arbitrations that differed from one profession to another and imposed increases that differed as well . . . Then came standardization at much higher rates after the law of 1938 . . . inaugurating much closer [state] control of *caisses*."[77] Cheylus' resumé of state intervention indicates waning support for employer control over family welfare. Without doubt, arbitration and the decree of 1938 delivered a serious

---

74 Data from "Règlement intérieur de la Caisse de Compensation des Mines et Usines de la Moselle," 17 June 1933, AN F22 1550; "Arbitration Rist," Archives Départementales de la Moselle (hereafter ADM) 310 M 75; "Arbitration Crussard," *Le Lorrain*, 24 February 1938.
75 *Lothringer Volkszeitung*, 20 March 1937; *Le Lorrain*, 10 April 1937, "Arbitration Suquet," ADM 310 M 27 and "Arbitration Jarlier," ADM 310 M 83. Also see AN F22 1572.
76 See Lisa Pine, *Nazi Family Policy, 1933–1945* (Oxford University Press, 1997).
77 CCRP Assemblée générale, *procès-verbaux*, 27 February 1941.

blow to employer control. But an even more grave threat arose with the
extension of family allowances to the countryside.

FAMILY WELFARE FOR THE COUNTRYSIDE

Leaders of the Popular Front knew that those who worked the land
could ultimately prove decisive to their success or failure. But their actions illustrate how little they understood the lives of rural country men
and women. Unlike Jean Jaurès, who forty years before had played a
critical role in steering the socialist party toward a mutually beneficial
accommodation with the smallholding peasantry, Blum and his agriculture minister, Georges Monnet, imposed a family welfare system on
agriculture that created havoc and bred mistrust of the government. Of
course, this is hardly what Popular Front leaders set out to do. They
were painfully aware that their initiatives on behalf of urban workers
had triggered large price increases in manufactured products and bred
resentment in the countryside. A rural newspaper captured the sentiment well in its reaction to Popular Front legislation in favor of industrial
workers: "What we don't want is to purchase supplies and everything
else based on the 40-hour [work week] law, and sell our products based
on the return established at 90 hours; we're human beings just like they
are."[78] Small- and largeholding peasants alike were already reeling from
overproduction and a slump in agricultural prices.[79] Wage-earning laborers continued to suffer from low pay and relatively difficult working
conditions while they watched their urban brothers and sisters obtain
large pay increases. Agrarian Party Deputy Joseph Cadic sought to exploit rural resentment of the Popular Front. He accused the government
of forsaking rural France: "Every society, they say, needs slaves so that
the rest may be wealthy. The Popular Front, too, has chosen its slaves –
the peasants!"[80] Cadic's attack drew thunderous applause from the right,
but his charge that the Popular Front was purely an urban phenomenon
and bent on exploiting rural France was inaccurate.

In fact, misfortune in French agriculture provided the left with important electoral support from rural districts of the center and southwest.[81]

---

[78] *Le Paysan Lorrain*, 12 July 1936.
[79] Agricultural prices fell approximately 50 percent between 1930 and 1935, leaving most agricultural workers with annual incomes of only 3,000 to 5,000 francs, barely enough to live on. See
the report by the Corporation Nationale Paysanne, Service Social, "Pour une amélioration de
la condition des ouvriers agricoles," pp. 11–12, AN F10 4970.
[80] Joseph Cadic, Deputy from Morbihan, *JO*, Débats parlementaires, Chambre, 19 February 1937,
p. 643, cited by Wright, *Rural Revolution in France*, p. v.
[81] Cleary, *Peasants, Politicians and Producers*, p. 85. Also see Laird Boswell, *Rural Communism in France,
1920–1939* (Ithaca, NY: Cornell University Press, 1998), p. 31.

In the departments of Cher, Allier, Lot-et-Garonne, and along the Mediterranean coast, communists garnered over 20 percent of the vote. Socialist support in these regions was even higher.[82] Many of these votes were cast in support of a single plank of the Popular Front platform: the reform of cereal marketing. Wheat prices, in particular, suffered from chronic instability and had been the ruin of many peasants. In 1935, the price of wheat stood at 85 francs per quintal, up 5 francs from 1934, but down from 150 francs in 1931.[83] The price instability of such an important agricultural product, coupled with growing import competition, also helped to fuel the membership in radical agrarian groups to unprecedented heights. Rural unrest and market uncertainty no doubt played a role in Blum's decision to appoint Georges Monnet, whom many regarded as Blum's heir apparent, as minister of agriculture. Monnet immediately set upon the creation of the Office du Blé, which, while controversial among peasants, succeeded in restoring stronger and steadier prices in the cereals market.[84]

The Popular Front was also anxious to redress the conditions of agricultural wage earners who felt betrayed by the initial social reforms of the Popular Front. Application of family allowance laws to the countryside appeared as an easy option. War allowances for dependents of mobilized men between 1914 and 1918 had been well received in rural departments. Pensions to widows and disabled veterans also provided a measure of economic relief to rural villages that had been especially hard hit by the high human cost of the First World War.[85] Moreover, the extension of family allowances to agriculture required no parliamentary approval since legislators in 1932 had foreseen such an eventuality. All that was needed was an administrative ruling that declared the government's intention to subject agricultural employers to the law. But this seemingly facile gesture, announced by Monnet on 5 August 1936, demonstrated an appalling ignorance of rural society.[86]

The industrial model of family welfare relied on the distinction between employers and workers and between wages and allowances. When

[82] Maurice Larkin, *France Since the Popular Front* (Oxford University Press, 1988), p. 45.

[83] Juliette Clément *et al.*, *Eure-et-Loir* (Paris: Editions Bonneton, 1994), p. 77.

[84] By the end of 1936, wheat prices rebounded to 160 francs per quintal. Clément *et al.*, *ibid.*, p. 77. Monnet discusses his plans for agriculture in "The Place of Agriculture in the Economic Policy of the French Government," *International Affairs* 16 (1937), 418–439.

[85] See chapter 1 and Moulin, *Peasantry and Society in France*, pp. 137–38.

[86] The designation of employer included non-land-owning share croppers. "Décret du 5 août 1936 portant règlement d'administration publique relatif à la mise en vigueur des allocations familiales en agriculture," *Documentation Générale* (Paris, 1940), pp. 7–15. Also see "Discours de M. Georges Monnet," Assemblée Permanente des Présidents des Chambres d'Agriculture, Session extraordinaire, *compte rendu*, 4 February 1937, pp. 27–38.

the Popular Front generalized this model to agriculture, where economic status and class relations were ambiguous, they triggered a revolt against employer-controlled family welfare that opened the door to large-scale state intervention. Our examination takes us to three rural departments, each of which represents an example of the diverse types of agricultural production during the period. The primary variable among the departments is farm size. The south-central department of Aveyron furnishes an example of *la petite culture*, where most plots were less than ten hectares and many constituted less than one hectare.[87] The Lorraine department of Meuse provides a second example. There we analyze the application of family allowances to medium-sized farms of the period, about twenty hectares. Third, we look at how well employer-paid allowances took root in France's granary, the Beauce, especially the department of Eure-et-Loir, where most peasants cultivated plots in excess of fifty hectares and many were much larger. Each of the three departments possessed a wide range of produce, including cereals, legumes, livestock, and dairy products. However, farm size proved overwhelmingly decisive to the success of employer-paid family support. This is because large farms resembled most closely the industrial factories where family allowances were born. In contrast to small and medium-sized operations, large farms tended to employ high numbers of wage-earning workers, which drew clear socio-economic distinctions between employer and employee. Workers on large farms also exhibited a relatively narrow range of job tasks and in-kind compensation, common on small farms, was exceedingly rare. Once again, we find the Popular Front, albeit unknowingly, at the origin of a major transformation in family welfare.

FAMILY ALLOWANCES IN AVEYRON, MEUSE, AND EURE-ET-LOIR

Located on the Massif Central of south-central France, Aveyron was and remains primarily an agricultural region. Despite the existence of an industrial island in the center of the department at Decazeville, most of Aveyron's 323,000 inhabitants worked on small plots and in related agricultural occupations, producing a variety of field and livestock products, including the renowned Roquefort cheese.[88] Only a few weeks after Monnet's decision to require agricultural employers to pay family allowances, Aveyron's prefect constituted a commission on the matter. Its membership included the director of agricultural services, the

---

[87] One hectare equals 10,000 square meters or 2.47 acres.

[88] Etienne Bastide, "La Vie commerciale et industrielle, 1900–1950," *Revue de Rouergue* 4 (October–December 1950), 567–591, especially pp. 579–580.

department's labor inspector, and representatives from the chamber of agriculture and local *syndicat agricole*. As directed by Monnet, the first task of the prefect, supported by members of the commission, was to conduct a census in order to identify candidates for mandatory affiliation to a new agricultural family allowance *caisse de compensation*.[89] This was a massive undertaking and required the aid of dozens of mayors and communal officials who soon revealed their opposition to the law.

The municipal council (*conseil municipal*) of the commune of Bozouls, for example, voted unanimously to protest imposition of the law. In reference to the dire state of agricultural markets, they objected to the "injustice of assimilating agricultural employers with commercial entrepreneurs and industrialists who can recuperate the costs of social policy."[90] Other local leaders repeated this charge. Even the general council (*conseil général*) of Aveyron rejected the law, noting its unfair treatment of peasants' children whom the law classified as dependants of employer and therefore ineligible for allowances.[91] A chorus of departmental officials thus enjoined the prefect to delay the law's imposition. Leaders in Bozouls typified local officials' protests to the prefect: "[We] hope that you will join with Aveyronnais members of parliament to force the government to recognize the legitimate claims of peasants who demand not to be excluded from family allowances . . . The current crisis makes it impossible to accept onerous new costs."[92] The prefect neither joined with the department's deputies and senators, as local officials wanted, nor carried out the directives of the minister of agriculture. In July 1937 prefect Maurice Beillard wrote to Monnet to report his failure at establishing a census of *caisse* candidates and beneficiaries. "Many mayors carried out no investigations of their inhabitants, making it difficult to establish verification lists."[93] As late as January 1939, 137 of the department's 306 communes had not even provided an accounting of their inhabitants for implementation of the law.[94]

Events on the cereals and dairy producing farms of Meuse followed a similar course. The prefect took *pro forma* actions to comply with

[89] Comité Départemental des Allocations Familiales Agricoles, *procès-verbaux*, 24 December 1936, Archives Départementales de l'Aveyron (hereafter AD Aveyron) 5 X 11.
[90] Conseil Municipal de la Commune de Bozouls, *procès-verbaux*, 2 May 1937, AD Aveyron 5 X 12.
[91] Conseil Général, Préfecture de l'Aveyron, *procès-verbaux*, 19 April 1937, AD Aveyron 5 X 12.
[92] Conseil Municipal de la Commune de Bozouls, *procès-verbaux*, 2 May 1937, AD Aveyron 5 X 12.
[93] Prefect to Minister of Agriculture, 5 July 1937, AD Aveyron 5 X 12.
[94] Commission Départementale des Allocations Familiales Agricoles, *procès-verbaux*, 17 January 1939, AD Aveyron 5 X 11.

directives from Paris but made little headway on enforcing the law.[95] Departmental officials were especially reticent to compel smallholding peasants to join family allowance *caisses*. One 78-year-old smallholder wrote to the prefect of the Meuse to exclaim his outrage at having to pay allowances for the children of his occasional day laborer. "I had three kids, now I have nothing, having suffered serious losses, but we worked and we raised our kids without help from anyone, I think they should pay me."[96] Strong resistance to the law also came from those who employed family members on their small farms. In 1938, the state modified its instructions in an effort to blunt resistance to the law. Peasants who employed family members could avoid paying into a *caisse* if the owner and his family workers jointly proclaimed that they shared all profits and losses of the enterprise. This modification of the law marked an implicit recognition that the line between employer and employee, upon which employer-based welfare in industry and commerce rested, was not so easily determined in agriculture.[97]

Despite this reform, enforcement proved virtually impossible in Aveyron and Meuse. Enforcement of *caisse* affiliation in the departments usually fell to the director of agricultural services. Other responsibilities of this official, however, such as the dissemination of advanced farming techniques, demanded close cooperation with peasants. This placed the director in a difficult position. In Aveyron, the chamber of agriculture pressured him to assume a benevolent attitude toward employers who ignored the law. To this request, he acquiesced, informing the prefect that "I think that we will obtain the desired results by persuasion more easily than by force."[98] Only after an agricultural worker filed numerous complaints did the director attempt to compel an employer to affiliate with a *caisse*. Results from these efforts were mixed. In Aveyron, a farmworker named Louis Jammes repeatedly complained that his employer denied allowances for his four children. The director contacted Jammes' employer, informing him of the complaint and attempted to persuade him to join a *caisse*. The result: Jammes was fired. In cases such as these the director transferred prosecution of the case to the prefect, who sent gendarmes – pen and *caisse* application in hand – to the farm. But forced

[95] Commission Départementale Agricole des Allocations Familiales, *procès-verbaux*, 22 December 1936, 22 October 1936, and 17 June 1937, Archives Départementales de la Meuse (hereafter AD Meuse) 415 Mp 8.
[96] Renouyer Prosper to Préfet de la Meuse, 1 April 1941, AD Meuse 236 Xp 26.
[97] "Instructions: Allocations Familiales aux exploitants utilisant des ouvriers salariés ainsi qu'aux membres majeurs de leur famille," AD Meuse 236 Xp 33.
[98] Memo, Directeur des Services Agricoles to the Prefect, 6 April 1938, AD Aveyron 5 X 12.

affiliation of employers with *caisses* did not necessarily mean continued compliance with the law. In the Jammes case, records do not indicate whether he was ever rehired or if his employer actually followed through with payments to the *caisse*.[99]

The attempt to bring employer-paid allowances to agriculture resulted in another sort of hardship for workers. Peasants who needed help on their land but did not want to run afoul of authorities turned to hiring childless men. As in industry and commerce, the law required all agricultural employers to join a *caisse* regardless of the eligibility of their workers. Enforcement of the law in agriculture, however, was so lax that these employers were rarely pursued. The wife of an agricultural worker and mother of five, Juste Chaliez, wrote to the prefect, describing the circumstances under which her husband had been denied work. "The law on family allowances has wronged fathers in our region. Peasants no longer want to hire them seeing how they have to pay the *caisse* for them. They like better to pay boys because they don't have any children and don't claim anything... One has got to either abolish the law or apply it."[100] Chaliez's letter is typical of dozens of families who wrote to authorities, hoping for relief. Given the treatment of Louis Jammes described above, it is likely that countless others were victims of lax enforcement but feared to contact authorities.

In the summer of 1939, a full three years after Monnet's announcement to compel family allowances in agriculture and despite the continued attempts by subsequent governments to apply the law, less than 50 percent of eligible agricultural employers in the Meuse had joined a family allowance *caisse*.[101] Results in Aveyron were even more dismal. There, the director of agricultural services estimated that only about 2,000 of the department's 60,000 eligible peasants were affiliated with a *caisse*.[102] In fact, large-scale non-compliance eventually eroded what small support for family allowances actually existed. *Caisses* were based on the principle of burden-sharing. Employers with workers who had children were subsidized by those whose workers had few or none. Non-compliance hence created a vicious cycle. When only employers who had workers

---

[99] A total of twenty-one letters written between September 1937 and April 1938 document the director's efforts to force the affiliation of Jamme's employer with a *caisse de compensation*. AD Aveyron 5 X 12.

[100] Letter, Juste Chaliez to the Prefect, 5 February 1939, AD Aveyron 5 X 10. Madame Chaliez's letter is among several in this file. In translating it, I have attempted to retain the somewhat awkward syntax.

[101] Comité Départemental des Allocations Familiales Agricoles, *procès-verbaux*, 16 May 1939, AD Meuse 236 Xp 50.

[102] Directeur des Services Agricoles de l'Aveyron to the Prefect, 6 April 1938, AD Aveyron 5 X 12.

with children joined a *caisse*, premiums remained high, which, in turn, encouraged more hostility towards family allowances and prompted further non-compliance.[103] The only regions where employer-paid allowances met with substantial success were those where farms resembled the urban factories where family allowances had originated. These conditions were amply found in the Beauce.

The Beauce, which covers most of the department of Eure-et-Loir, is a vast plain of cultivable land that has long served as France's granary. Large farms of over 50 hectares were typical and many operations covered well over 100 hectares, producing cereals, beets, and livestock. The department exhibited one of the highest ratios of wage-earning agricultural workers. Just under 17,000 wage-earning agricultural laborers worked on the largest of the department's 9,000 farms.[104] In Aveyron, by contrast, 11,000 agricultural workers helped to tend over 60,000 plots.[105]

Moreover, wage-earning farm workers in Eure-et-Loir share an important trait with their industrial counterparts: they were organized. Taking advantage of Popular Front legislation that bolstered collective bargaining rights, workers in the department flocked to the Fédération des Travailleurs Agricoles, which had been launched by the Confédération Générale du Travail (CGT) to organize farm workers.[106] In response, membership in the Association Centrale des Employeurs Agricoles skyrocketed. Although the association proclaimed itself to be "purely professional and independent of all politics," its leaders attacked the CGT for "stoking class conflict" in the department and expressed their unwillingness to negotiate with the local Fédération syndicate.[107] Ultimately, however, with the help of the prefect, agricultural workers forced their employers to the bargaining table. The resulting contract granted workers substantial raises and created a mixed commission to examine grievances.[108] While tensions between employers and employees clearly rose, the well-drawn socio-economic distinction between

---

[103] Interview with M. Chibois, Director of the Caisse Mutuelle de la Haute-Vienne, 1937–1939, Comité d'Histoire de la Sécurité Sociale, AN 37 AS 3. Chibois remarked that "in order to fully enforce the law, we would have needed a gendarme for every peasant." Also see remarks of M. Sangnier of Pas-de-Calais, Assemblée Permanente des Présidents des Chambres d'Agriculture, Session extraordinaire, *compte rendu*, 4 February 1937, pp. 162–163.

[104] Chambre d'Agriculture d'Eure-et-Loir, *procès-verbaux*, 9 October 1937, Archives Départementales d'Eure-et-Loir (hereafter AD Eure-et-Loir) 7 M 162.

[105] "Recensement," Département de l'Aveyron, 28 July 1937, AD Aveyron 7 M 105.

[106] For a comprehensive treatment of communist organizing in the countryside, see Boswell, *Rural Communism in France*.

[107] Memo, Subprefect of Dreux to the Prefect of Eure-et-Loir, 11 May 1937, AD Eure-et-Loir 7 M 152.

[108] "Accord du Travail dans l'agriculture en Eure-et-Loir," 17 June 1937, AD Eure-et-Loir 10 M 34.

these groups aided the application of employer-paid family allowances in the department.

In April 1937, the prefect received the first of several reports on agricultural employer compliance. At this early date, the subprefect reports that 3,200 farms, representing some 9,300 wage earners, had joined one or another of the department's family allowance *caisses* and that new applications were being received daily. Especially revealing is the subprefect's discussion of a single region in the southwest corner of the department, known as the Perche. While praising "the spirit of compliance" found in the Beauce, he singles out the Perche for its much higher rate of noncompliance and explains to his superior "in contrast to the Beauce, it is a region of smallholders where one finds very few farms that employ many workers . . . peasants there complain that they don't collect allowances for their children while they must pay for the children of workers of other farms."[109] The subprefect goes on to comment that he does not believe difficulties in the Perche will influence farmers in the Beauce. In fact, the reverse came to pass. The local chamber of agriculture, controlled by the largeholding peasants of the department, insisted that "all eligible employers pay their full premiums so that the *caisses* may function without family allowance costs becoming too burdensome."[110] Thus, in contrast to the vicious cycle observed in Aveyron where non-compliance drove up costs, causing abandonment of family allowance *caisses*, in Eure-et-Loir a virtuous cycle was established whereby *caisse* participants were numerous and powerful enough to compel widespread adherence to the law. This outcome is apparent in the annual report of 1939 where the director of agricultural services gleefully notes that "inspectors from the ministry of agriculture have verified perfect application of the law in Eure-et-Loir."[111] The success of family allowances in Eure-et-Loir and a handful of other departments where large agricultural enterprises were common, however, represented only a small victory for state officials.

Most rural inhabitants were denied family welfare because so much of the countryside resembled Aveyron and Meuse where small and medium-sized agricultural enterprises predominated. Figure 9 depicts the distribution of farm sizes.

[109] Subprefect of Chateaudun to the Prefect of Eure-et-Loir, 23 April 1937, AD Eure-et-Loir 7 M 152.
[110] "Proposition de M. Leroux," Chambre d'Agriculture d'Eure-et-Loir, *procès-verbaux*, 21 February 1937, AD Eure-et-Loir 7 M 162.
[111] Memo, Directeur des Services Agricoles d'Eure-et-Loir to prefect, 17 August 1939, AD Eure-et-Loir 7 M 180.

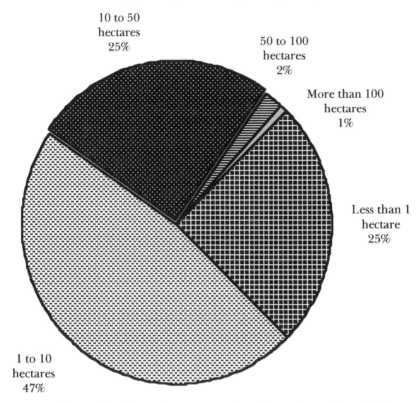

Figure 9   Distribution of farm size as a proportion of the total 1929. Marcel Braibant, *La Tragédie paysanne* (Paris: Gallimard, 1937), p. 38.

On small and medium-sized farms the line between agricultural workers and their employers was difficult to distinguish. These farms relied on shared labor depending on the job at hand. Some workers were paid in kind, either with meals and lodging or, if they were smallholders themselves, with help on their own land at a later date. Employer-paid allowances also failed because of the overwhelming proportion of employers to workers. In fact, fully 55 percent of French farms were run entirely by family members; 44 percent employed between one and five workers, leaving only 1 percent of farms employing more than six workers.[112] The predominance of small and medium-sized enterprises in

[112] "Les Allocations Familiales en Agriculture," Rapport d'information pour les Présidents des Chambres d'Agriculture, Assemblée des Présidents des Chambres d'Agriculture, 23 April 1936, *compte rendu*, pp. 271–275. Also cited by Louis Salleron, "L'Agriculture et les allocations familiales," *Revue Politique et Parlementaire* 521 (10 April 1938), p. 25.

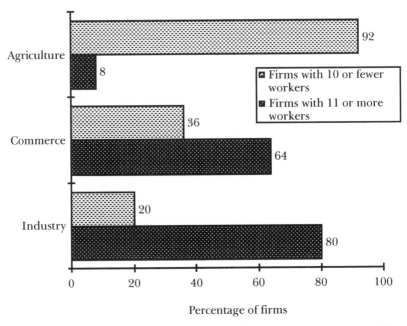

Percentage of firms

Figure 10   Industry, agriculture, and commerce by firm size in percentages 1931. Data from XVe Congrès National des Allocations Familiales, *compte rendu*, 1936, p. 95.

agriculture contrasts sharply with firm sizes in commerce and industry. Figure 10 illustrates this contrast.

The overwhelming presence of smallholding peasants who occasionally employed wage (or in-kind) labor made application of the law exceedingly difficult. Since employers' children were denied allowances, the vast proportion of those who worked the fields did not benefit from the law. This was especially problematic in the countryside where there often existed little difference between the standard of living of smallholding peasants and their hired help. At times they literally lived under the same roof and ate from the same table. In fact, the predicament of depression-era smallholders was sometimes worse than their laborers, whose mobility and freedom from debt provided advantageous flexibility in difficult economic times.[113] The law also ignored the ideal occupational progression of a male agricultural worker, according to which one

[113] See the remarks of President of the Chamber of Agriculture from Deux-Sèvres, Naslin, to Monnet, Assemblée des Présidents des Chambres d'Agriculture, Session extraordinaire, *compte rendu*, 4 February 1937, p. 48. Also see Memo, Directeur de la Caisse Centrale d'Allocations Familiales Mutuelles Agricoles to Pinel, Chef de Bureau, Ministry of Labor, 21 February 1938, AN F22 1516.

inherited or saved money to purchase land, married, and then had children. As enacted, the law withdrew eligibility for family allowances just at the stage when many farm laborers foresaw fatherhood.[114] Clearly, an employer-based system that had been created by and for industrialists as part of a wage strategy against highly organized urban workers could not succeed in the diverse smallholder world of French agriculture.

THE BATTLE OVER FAMILY WELFARE IN AGRICULTURE

By 1938, even the strongest proponents of employer-controlled family allowances conceded that agriculture required a departure from the system that had evolved in commerce and industry. In order to bring allowances to the countryside in any meaningful way, smallholding peasant *chefs de famille* had to be entitled to allowances alongside wage-earning workers. Yet given the overwhelming proportion of financially strapped peasant families, a new source of revenue and structural change to agricultural allowances would be required.[115]

Two principal options and some unlikely political bedfellows emerged in the ensuing fight over reform. Radical agrarian leader Henri Dorgères and leftist politicians argued for a new system that would be funded entirely by state subsidies. In opposition stood the clerical and corporatist Union Nationale des Syndicats Agricoles (UNSA), which represented the collective weight of the country's conservative local *syndicats agricoles*. UNSA had been created by former leaders of the UCSAF, which had collapsed from depression-induced financial distress in 1931. UNSA railed against proposals that called for state funding as a sacrilegious *étatisation* of family life, advocating instead a special tax on agricultural products whose proceeds would be dedicated uniquely to supporting rural family welfare. The question of funding inevitably raised the issue of management. What was to become of the departmental family allowance *caisses*? Would *caisse* managers remain local or would allowances henceforth be paid from Paris? Here too significant controversy arose. UNSA resisted any form of management from Paris while the leaders of the left were disposed to central control. Henri Dorgères' attitudes were more ambiguous, yet an examination of his flamboyant politics and his rivalry with UNSA casts considerable light on the debate over family welfare reform.

---

[114] Henry Chatenay, *Les Allocations familiales en agriculture* (Poitiers: Imprimerie Moderne, 1939), p. 56.

[115] Deliberations and resolutions of the Assemblée Permanente des Présidents des Chambres d'Agriculture reveal a marked frustration among agricultural leaders with employer-paid allowances. See especially *compte rendu*, session extraordinaire, 4 February 1937, when the presidents confronted Georges Monnet with their complaints.

Dorgères led peasants in a series of direct action campaigns against what he deemed the concrete manifestations of the Republic's malicious neglect and disrespect of rural France. Among his favorite targets were the social insurance and family allowance laws of the 1930s.[116] Dorgères encouraged peasants to boycott family allowance *caisses* and sought to intimidate departmental officials who attempted to prosecute peasants for non-compliance.[117] To support these endeavors, Dorgères employed local bands of young men, known as Green Shirts (*chemises vertes*), who could be quickly convoked by a simple newspaper announcement.[118] Actions against the imposition of employer-paid family allowances were lauded in most rural departments, but not necessarily those where Dorgères boasted his largest followings. Despite Dorgères' clear strongholds in the north and west, his denunciation of employer-paid family allowances elicited little action in Eure-et-Loir. Largeholding peasants of the Beauce may have applauded much of Dorgères' anti-Paris platform, yet they simultaneously found little difficulty in adapting an industrial wage strategy for use on their farms. However, a strong Dorgèriste following was not required for a department to exhibit resistance to the law. Indeed, Dorgères was relatively weak in the south, yet, as we have seen, Aveyron showed a marked hostility to the law. Thus, although Dorgères' invective against agricultural family allowances was well received throughout much of rural France, his actual followers exhibited a much narrower political sociology. They tended to be found in areas where more staid agrarian organizations, such as the local UNSA *syndicat* or crop-specific associations, were weaker and peasants consequently felt more exposed to the dictates of Paris. The map of Dorgèrisme does not correspond to any single crop, farm size, or socioeconomic situation, but rather to the more emotional, social, and political perceptions of peasant vulnerability to urban politicians.[119] Notwithstanding these limitations, Dorgères played an influential, albeit problematic, role in the debate over reform. He proclaimed that family allowances should be a "national expense,"

[116] Dorgères, *Haut les fourches*, pp. 182–188.
[117] *Le Cri du Sol*, 18 December 1937; *Paysan du Centre-Ouest*, 16 April 1939; Also see the analysis of André Parsal's resolution (*JO*, Chambre, Annexe no. 3581, 4 February 1938) by the Directeur Adjoint, Ministry of Labor, 21 February 1938, AN F22 1511.
[118] *Le Paysan Lorrain*, 21 March 1937; *La Croix Meusienne*, 5 March and 14 May 1938.
[119] The most notable crop-specific organizations included the Association Générale des Producteurs de Blé (wheat growers), the Confédération Générale des Planteurs de Betteraves (sugar beet growers), and the Confédération Générale des Vignerons (vintners' association). On rightist groups in Eure-et-Loir, see Clément *et al.*, *Eure-et-Loir*, p. 77.

paid directly from the state budget, insisting that peasants should be treated no differently than *fonctionnaires* (state employees), whose employment benefits included allowances.[120] Despite this rhetoric, Dorgères' real motivations lay more in his battle to maintain leadership of rural radicalism. After several heady years of cooperation between Dorgères and conservative *syndicats agricoles*, a split over strategy emerged in late 1937.

The *syndicats*, led by Jacques Le Roy Ladurie of their national federation (UNSA), favored the building of a corporatist agricultural economy that would make state regulation and intervention unnecessary. UNSA emerged from Le Roy Ladurie and Louis Salleron's vision of a new agricultural association that focused on modern and technocratic solutions to production and social welfare. Like its predecessor, UCSAF, UNSA's strength lay in its regional unions, which Le Roy Ladurie skillfully expanded into the largest national peasant organization by 1938. UNSA generally attracted young, technically skilled peasants from all regions who represented a full array of agricultural production. The attraction of UNSA for many was twofold. First, a national grouping appeared imperative in order to engage the Popular Front on agricultural and rural issues. Indeed, UNSA played an influential role in the creation of the Popular Front's Office du Blé. Second, Le Roy Ladurie sought to broaden UNSA's scope of activity and thereby transform it into a truly corporatist venture. As one regional UNSA newspaper put it, the association must not only protect economic interests but also "defend the profession and sustain the peasant family."[121] Whereas Dorgères attacked the state for not intervening more forcefully, Le Roy Ladurie hoped to place UNSA in a pivotal role between the state and rural families, thereby safeguarding peasant autonomy. Le Roy Ladurie eventually found Dorgères' unremitting denunciation of employer-paid family welfare and advocacy of a fully state-subsidized regime contrary to UNSA interests.[122] For UNSA, the failure of the government's family policy in agriculture presented an opportunity. Le Roy Ladurie proposed that UNSA's *syndicats agricoles*, which already administered some *caisses*, assume control of all of them and that revenue for family allowances be provided by a new tax on the first purchase of agricultural products. Dorgères' promotion of state-funded agricultural allowances was motivated at least in part then, by a

[120] Henri Dorgères, *Révolution paysanne* (Paris: Jean Renard, 1943), p. 88; Paxton, *French Peasant Fascism*, p. 84.
[121] Cleary, *Peasants, Politicians and Producers*, p. 75.   [122] Paxton, *French Peasant Fascism*, p. 139.

reticence to see his rival, UNSA, expand its constituency by taking over such an important institution of rural social welfare.[123]

In announcing his belief that the state should assume responsibility for allowances, Dorgères found himself in the same corner as leftist politicians and union leaders whom he regularly criticized as miscreants.[124] Working-class leaders, of course, came to their position by a very different path. The left had been calling for a state takeover of family allowances since they first emerged as an industrial wage strategy in the early 1920s. It is not surprising then that when the full scope of failure in rural allowances became apparent, leaders of the left sought to enact in agriculture what they had been unable to effect in commerce and industry: full state funding and control. Indeed, the leadership of organized agricultural workers was as wary of local employer-controlled *caisses* as their industrial counterparts had been fifteen years earlier. Hence, complete state responsibility for family allowances appeared the most prudent path to social justice.[125]

Advocates of corporatism, on the other hand, represented by UNSA, opposed any form of employer-paid allowances or the state-funded scheme proposed by Dorgères and the left.[126] UNSA's plan for allowances in agriculture was widely disseminated in their newspaper, *Les Syndicats Paysans*. It rested on three interrelated principles: the fundamental difference between allowances and insurance, the highly competitive nature of agricultural markets, and the pernicious effect of state control. First, UNSA argued that family allowances were not a form of insurance, such as that offered by local mutual insurance societies. Confusion between these fundamentally different sorts of social welfare, according to UNSA, explained the failure of rural family allowances. As one UNSA circular put it, insurance relied on the "law of large numbers" where individual premiums provided a "social basis" for protection against catastrophic weather, accidents, illness, or other calamities. Insurance, UNSA contended, was successful and popular because individuals were willing to contribute to a capitalized fund that could eventually render

---

[123] *Ibid.*, p. 83.
[124] *Le Paysan Lorrain* summed up well the outrage of Dorgèristes at the course of the Popular Front: "Equality. When the CGT launches a strike affecting hundreds of thousands of workers Monsieur Jouhaux [leader of the CGT] is appointed Regent of the Bank of France. When the Comités de Défense Paysanne unleash a strike of truck farmers, Monsieur Dorgères is put in prison." *Le Paysan Lorrain*, 31 January 1937.
[125] Renaud Jean, "Les Devoirs du Front Populaire envers les paysans de France," 9ème Congrès du Parti Communiste Français, Arles, 25–29 December 1937, *compte rendu*, pp. 26, 61.
[126] For UNSA attacks on Dorgères and leftist leaders see, respectively, *Syndicats Paysans*, 1 January 1939 and 19 January 1939.

them benefits. Family allowances, on the other hand, also relied on individual premiums to *caisses*, but were both psychologically and financially untenable because they penalized peasant families at the expense of wage-earning workers. Instead of individual premiums, UNSA leaders advocated broad social funding for allowances, i.e. a tax on agricultural products whose revenues could be redistributed to land-owning peasants, wage-earning agricultural workers, and rural artisans alike, based not on some urban notion of class, but rather on their status as *chefs de famille*.[127] UNSA officials' preference for tax-generated funding was tied to their perspective on agricultural markets.

UNSA leaders held a classical view of the market for farm products in which producers were price-takers in highly competitive, volatile market places. Large numbers of small producers with identical products, such as wheat, meant that prices were largely dependent on total demand and supply. Extraordinarily good wheat-growing weather of 1934–1935, for example, resulted in record harvests but coincided with a fall in demand. The consequence was a 40 percent drop in wheat prices and financial disaster for many smallholders. UNSA contrasted this producer vulnerability to the industrial sector where differentiated products and relatively few producers meant that firms could more effectively increase prices to compensate for additional social costs. Indeed, as noted above, the Matignon accords and the resultant wage increases prompted industrial employers to raise prices, which were paid by all consumers of industrial products, including peasants. UNSA leaders thus reasoned that if industrialists were recouping the cost of family allowances through price increases, agricultural producers should do likewise. And if the nature of agricultural product markets did not permit such a solution, then a tax would have to be levied in order to achieve the same ends. UNSA calculated that approximately 2.5 billion francs would be required annually to provide agricultural family allowances on par with rates found in industry.[128] UNSA further estimated the annual value of domestically produced and imported agricultural products at approximately 100 billion francs at the time of first sale. Thus, a tax of 2.5 percent levied on the commercial and industrial consumers of agricultural products would cover the entire cost of rural family welfare.[129] UNSA leaders

---

[127] Circulaire, Union Nationale des Syndicats Agricoles, 29 April 1938, AN F10 5049.
[128] *Les Syndicats Paysans*, 15 February and 2 March 1939.
[129] *Les Syndicats Paysans*, 16 March 1939. Some UNSA officials favored a much higher tax on imported products. Also see the comments of the Deputy from Meuse, Chanoine Polimann in *La Croix Meusienne*, 6 May 1939 and *Le Paysan Lorrain*, 21 November 1937.

also favored a dedicated tax because it would tie revenues from agricultural production to peasant welfare funding. *Les Syndicats Paysans* announced that "peasants will not tolerate the purchase of their children by the State, nor a threat to their familial independence by the exigencies of the Government."[130] UNSA's insistence on control over funding stemmed from its corporatist philosophy. To permit state intrusion, even if it was to fix an unjust and failed system of family welfare, would constitute a serious blow to the peasant movement, especially in the light of the persistence of employer-controlled family allowances in commerce and industry.[131] While the opposing views of rural family welfare held by Dorgères, leftist leaders, and UNSA might have complicated legislative action on agricultural allowances, another force was at work that virtually assured reform. History bound French political leaders into a special pact with those who worked the land.

Mindfulness of peasant sensibilities and a notion of the rural ideal have deep roots in the Third Republic. In 1884, one of the founders of the Republic, Jules Ferry, observed that "the Republic will be a peasants' republic or will cease to exist."[132] This dictum remained a salient imperative across the political spectrum well into the twentieth century. The sheer electoral weight of the rural population fortified this attention.[133] In contrast to the speed of urbanization in some other European countries, two-thirds of the French were classified as rural in 1870 and this proportion did not fall below half until the census of 1931.[134] Table 5.2 shows the importance of those occupied in agriculture as a proportion of the active population in 1936.

Although farm-to-city migration steadily eroded rural electoral influence during the first half of the twentieth century, the peasantry's disproportionately large sacrifice for the nation during the First World War spurred support for rural interests.[135] Rural villages supplied many of the infantry regiments that suffered the most severe losses and, unlike industrial workers, peasants were not recalled from the front to work in munitions factories. After the war the image of the hardy *paysan–poilu* (peasant–soldier) joined that of a bountiful rural hinterland as an indispensable element of French national identity. Government policies

---

[130] *Les Syndicats Paysans*, 4 August 1939.
[131] *Ibid.* Also see Louis Salleron, *Un Régime corporatif pour l'agriculture* (Paris: Dunod, 1937), pp. 20–21.
[132] Wright, *Rural Revolution in France*, p. 13.
[133] Moulin, *Peasantry and Society in France*, pp. 129–131; Wright, *ibid.*, p. 14.
[134] Wright, *ibid.*, p. 13.
[135] The peasantry could claim 41.5 percent of the dead after the war. See Fabrice Abbad, *La France des années 20* (Paris: Armand Colin, 1993), p. 6.

Table 5.2. *Population and employment by occupation 1936*

Sector	Workers (in millions)	Percentage
Industry and transport	7.4	38.3
Agriculture	6.3	32.5
Commerce	2.8	14.6
Domestic servants	.75	3.9
Liberal professions and staff	.74	3.8
State employees	.81	4.2
Armed services	.55	2.7
Total active population	19.35	100
Total population	41.18 million	

Source: Maurice Larkin, *France Since the Popular Front: Government and People, 1936–1986* (Oxford University Press, 1988), p. 3. Statistics for agriculture include fishing and forestry.

that supported this representation followed immediately after the war. Accession to land ownership and the improvement of rural properties were encouraged through the availability of low-interest, long-term loans, and low taxes. By the late 1920s the Third Republic's rural ideal of a fecund countryside, teeming with family farms, approached reality.[136] Indeed, political leaders, publicists, and social theorists commonly extolled the smallholding peasantry as the keel of the nation, and fought initiatives that would force agricultural consolidation or threaten the preservation of a rural lifestyle. In 1934, Edouard Herriot, Radical party leader and future president of the Republic reaffirmed the saliency of Jules Ferry's observation of a half century earlier, proclaiming that the peasant "ranks as the greatest of French philosophers, who might be described as our silent master."[137] What is more, this popular sympathy for traditional peasant life coincided with the apex of the interwar pronatalist movement, whose propaganda and social policy initiatives led to a further veneration of France's rural ideal.

Pronatalists had long viewed the countryside as more wholesome and fertile than urban areas, which they accused of breeding anti-family attitudes, egoism, and barrenness. Indeed, Jacques Bertillon, the founder of the Alliance Nationale, proclaimed in 1901 that country-to-city

[136] Moulin, *Peasantry and Society*, pp. 136–141.
[137] As quoted by Wright, *Rural Revolution in France*, pp. 13–14.

migration was accentuating France's already serious demographic crisis.[138] The rural exodus continued unabated during the interwar years, causing heightened concern within the pronatalist movement.[139] Alliance Nationale Secretary-General Fernand Boverat called for family allowance mandates in agriculture as early as 1924. He believed that the voluntary adoption of allowances in commerce and industry caused fathers of large families "to abandon their working of the earth and go to our urban agglomerations and work in factories for the express purpose of collecting allowances."[140] Agricultural leaders corroborated this view during the Popular Front. They complained that leftist programs of improved pay and a forty-hour week caused agricultural labor shortages in many regions.[141] By the late 1930s virtually all pronatalist groups strongly favored whatever measures were necessary, including state funding, to stem the rural exodus and encourage population growth in the countryside.[142] In order to rally support for state action, pronatalists focused public attention on family policy by linking the nation's demographic crisis to German revanchism. Pronatalists effectively portrayed France's stagnant population growth as a fatal chink in the country's armor, which had invited Hitler's remilitarization of the Rhineland, the *Anschluss*, and the Sudeten crisis of 1938.[143]

Demographers conferred scientific legitimacy on pronatalist harangues in favor of large families. In 1937, the Alliance Nationale commissioned Alfred Sauvy to study long-term trends of the French population. Sauvy presented his findings to the Conseil Supérieur de la Natalité in 1937. Figure 11 illustrates Sauvy's projections.

Sauvy predicted a steady rise in surplus deaths, mostly caused by a falling birthrate, resulting by 1985 in a decrease in the French population

[138] Assemblée générale de l'Alliance Nationale, *procès-verbaux*, 14 June 1901.
[139] Maurice Garden and Hervé Le Bras, "La Population française entre les deux guerres," in Dupâquier, *Histoire de la population française*, vol. IV, p. 88.
[140] Fernand Boverat, "Les Allocations familiales et l'émigration vers les villes," *Revue de l'Alliance Nationale* 142 (May 1924), 141–144. Also see the report by Henry Girard, IVe Congrès National de la Natalité, *compte rendu*, September 1922, pp. 144–146. Beginning in the 1920s political leaders also became concerned that family allowances in commerce and industry would exacerbate the rural exodus. See Commission d'Assurance et de Prévoyance Sociales, *procès-verbaux*, 12th legislature (1919/1924), Archives de l'Assemblée Nationale A13, Dossier 1105, vol. 2, 4 March 1921.
[141] Remarks of President of the Haute-Marne Chamber, Dumaine, Assemblée Permanente des Présidents des Chambres d'Agriculture, Session ordinaire, *compte rendu*, 28–29 May 1936, p. 195.
[142] Conseil Supérieur de la Natalité, "Rapport Général," September 1938.
[143] See especially Fernand Boverat, *Comment nous vaincrons la dénatalité* (Paris: Editions de l'Alliance Nationale, 1939).

Population (in millions)   Surplus deaths (in thousands)

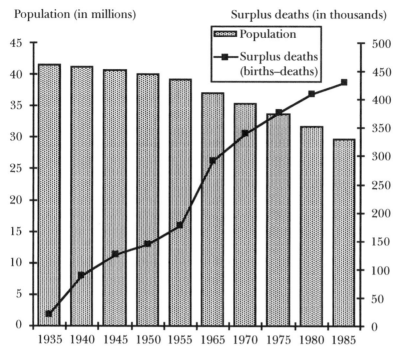

Figure 11   Population projection according to Sauvy 1937. "Rapport sur les nouvelles
perspectives démographiques," Conseil Supérieur de la Natalité, 30th Session,
Rapports et voeux, no. 1, 1 February 1937, p. 22. Sauvy founded the Institut National
d'Etudes Démographiques (INED) in 1945. See Dupâquier, *Histoire de la population
française*, vol. IV, p. 24.

of seven million. These statistics, which were widely distributed by the
Alliance Nationale, contributed to public anxiety over France's ability to
protect itself in the face of a German threat. By 1939 the French public
viewed family allowances not just as welfare but as a vital provision of
national defense.[144] The horrific losses of the First World War supported
this logic. Most people believed that if war came, it would resemble the
conflict of 1914–1918 in which millions of young Frenchmen were needed
to protect the Republic.[145]

[144] After the Munich Agreement, the mainstream press increased its coverage of demographic
issues, dramatically fueling public concern. One of France's largest dailies published a series of
investigative articles on the population question and its bearing on France's place in Europe,
especially its relationship with Germany. See *Le Temps*, 4, 8, 11, 13, 14, 16–19, 29 July 1939.
[145] This view also appeared prevalent in French diplomatic circles. See memo, French ambassador
in Berlin to the minister of foreign affairs, 25 May 1939, AN F60 495. Also see Spengler, *France
Faces Depopulation*, p. 251.

Spurred into action by pronatalist fervor, the Daladier government established the Haut Comité de la Population (HCP) in February 1939 and charged it with preparing reforms that would encourage population growth, especially in the countryside. The work of the High Committee was heavily swayed by pronatalists, especially the Alliance Nationale's Fernand Boverat and the president of the Fédération des Associations des Familles Nombreuses, Senator Georges Pernot, as well as Adolphe Landry. After deliberations that lasted throughout the winter and spring, the government blended the High Committee's proposals, many of which were simply long-standing pronatalist demands, into a sweeping decree known as the Code de la Famille.[146] The Code brought family allowances to agriculture by creating a state-sponsored entitlement program. It also made important modifications to family allowances in commerce and industry. But its preoccupation with rural family welfare cannot be overemphasized. We turn now to an examination of the Code, taking up first its directives for urban workers, followed by its initiatives in rural family welfare.

THE CODE DE LA FAMILLE OF 1939

The Code marked a rapprochement between pronatalists and employers of the family allowance movement after their acrimonious disagreement over the Popular Front's arbitration law. Reconciliation is evident in the Code's compromise between pronatalist goals and employer wishes to cut their family allowance expenses. It was achieved through a redistribution of benefits away from the numerous small families at employers' charge and toward large ones whose formation pronatalists sought to encourage. The Code replaced the first-child allowance with a birth bonus equal to two times the administratively determined average monthly departmental wage, but only if the birth occurred during the first two years of marriage.[147] The Code also decreased allowances for second children by one third and divided the departmental wage into urban and rural categories. Regardless of their occupation, residents who lived in communes of less than 2,000 inhabitants were assigned a lower average wage for the calculation of their allowances.[148]

---

[146] *Revue de l'Alliance Nationale* 324 (August 1939), 264–297. Also see Tomlinson, "The Politics of 'Dénatalité'," chapter 9.

[147] During deliberations, the Alliance Nationale's representative on the High Committee opposed abolishing the first-child allowance but acquiesced in order to assure approval of the Code. Haut Comité de la Population, *procès-verbaux*, AN F60 494, p. 58.

[148] *JO*, Lois et décrets, 30 July 1939, pp. 9607–9626. For allowance rates, see chapter 2, section 1, article 13, which begins on page 9610.

Prior to the announcement of the Code, the political left had high hopes for the HCP's family welfare measures. Indeed, the left rallied to the pronatalist cause, demanding government action to solve the demographic crisis. Maurice Thorez, secretary-general of the Communist Party, voiced his concern at the Congress of Villeurbane and Arles in November 1938. Remarks in the party's official press also indicated the adoption of pronatalist views. The *Cahiers de Bolchevisme* proclaimed that "to diminish infant mortality is not enough . . . We have to increase the birth rate and family allowances."[149] Upon the Code's unveiling, however, workers' union leaders denounced it as a deception and a retreat from efforts to help French families. They noted that abolition of the first-child allowance and the designation of lower average wages for workers in rural communes would actually mean lower benefits for most families.[150] Statistics on total allowance payments to steel workers in the Moselle supported their contention. Before the Code, 13,282 steel workers received allowances. However, 5,570 or 42 percent benefited only from the single-child allowance. These families lost all benefits under the Code. A further 3,944 families with two children, or 30 percent of the total, suffered a one-third decrease in allowances for these children. The one-time birth bonus of 2,100 francs for urban residents was a significant sum. But its value paled beside the abolished monthly first-child allowance of 50 francs, which was customarily paid until the child reached the age of fourteen. In fact, less than 13 percent of the department's steel workers saw an increase in their family welfare as a result of the Code de la Famille and most saw their benefits decline substantially.[151] Lorraine's CGT leader Schwob protested to Prime Minister Daladier that "the creation of the birth bonus along with the abolition of the first-child allowance constitutes a step backward in the encouragement of families in our society."[152] By "society" Schwob no doubt meant all French families not just those of his workers in Lorraine. The triumph of pronatalist ideals over family welfare represented a particularly serious reversal for working-class families. The ascendant constructions of motherhood and the family, which drove the Code de la Famille, rewarded large families at the expense of their less prolific but more typical neighbors. Although the

---

[149] *Cahiers du Bolchevisme* 16:3 (March 1939), 370–371.   [150] *L'Humanité*, 4 August 1939.

[151] Letter, Secrétaire-Général de l'Union des Ouvriers Métallurgistes de la Moselle, Schwob, to Prime Minister Daladier, 9 August 1939, ADM 6 X 10. Birth bonuses in the department's urban areas were 2,100 francs. But CGT steel workers' syndicate leader Schwob estimated that between 45 and 50 percent of metal workers lived in rural communes where birth bonuses were only 1,700 francs. For average departmental wages according to the Code de la Famille, see AN F22 1511.

[152] *Ibid.*

Code reinforced a loss of discretion over allowance schedules by *caisses de compensation*, it nevertheless reduced employers' total outlays significantly while maintaining family allowances as a wage supplement.

The Code's provisions for industrial and commercial workers proved far less innovative than those foreseen for agriculture. Adolphe Landry provided the High Committee on Population with ample statistics on the difficulties of employer-based family allowances in agriculture. 2.9 million smallholders and sharecroppers, i.e., those that were classified as employers under the current system, had 2.4 million dependent children in their households. Meanwhile, the nation's 2 million agricultural workers had only 462,000 dependent children.[153] These bedeviling statistics were joined by the urgent appeal of Georges Pernot who insisted that "the rural milieus are extremely preoccupied by family allowances and expect the government and the High Committee on Population to act."[154] And act they did. The Code boldly dispensed with the distinction between employer and worker in the determination of beneficiaries for agricultural allowances. In order to pay for the large number of now allowance-eligible employers, the Code committed the state to cover two-thirds of the costs of rural allowances, or about 1.65 billion francs annually. The remaining third continued to be paid by agricultural employers with premiums calculated according to the size and value of their farms. The Code also created generous marriage loans (*prêts au marriage*) for peasants who pledged to continue farm work for ten years.[155] Indeed, the bulk of funds required by the Code were to be spent on rural family welfare. Reflecting this priority, the Code's preamble is largely devoted to the notion of the rural ideal and the primacy of the peasant family to the nation. It rejects the charge that state subsidies will simply bail out peasants who refuse to pay family allowances to their workers. Instead, the framers of the Code proposed a Listian ethic whereby the government's fiscal commitment to keep peasants on the land stems from a "profound interest that we attach to the maintenance of a traditional equilibrium in our nation that in bygone days has always been more agricultural than industrial."[156] Thus, in the name of national solidarity,

[153] Haut Comité de la Population, *procès-verbaux*, 22 April 1939, AN F60 494.
[154] *Ibid.*, 3 June 1939.
[155] *JO*, Lois et décrets, 30 July 1939, pp. 9607–9626. See especially section 3: "Des allocations familiales agricoles," Articles 25–33, pp. 9611–9612.
[156] *Ibid.*, pp. 9607–9609. Writing in the early nineteenth century, Friedrich List favored a commercial association of German states and policies that would preserve their agricultural sectors. See Friedrich List, *Das nationale System der politischen Ökonomie* (Berlin: Akademie-Verlag, 1982), especially chapter 13.

the Code called upon all French to contribute to a renovation of social policy and especially to the improvement of living standards for peasant families.

The government's refusal to heed calls by UNSA for a new tax on agricultural products to fund rural family welfare illustrates the collusion of pronatalists and industrialists that had characterized the family allowance movement since the early 1920s. Pronatalists had long sought the kind of influence on family policy granted them by the HCP.[157] To permit UNSA's tax on agricultural products, whose proceeds were to go directly to local *syndicats agricoles*, would have meant a paring of state control over family welfare just at the moment when pronatalists had succeeded in attaining a predominant position in the state's primary family policymaking body, the High Committee on Population. Second, industrialists' successful use of family allowances as a wage strategy since the early 1920s gave rise to close relations, both financial and administrative, between industrialists and pronatalists. Industrialists opposed UNSA's tax proposal on grounds that it would fall heavily on industrial consumers of agricultural products and lead to economic instability.[158] They thus utilized their influence within the pronatalist movement as a hidden lobbying position from which to attack UNSA's tax. Because of the pronatalist influence under which the Code de la Famille was drafted, UNSA's vision of a corporatist, self-funding regime for rural family welfare could not succeed. But, on the other hand, nor could the Daladier government continue to ignore the failure of a class-dependent, employer-paid system. The remaining choice was a large state commitment to family welfare and a big step in the development of the nation's welfare state.

On the issue of management, the Code continued to rely on local family allowance *caisses*. In areas of republican allegiance, the local *caisse* was associated with the local republican *syndicat* and the FNMCA. In regions of conservative control, the local family allowance *caisse* harbored a clerical alignment and held ties to the local UNSA *syndicat*. Thus, UNSA stood to gain as its local affiliates obtained substantial funding from the state, but it nevertheless treated the Code as an injurious reform. Corporatists believed that Paris would never treat UNSA *caisses* with the same regard as republican *caisses* that openly declared their loyalty to Paris. Shortly after the Code was promulgated, *Les Syndicats Paysans* announced

---

[157] Pedersen, *Family, Dependence, and the Origins*, p. 386.
[158] "Rapport Chaland," Secrétaire-membre, Chambre de Commerce de Sainte-Etienne, 5 April 1938, AN F22 1516.

that "[peasants] want their allowances financed by their products and managed by their own *caisses*... on this point the battle continues."[159] UNSA leaders did not have to wait long. The French defeat of June 1940 ushered in a new regime that appeared, at least at first blush, wholly sympathetic to the corporatist movement headed by UNSA.

CONCLUSION

The 1930s were a tumultuous but formative decade for the French welfare state. After nearly ten years of political maneuvering and debates, France witnessed the implementation of the most comprehensive social protections in the nation's history. Challenges to this undertaking emerged from diverse quarters among rural and urban constituencies. Rural radicals menaced social insurance from its inception while more moderate agrarian syndicalists demanded local control and substantial state subsidies. Once again, the flexibility of the mutual model of social welfare proved advantageous. Legislators could refuse to concede to radicals on the principle of obligation while essentially caving in to moderate agricultural groups on issues of management and money. Popular concern over country-to-city migration, coupled with lower wages and standards of living in the countryside, helped make possible a national commitment to the peasantry. But creation of an autonomous agricultural social insurance system that benefited from unprecedented state subsidies did not dominate rural newspaper headlines as one might have expected. Ink was much more likely to have been spent on boisterous rallies led by Henri Dorgères. We can now see that the achievement of agricultural social insurance marked a significant milestone in the creation of France's welfare state. It further demonstrated the viability of the mutual model of social welfare and opened the door to legislators who, when confronted with the abject failure of agricultural family allowances later in the decade, would again reach for state subsidies.

Similarly, a contemporary observer of the Popular Front's short time in power would have concluded that its leaders were incapable of a frontal attack on employer control of family welfare. Nevertheless, the changes that the Popular Front set in motion had a far greater effect on family welfare than any all out assault on employer family allowance *caisses* could have ever achieved. Through binding arbitration, the

---

[159] *Les Syndicats Paysans*, 4 August 1939. Letter, UNSA Délégué Louis Salleron to Prime Minister Daladier, 2 November 1939; letter, Président d'Union du Sud-Est des Syndicats Agricoles, F. Garcin, to Sénateur Maupoil (Sâone-et-Loire), 7 November 1939.

Popular Front not only severely disrupted the function of employer *caisses de compensation* and forced substantial allowance increases, it also instigated the most significant state intervention into family welfare since 1932. Binding arbitration succeeded in cracking what had theretofore been employers' impenetrable defense of their prerogative to set allowance rates. The fissure, once exposed, brought Radical legislators, such as Adolphe Landry, to enter the breach in order to reestablish order. To be sure, employers benefited in the short term from succeeding legislation, especially the Code de la Famille, because it lowered allowance rates for most workers. But the Code also pushed the boundaries of state intervention well beyond previously defined limits in order to provide allowances to peasant smallholders and agricultural workers. Here too we can trace the instigation of far-reaching reforms to the Popular Front. Agriculture Minister Monnet could not have realized that his attempt to reward agricultural laborers for voting on the left would lead to such an important milestone in the struggle for French social welfare. Nor is there any evidence that Popular Front leaders purposefully set out to destroy German-style family welfare in Alsace-Lorraine. Rather, Popular Front reforms were contingent on contemporary challenges from the city and countryside during a decade of intense social and economic change.

6

Retrenchment and reform, 1939–1947

Developments in family allowances and social insurance during the Second World War virtually assured massive welfare reforms after the liberation in 1945. Strife between different kinds of industrial and commercial employers over the burden of family allowances continued to attract the attention of state officials until the final days of the Third Republic. As we saw in the previous chapter, employers whose workers had relatively few children increasingly grouped themselves in professional *caisses* in order to decrease their expenditures. This resulted in higher costs for employers of more typical working populations who relied on burden sharing between firms with varying numbers of parents. In 1938 the state proposed a national compensation fund that would equalize employer expenses across *caisses* throughout France. Industrialists were the greatest proponents of national compensation – as long as administration remained in private hands – because eligibility among their workers was relatively high. Pronatalists also supported this measure in order to lighten the burden of employers in departments where birthrates were above average. Detractors of national compensation were concentrated in textiles and commerce where workers tended to have fewer children. The resulting altercation between these constituencies of the family allowance movement was so fierce that it cast doubt on the efficacy of autonomous *caisses de compensation*. Indeed, by 1940 state officials began to wonder aloud whether a national state-managed system might be necessary to overcome the inherent problems of employer-controlled family welfare. Discord among employers over family allowances was matched by further conflict between the mutual movement and physicians. The FNMF's decision to take advantage of the favor it enjoyed under Vichy to pursue its attack on doctors eroded the mutual movement's capacity to protect itself during post-liberation reforms.

Vichy leaders also promulgated significant changes to welfare, especially during their first year in power. The government's promotion of a domestic ideal for women and its repression of independent labor unions marked a period of significant retrenchment. Reactionaries restricted women's professional opportunities and condemned birth control and abortion with ever-greater penalties.[1] The PCF had already been repressed by the Daladier government during the *drôle de guerre* because of its support for the Molotov-Ribbentrop pact and its dissemination of defeatist propaganda. Vichy expanded repression well into the center of the political spectrum, outlawing the CGT and the CFTC. This left only state-approved labor unions whose independence was gutted by their inability to strike. The regime also sought to reorganize welfare along corporate lines, an effort that ran headlong into a reticent mutual movement without whose cooperation such a reform could not succeed. Meanwhile, Vichy continued structural reforms to rural family welfare that had been enacted by the Third Republic, using the Code de la Famille as a starting point.

FAMILY WELFARE: THE DEBATE OVER
NATIONAL BURDEN SHARING

In February 1940, with France technically at war, the controller at the ministry of labor issued a report that advocated a sweeping consolidation of family allowances. In his conclusion, he stated: "I believe a single *caisse* for all of France would be the ideal. This *caisse* would equalize costs between *caisses de compensation* . . . Existing *caisses* would be but administrative sections."[2] This radical prescription for family allowances was prompted by a growing inequity of costs between *caisses* and employers' inability to resolve the issue. Landry and others called for the equalization of employer expenses through the establishment of a "National Compensation Fund that would aid *caisses de compensation* whose costs are abnormally high due to high eligibility rates of workers who are employed by members of these *caisses*."[3] Revenue for the new fund was to come from all *caisses* whose costs fell below average. In effect, the new fund would be a state-run super *caisse* capable of equalizing the cost of family allowances between employers nationwide. However, formidable technical difficulties of implementing such a measure remained. Employer-run *caisses* exhibited varied accounting and compensation practices, making

---

[1] Miranda Pollard, *Reign of Virtue: Mobilizing Gender in Vichy France* (University of Chicago Press, 1998). Also see Muel-Dreyfus, *Vichy et l'éternel féminin*.
[2] "Rapport," Contrôleur au Ministère du Travail, 2 February 1940, AN F22 1511.
[3] XVIIIe Congrès National des Allocations Familiales, *compte rendu*, 1938, pp. 28–31.

an equalization of costs among them a serious logistical challenge. But political considerations proved a far greater obstacle. The proposal ran headlong into the divisive issue of interprofessional versus professional compensation, which had been festering within the family allowance movement for nearly two decades.[4]

The initiative for national compensation originated from employers who wished to equalize *caisse* costs from department to department. These efforts were supported by pronatalists who condemned the current situation whereby employers in departments with high birthrates had to bear a greater burden for rescuing the country from demographic demise.[5] As the Chamber of Commerce of Brest noted: "It is unfair that other departments pay the same allowances but employer costs are often half of ours... [W]ithout national Compensation [the law] penalizes those departments that make the greatest contribution to increasing the French birthrate; this is indeed a paradox."[6] Similar pleas came from the Moselle, Manche, Pas-de-Calais, Calvados, and other departments where birthrates exceeded the national average. Employers in these regions insisted that if the state wanted allowance increases for large families, then special compensation must be paid to *caisses* in departments where children were more numerous.[7]

Whereas widely differing birthrates between departments were important to the issue of national compensation, they alone did not draw the lines of the debate. The state's proposal specified that equalization of costs should take place between *caisses*, and not necessarily between departments. Thus, many low-cost professional *caisses*, regardless of whether they were located in departments with high birthrates, were liable for contributions to the proposed national compensation fund. We saw earlier that two basic types of *caisses* evolved in the 1920s and were sanctioned by the 1932 law: interprofessional and professional. Interprofessional *caisses* accepted the affiliation of all kinds of employers, thus sharing the costs of workers' dependent children across diverse sectors of economic activity. Professional *caisses*, on the other hand, were established strictly among firms of similar professions. These *caisses* were found in a variety of sectors, including mining and metals that employed large numbers of family-age men. But professional *caisses* were far more common in

---

[4] See chapter 4.   [5] Alliance Nationale, Conseil d'administration, *procès-verbaux*, 14 March 1939.
[6] Chambre de Commerce de Brest, Extrait du Registre des Délibérations, 26 January 1939, AN F22 1511.
[7] Commission Départementale des Allocations Familiales de la Moselle, *procès-verbaux*, 28 April 1937; Memo, Guermont to the Prefect, 13 January 1939, Archives Départementales de la Moselle 6 X 12; Georges Maignan, "Note au sujet de la surcompensation," 18 April 1939, AN F22 1511.

light industry, commerce, and financial services, where the employment of women and young men kept employer costs significantly below the national average.[8] In 1939 professional *caisses* in textiles exhibited costs that were one-third the level found in heavy industry. The proposal for national compensation would make employers who were affiliated with such *caisses* subsidize allowances in sectors where eligibility among workers was much higher.[9]

Leaders of low-cost professional *caisses* adamantly opposed any sort of national compensation. They argued that family allowances should be viewed no differently than other employer expenses, which inevitably varied by region and by sector. State efforts to equalize the burden of family allowances, they asserted, would result in a suffocating bureaucracy and destroy healthy competition. One detractor of national compensation wrote facetiously: "Why stop half-way? There are other costs that could be equalized, starting with wages . . . We also need to place everyone the same distance from his raw materials and markets, regulate his transport costs, equalize all local taxes, and give all employers the same level of intelligence . . . so that no one can take advantage of another."[10] Critics of national compensation also maintained that employers who paid more in family allowances benefited from work forces with large numbers of parents. Parents, they argued, were more stable than single workers, thus reducing turnover and training expenses. Proposals for national compensation, they charged, ignored these benefits.[11]

Leaders of high-cost interprofessional *caisses* supported national compensation and hotly disputed the assertions of its opponents. They accused their colleagues in textiles and commerce who subscribed to professional *caisses* of shirking their responsibility for workers' children and forcing other employers to pay higher allowances. They pointed out that children did not necessarily adopt the professions of their parents. Hence, family allowances were not like other employer costs, but a burden that had to be shared by all employers. National compensation, they argued, provided the fairest mechanism of sharing allowance costs across diverse economic sectors while preserving local *caisses de compensation*. Virtually all supporters of national compensation insisted that the

---

[8] Women were eligible for family allowances but only under circumscribed conditions. See chapter 2.

[9] Maignan, "Note au sujet de la surcompensation," 18 April 1939, AN F22 1511; CCRP Commission de gestion, *procès-verbaux*, 23 March 1939.

[10] XIXe Congrès National des Allocations Familiales, *compte rendu*, 1939, p. 36.

[11] *Ibid.*, p. 35. Also see Letter, Director of the Caisse d'Allocations Familiales des Industries du Vêtement de Rouen et de la Région to the Minister of Labor, 24 February 1940, AN F22 1511.

CCAF, not the state, manage the proposed fund. But this caveat did not improve the appeal of national compensation among its opponents.[12]

The debate over national compensation tore the employer family allowance movement apart in the final year before the Second World War. During the previous two decades CCAF leaders had favored the creation of interprofessional *caisses* but had also accepted the choice of employers to group themselves by profession. By 1938, however, they recognized that the proliferation of professional *caisses* threatened to instigate massive state intervention, which would greatly curtail the autonomy of all *caisses*. But by then it was too late to alter course. Instead, the CCAF criticized state officials for wanting to bureaucratize family allowances and of having "snatched national compensation on the fly without really knowing all the risks it entailed."[13] Yet CCAF leaders themselves could offer no solution to the problem. Their lack of leadership testified to the limits of employer-controlled welfare. Throughout the interwar period, the lobby had been highly effective at minimizing the state's role in family allowances. Ironically, the very freedom that the CCAF had fought so hard to protect led to its downfall. Employers who insisted on grouping themselves by profession in order to minimize expenses repeatedly invoked the liberal principles upon which the family allowance movement had been founded. The result was a deadlock among employers over the fundamental role of *caisses de compensation*. The CCAF's failure to mediate the crisis led the government to bring the various factions together in order to impose a settlement.[14]

In January 1940, Labor Minister Paul Ramadier appointed a commission and charged it with resolving cost inequities between *caisses de compensation*. Members included representatives of the opposing factions in the family allowance movement as well as state officials. Commissioners worked throughout the Phony War but made little progress, meeting for the last time on 10 May 1940, the day of Germany's attack on France. The commission remained far from resolving the issue of national burden sharing and, in the words of one of its members, once the war had begun "nobody talked about it anymore."[15] The impasse at the commission could not have been entirely unexpected. Employers had created *caisses* out of their own interests to pay allowances to a specific population

---

[12] CAFM Commission de gestion, *procès-verbaux*, 21 March 1939.
[13] Fernand Rey, "La surcompensation nationale," XIXe Congrès National des Allocations Familiales, *compte rendu*, 1939, p. 31.
[14] CCAF Assemblée générale, *compte rendu*, 24 May 1938.
[15] Interview with Aymé Bernard, Third phase, 19 February 1976, Comité d'Histoire de la Sécurité Sociale, AN 37 AS 2.

of workers. The 1932 law that mandated allowances, and subsequent legislation in 1938 and 1939, had not fundamentally altered these circumstances. National compensation would have broadened employers' responsibility to virtually all workers in society. It would have violated the inherent parochialism of the *caisse* system, which many employers clung to in the hope of maintaining family welfare as an instrument of labor pacification. Vichy leaders were much too close to the *grand patronat* to impose a solution. Hence, during the war, the issue of burden sharing stewed, further justifying the arguments of postwar reformers then deliberating in London that employers should be stripped of their control over family welfare.

VICHY SOCIAL INSURANCE INITIATIVES AND THE FNMF

After June 1940, most provincial mutual leaders continued their service to local societies while trying to avoid changes that were invoked by the National Revolution. The FNMF, on the other hand, was much more willing to engage Vichy as a partner, albeit a cautious one. The Fédération's collaboration stemmed from traditional mutualists' corporate vision of social relations, which corresponded with Vichy's own. Prior to the creation of social insurance, traditionalists had taken pride in the fact that their associations represented "the solidarity of . . . workers, bosses, foremen, customers, and suppliers."[16] As we saw earlier, traditionalists, such as Henri Vermont, fought the movement's participation in social insurance in part because of its recognition of class relations under the auspices of mutual aid. Traditionalists refused to grant credence to notions of class struggle, preferring to view mutual aid as a beneficial social practice that could be adapted to the world of industrial labor without penalizing employers and without the participation of the state. During the Vichy years, traditionalists enjoyed a resurgence within the FNMF. Fédération President Heller's ability to command the movement suffered from his previous association with free masonry, whose societies were suppressed by Vichy.[17] Although resurgent traditionalists prudently resisted elements of Vichy's National Revolution that might undermine the authority of mutual societies, their disposition toward corporatism resulted in significant collaboration on social welfare, especially in the provision of medical care.

[16] Porte, *Assurances sociales*, pp. 8–9. Also see chapter 2.
[17] Letter, Le Secrétaire général auprès du Chef du Gouvernement, Renand, to Le Secrétaire d'Etat au Travail, Hubert Lagardelle, 7 August 1943; Lagardelle to Renand, 25 September 1943, both in AN F60 651.

Vichy corporatists believed that workers and employers throughout the economy would cooperate to ensure their mutual success once the basic structure of Vichy's National Revolution was erected. Pursuant to this goal, on 9 November 1940, the head of the Vichy state, Philippe Pétain, dissolved all economic interest groups, including employers' associations and workers' unions. In one fell swoop, the CGT and the CFTC were declared illegal. The principal employers' organization, the CGPF, was also disbanded. But, in preparation for the transition to a corporatist economy, employers were called upon to create organization committees (*comités d'organisation*), which quickly became *de facto* employer associations. Organization committees were established for each economic sector during the first months of 1941, and they quickly became dominated by the same large employers who had ruled the CGPF. Meanwhile, to workers Vichy offered only state-supervised associations, known as social committees (*comités sociaux*), which possessed no power to strike. Many workers believed that Vichy labor policies constituted revenge, pure and simple, for the social advances forced on employers by the Popular Front. But Vichy officials insisted that the National Revolution would open a harmonious era of labor relations and that there would be no need to strike since disputes would be settled cooperatively under the terms of Vichy's new Labor Charter (*Charte du Travail*).

In addition to governing labor-management relations, the Labor Charter envisioned substantial reforms to social welfare.[18] The FNMF cautiously declared that "the supreme purpose of the Labor Charter is to do away with the principal cause of division among the French, bringing employers and workers together for the sake of national unity, which is absolutely imperative for the future of our country. This purpose is in complete harmony with the doctrine and action of the mutual movement which has always worked for the development of an active union and solidarity between diverse categories of workers."[19] Yet mutual leaders remained anxious about the practical effect of the Labor Charter. The Labor Charter dictated that management of social welfare would henceforth be reorganized along corporate lines and administered

---

[18] Robert O. Paxton, *Vichy France: Old Guard and New Order* (New York: Knopf, 1972), pp. 215–217. On the Labor Charter, see *Colloque sur le Gouvernement de Vichy et la Révolution Nationale*, Fondation Nationale des Sciences Politiques, 6–7 March 1970 (Paris: Armand Colin and Fondation Nationale des Sciences Politiques, 1972), pp. 158–210.

[19] Fédération Nationale de la Mutualité, "La Mutualité et la Charte du travail," February 1941, p. 3. On the CCAF's endorsement of the Labor Charter, see *L'Actualité Sociale* 167 (November 1941), 1.

by workers and employers' representatives who together made up so-cial committees. Social committees would assume responsibility for the full gamut of social protections and assistance: social insurance, worker housing, family allowances, assistance to unemployed workers, as well as leisure-time activities such as sports leagues, special theaters, camp-ing facilities, the arts, etc. Yet hopes that workers might gain control over social welfare under the new regime were quickly dashed. The Charter set out a tripartite corporate representative system that de-prived the mass of wage-earning workers of their due weight. Each social committee contained between twelve and twenty-four members, divided equally between three constituencies: employers, wage-earning workers, and a third group of master artisans, engineers, and mid-level managers. In adding mid-level managers, who usually sided with man-agement, Vichy officials borrowed a tactic from Italian Fascists who had succeeded in diluting working-class power in their social committees.[20] Yet even this inequitable slice of power for wage earners remained but a promise since so few social committees were ever constituted.[21] Of course, mutual leaders were more concerned about the absence of di-rect mutual society representation on social committees than the division of workers. Vichy officials quickly reassured FNMF leaders of the con-tinued importance of the mutual movement. In fact, the Labor Charter explicitly required social committees to respect existing legislation, in-cluding the social insurance laws of 1928 and 1930. And the secretary of state for industrial production and labor – the Vichy designation for the minister of labor – who became the final arbiter of social committee initiatives, promised to uphold this commitment.[22] During Vichy's early months, this ministry was in the hands of a former CGT official, René Belin, who believed that Vichy offered the working class an opportu-nity to improve social welfare in exchange for collaboration in the new order. Belin promptly proposed sweeping reforms that would have en-tirely recast the administration of social insurance and family allowances, sparking considerable consternation among mutual leaders and employ-ers. Belin's proposal constituted the first test of Pétain's commitment to improve worker welfare.

[20] Alexander De Grand, *Italian Fascism: Its Origins and Development*, third edn. (Lincoln: University of Nebraska Press), 1989.
[21] Commission des Affaires économiques et sociales, Comité sur les Problèmes sociaux de la France libérée, Rapport sur les principales mésures sociaux à prendre dès la libération, January 1944, AN F22 2050. In this report, Albert Gazier uses Vichy's own statistics to conclude that the number of social committees ever created was "infime."
[22] See Charte du Travail, especially articles 3, 36, 45, and 48.

Belin had served as an official for the telephone workers' union, rising to the post of deputy secretary-general of the CGT in 1933. He was one of the highest ranking working-class leaders to participate in the Vichy government. Belin's pacifism led him into early opposition to the war and to support the June armistice. Thereafter his enthusiasm for Vichy was stoked by Pétain's early addresses that denounced liberal capitalism alongside class struggle as ideologies that had oppressed and divided the nation. Belin thus took Pétain at his word when he promised an orderly and social regime that would improve living conditions and welfare protections for the working class.[23] In July 1940 Belin recruited Pierre Laroque, a former high-ranking official at the labor ministry and the Conseil d'Etat. Laroque immediately set to work on the problem of workers' rights and social insurance.[24] By late summer, Laroque had drafted a plan for the unification of social insurance and family allowances into a single, state-directed system of social welfare. Laroque's proposal, which was forwarded by Belin to Pétain in September, was nothing short of revolutionary.

Laroque called for the elimination of all 800 social insurance *caisses* and their replacement with regional *caisses* whose circumscriptions would range from a single department or an *arrondissement*, depending on population density. Laroque foresaw a continued division of social insurance premiums between workers and employers, but in order to bolster pension reserves, rates would be raised. The cost of family allowances would remain exclusively on the shoulders of employers, but they would lose all administrative control to the new regional *caisses*. Eventually, the regional *caisses* would assume control over accident insurance as well, which employers were currently required to purchase from private insurers. Belin and Laroque justified their proposal on several grounds. The first of these referred to Vichy's announced goal of reorganizing social welfare along corporate lines. The proposal argued that current social insurance practices were neither sufficiently mature nor perfected to permit a wholesale switch to corporate organization under social committees. Belin and Laroque observed that the mutual movement's professional framework had been substantially deformed by its participation in mandatory social

---

[23] Pétain made a major address on social policy that had been drafted by the leader of the 1930s Frontist movement, Gaston Bergery on 12 October 1940. The Frontists opposed communism and the power of industrial and commercial magnates. See Paxton, *Vichy France*, pp. 213–214. On Belin, see "M. René Belin a défini la politique sociale du gouvernement," *France Socialiste*, 8 December 1941, in F7 15287.

[24] Pierre Laroque, *Au service de l'homme et du droit* (Paris: Association pour l'Etude de l'Histoire de la Sécurité Sociale, 1993), pp. 124–126.

insurance since 1930. In the light of these circumstances, the best alternative would be the creation of a single state institution under whose
guidance a corporate organization of social welfare could be effected at
the appropriate time. Belin and Laroque also believed that their plan
held the additional benefit of removing employer influence over family
allowances, a situation about which they were clearly of two minds. A
summary of the proposal notes that "in the past they [employers] have
taken advantage of this process either for marvelous objectives or with
the purpose of battling against normal wage increases."[25] The authors
were unrepentant about their plan's contempt for employer-controlled
family allowances and mutual society social insurance *caisses*. They insisted that corporate – they preferred the term "professional" – bodies
that manage social welfare must be truly collaborative efforts by workers
and employers: "[T]hese organizations are, in effect, often limited to one
profession or sector, but their internal structure, on the contrary, never –
or almost never – presents a truly professional character. They are not
institutions created and managed collaboratively by employers and workers but are more often either purely employer institutions, purely worker
institutions, or mutual societies whose professional character is very
weak. Such institutions with such management in no way correspond to
the Government's conception of professional organization."[26] Clearly,
Belin assumed that Vichy's conception of corporate association corresponded to Pétain's early speeches, but he soon came to understand his
delusion.

Attacks on Belin and Laroque's proposal began even before Pétain
received an official copy. The director of the Chambres Syndicales du
Bâtiment wrote a long letter to Pétain in which he called the plan an
"*étatisation du Social*" whose realization would rob social welfare of its "soul
and family spirit" and "sterilize all planned rapprochement between
employers and their workers." The building lobby director offered no
concrete solutions for the problem of burden sharing that wracked family
allowance *caisses*, but he was certain that a centralization of administrative
and financial functions was wholly unwarranted. In a direct attack on
Belin, he urged Pétain to transfer responsibility for family allowances
to the newly created Secrétaire d'Etat de la Famille Française, which

---

[25] Hamelin, an official at the Conseil d'Etat, provided a summary of Belin's proposal. Hamelin
credits "M. Laroque du Cabinet Belin." See "Note pour le Secrétaire Général, Présidence du
Conseil," 30 September 1940, Dossier Assurances Sociales 1940–1944, AN F60 646.
[26] Memo, Secrétaire d'Etat à la Production Industrielle et au Travail to Secrétaire Général de la
Présidence du Conseil, 24 September 1940, Dossier Assurances Sociales 1940–1944, AN F60
646.

was headed by pronatalist Georges Pernot. Similarly, he recommended that reforms to social insurance should be drafted by officials in the department of public health rather than at the labor ministry.[27]

Rural mutual society leaders and UNSA constituted the other great opponents of Belin and Laroque's proposal. They conceded that the labor ministry's analysis of urban family allowance and social insurance *caisses* was accurate. However, they maintained that such difficulties did not exist in agriculture. As we have already seen, the rural mutual movement and family allowance *caisses* were more closely intertwined than their urban counterparts and their management was already coordinated with state subsidies. Belin and Laroque foresaw their objections and confided that agriculture, whose conditions they called "satisfactory," would mount the greatest resistance to the plan. In the hope of solving rural residents' remaining social welfare difficulties and providing an efficient and unified system, they insisted that agriculture must participate in the reform.[28] However, opposition from the *grand patronat* and rural interests persuaded Pétain to quickly kill the proposal. Retribution for its authors was swift.

Laroque was ousted from government service, using Vichy's "purification" law of 3 October 1940. That law barred anyone with at least three Jewish grandparents from public service or teaching.[29] Belin remained at his post until April 1942, but he lost many of his responsibilities to Pierre Pucheu, a former high official in the service of the metals employers' association, who assumed the post of Secrétaire d'Etat de la Production Industrielle et l'Intérieur in Februrary 1941.[30] With the passing of Belin and Laroque from government service, any hope that Vichy would bring control of social welfare closer to beneficiaries receded.[31] Laroque soon departed for London where he would begin work on yet another plan to bring a unified system of social welfare to his compatriots.

---

[27] Directeur du Comité du Groupe des Chambres Syndicales du Bâtiment, Michel, to Maréchal Pétain, 24 September 1930, Dossier Assurances Sociales 1940–1944, AN F60 646.

[28] Note pour le Secrétaire General, Présidence du Conseil, 30 September 1940, Dossier Assurances Sociales 1940–1944, AN F60 646.

[29] Laroque never professed adherence to Judaism, his mother being an Anglican Protestant. See Laroque, *Au Service de l'homme et du droit*, pp. 126–127.

[30] Both Belin and Pucheu were arrested at the time of the liberation. Pucheu was executed in Algiers. See Direction Générale de la Sureté Nationale, Liste des justiciables de la haute cour de justice, 13 December 1945, AN F7 15287.

[31] Deliberations of the mutual aid society at Renault indicate that only minor changes in statutes were forced on the society as a result of the Labor Charter. See Société de Secours Mutuels des Usines Renault, Conseil d'administration, *procès-verbaux*, 28 September and 13 November 1942. François Lehideux, Louis Renault's nephew, followed Pierre Pucheu in Belin's old job as minister of industrial production and labor.

Vichy's early popularity gave way to a second period during which the regime became increasingly authoritarian. With its fate so closely tied to German predominance, the wartime state's ability to enact welfare reform tracked the war's major turning points. The American landings in North Africa in November 1942 triggered a German occupation of south and central France that had previously been governed solely by Vichy. Three months later, the Soviet victory at Stalingrad indicated the probability of an Axis defeat. As fellow travelers in Vichy's National Revolution, FNMF leaders responded to these developments with a two-front offensive of their own. First, while continuing to pay *pro forma* respect to the Labor Charter, they insisted, more boldly than anytime since the French defeat, that the mutual movement would not serve as an instrument of the regime's social policy. FNMF Director-General Marc Degas expressed the changed attitude in June 1943: "In offering its loyal participation in all measures of the Labor Charter that fall within its domain, the mutual movement is formally committed – and I want to underline this – to remain within that domain. We do not want to become involved in corporate or syndical organizations nor substitute ourselves for social committees whose prerogatives far exceed our mission." Degas' reverence for the prerogatives of the Labor Charter's social committees was hardly genuine. By spring 1943, the government's brutal draft of workers for labor service in Germany had exposed the impotence of social committees.[32] Degas had an ulterior purpose. While remaining just within the bounds of acceptable allegiance to the regime, he sought to project the image of a neutral FNMF whose "proper activity [remained] the improvement of social protections and the implementation of mutual assistance."[33] Meanwhile, the FNMF sought greater freedom for mutual aid societies by attacking the constraints imposed upon them by the 1930 social insurance law.

FNMF Secretary-General Romain Lavielle led the charge by denouncing interwar advocates of social insurance for their "threats and unwillingness to collaborate with us . . . the movement only survived and at great cost," Lavielle contended, "because we were supported by our faith."[34] As we have already seen, such an account bears little resemblance to reality. During the late 1920s and early 1930s, when social

---

[32] Labor service in Germany was directed by the Service du Travail Obligatoire. For a compelling account of how the STO triggered widespread discontent and resistance to Vichy, see John F. Sweets, *Choices in Vichy France: The French under Nazi Occupation* (Oxford University Press, 1994).

[33] Marc Degas, "La Mutualité française," speech delivered at the Fondation Française pour l'Etude des Problèmes Humains, 2 June 1943 (Paris: Bernard Frères), p. 19.

[34] Cited by Gibaud, *De la mutualité à la sécurité sociale*, p. 111.

insurance legislation was drafted and implemented, the FNMF epitomized the "insider" Third Republic interest group. It enjoyed the support
and leadership of men like Gaston Roussel, Raoul Péret, and Georges
Petit, whose connections reached into the very heart of parliamentary
power. Indeed, it is just this involvement in the grubby infighting of the
Republican past that Lavielle and FNMF President Léon Heller wished
to dispel, replacing it with the image of a politically neutral and altruis-
tic mutual movement which had barely survived a depraved chapter in
French history. It should be noted that Vichy supporters and opponents
alike wondered aloud about the nature of the Third Republic and its
role in the humiliating defeat of June 1940. If historical revisionism had
been the extent of the FNMF's endeavors during the Vichy years, their
actions would hardly have been unusual. Most institutions adjusted their
rhetoric in order to survive under Vichy. But FNMF officials went further.
Under the guise of their newly refurbished image and working relations
with the wartime regime, they sought to expand their prerogatives at the
expense of their interwar adversaries.

Medical professionals constituted the FNMF's foremost target.
Throughout the 1930s doctors had fought a running battle with mutual societies over reimbursement for medical diagnoses and procedures.
Doctors resented the growing influence of mutual officials whom they
accused of disrupting proper medical practices by injecting financial considerations into patient care. As we saw in chapter four, the Confédération
des Syndicats Médicaux effectively defended doctors' prerogatives
under the 1930 law. Under Vichy, mutual leaders sought to settle the
score. FNMF Secretary-General Lavielle described the intransigence
of doctors in the 1930s as a direct result of the social insurance law
and "a certain change in character," a veiled accusation that physicians
placed profits ahead of their patients.[35] At the FNMF annual meeting in
October 1943, Lavielle reported that the FNMF had obtained the support of the ministry of labor in its conflict with doctors in several cities
and departments, including Montpellier, Jura, Pyrénées-Orientales,
and Bouches-du-Rhône. Once again, Lavielle argued that "the principal
difficulties which have arisen between the mutual movement and doctors
are founded in a code of ethics ... which opposes any hindrance to the
free choice [of doctor] ... and refuses any regulations that would force
adherence to a third-payer system." A delegate seconded this position,

[35] Conférence de Romain Lavielle, "L'Œuvre de la mutualité et des assurances sociales," Maison
de la Mutualité, Paris, 15 March 1944 (Paris: Imprimerie Municipale, 1944), p. 28.

insisting that physicians "have succeeded in creating a privileged situation based on their important services and on purely material interests."[36] The assembly approved a series of hard-hitting resolutions, including one that charged doctors with "abusive practices" and labeled as "unacceptable a doctor's judgment of a patient's condition in the sole pursuit of augmenting his personal profit." Other resolutions dubbed doctors' rate increases unfair and called for the spread of capitated medical payments.[37] Capitated payments require a physician to accept a fixed fee (*abonnement forfaitaire*) for all of an individual's medical needs for a set period whether he or she needs medical attention. Mutual societies preferred capitated medicine, especially for their elderly members who would most likely need health services, because it increased their ability to predict and reduce costs. Although the FNMF's offensive against doctors did not result in a major revision to social insurance, it nevertheless represented a bald use of Vichy's political favor to upset the balance between medical service providers and insurance *caisses* that had been painstakingly legislated in 1930. Vichy authorities ransacked the offices of the Confédération des Syndicats Médicaux and confiscated its property for use by a pro-Vichy association of physicians.[38] Meanwhile, the FNMF flourished under a cozy relationship with the government. Eighty-nine new societies were founded between June 1941 and March 1944, twelve of them serving government ministries, including justice, interior, labor, finance, and the office of the prefecture of the Seine.[39] Clearly, the FNMF was not an outsider to Vichy politics, but rather a strong-willed collaborator that carefully distanced itself as the outcome of the war became apparent. But even while it insisted on greater autonomy after 1943, the FNMF continued to use its close relations with the regime to expand its reach over social policy.[40]

RURAL FAMILY WELFARE UNDER VICHY

Vichy succeeded in enacting important systemic changes to rural family allowances even if the value of actual benefits proved disappointing. However, the regime also faced important setbacks. Most striking

---

[36] Remarks of Delegate Arnaud, Fédération Nationale de la Mutualité Française, Assemblées, *compte rendu*, 30 September to 2 October 1943, pp. 28–29.
[37] *Ibid.*, pp. 30–31.   [38] *Le Médecin de France*, 20 July 1945.
[39] Romain Lavielle "L'Œuvre de la mutualité et des assurances sociales," p. 8.
[40] Lavielle's *Histoire de la mutualité*, published in 1964, devotes only four pages to the Vichy period and ignores FNMF activities entirely, thus constituting yet another revision of the mutual movement's history.

among these was its failure to recast agricultural production and peasant life through the creation of a National Peasant Corporation (Corporation Nationale Paysanne). Similar to the Labor Charter for urban workers, this effort became essentially moribund after initial enthusiasm for the National Revolution subsided.[41] But enthusiasm was not the only thing that Vichy found in short supply.

Wartime exigencies and demands by German occupiers drastically limited Vichy's ability to improve the lives of rural families. Nowhere was this more evident than in agricultural production. Most peasants faced shortages of spare parts, fuel, fertilizer, and pesticides, resulting in dramatic falls in production during the war: 18 percent for wheat, 40 percent for potatoes, and 30 percent for milk. To make matters worse, by 1943 15 percent of French agricultural production was being shipped directly to Germany.[42] Therefore, much effort was devoted to merely avoiding serious food shortages and ensuring an equitable distribution of the reduced resources.[43] Indeed, evidence of widespread disaffection with the regime by 1943 was, in large part, due to the government's inability to deliver on its promises to improve family living standards.[44] These difficulties, however, did not prevent Vichy from implementing the rural family policy directives of the 1939 Code de la Famille.

Initially, responsibility for these reforms was to be assumed by an agricultural profession that had been reorganized along corporate lines. The December 1940 decree that created the National Peasant Corporation promised its membership a primary role in "the promotion and management of the common interests of peasant families in the moral, social, and economic realms."[45] Défense Paysanne leader Henri Dorgères and UNSA officials, such as Jacques Le Roy Ladurie, Louis Salleron, and Pierre Caziot, who had advocated agricultural corporatism since the 1930s, assumed prominent positions in state agencies and the new corporation.[46] Buoyed by Vichy's commitment to a rural revival, these leaders drew up an ambitious list of reforms. It included improving provincial transport, a decrease in peasant working hours, increases

---

[41] Chalmin, *Les Assurances mutuelles agricoles*, p. 205.   [42] Larkin, *France Since the Popular Front*, p. 95.

[43] Cleary, *Peasants, Politicians and Producers*, pp. 92–93.

[44] Pollard, *Reign of Virtue*, p. 197. Pollard treats the shortcomings of Vichy welfarism in chapter 5.

[45] "Loi du 2 décembre 1940 relative à l'organisation corporative de l'Agriculture" (*JO*, 7 December 1940), article 7. Text of law reprinted in annexe of Pierre Caziot, *Au service de la paysannerie* (Paris: Fernand Sorlot, 1942), pp. 116–126. See especially p. 119.

[46] Le Roy Ladurie served as Vichy's minister of agriculture and then joined the armed resistance in 1944.

in family allowances and social insurance benefits, and home loans.[47] Local UNSA *syndicats agricoles*, which formed the fundamental unit of the new corporation, had little difficulty in subduing rival family allowances *caisses* whose Republican tendencies had appeared so threatening under the Third Republic.[48] In theory, the *syndicats* were to have principal control over the coordination of agricultural production and marketing, as well as the determination of local social welfare priorities. In practice, however, most important decisions in agricultural family policy emerged from the agriculture ministry in Paris under the direction of Pierre Caziot.[49]

In fact, far from conceding control of family welfare to regional corporate bodies Caziot further established state responsibility for new entitlements and enacted reforms that went well beyond the Code de la Famille. In so doing, he ignored the wishes of local UNSA *syndicats* and Church leaders who had believed that Vichy would offer increased rural autonomy in welfare administration.[50] Vichy did, however, enact the tax on principal agricultural products to pay for family allowances, which corporatists had advocated earlier.[51] Meats were taxed at 1 percent, industrial beets and cereals at 2 percent, wines at 4 francs per hectoliter, and ciders at 2 francs per hectoliter. The resulting revenue, used entirely for family welfare and known as the National Fund for Agricultural Solidarity (Fonds National de Solidarité Agricole), covered 40 percent of the cost of allowances. The remaining 60 percent was split evenly between premium payments by agricultural employers and state subsidies.[52]

---

[47] Louis Salleron, "L'Agriculture et les lois sociales," 28 April 1941; President Pierre Lescop, Fédération corporative de la mutualité agricole to Guebriant, Vice President, Commission Nationale d'Organisation corporative paysanne, 19 March 1942. Also see "Pour une amélioration de la condition des ouvriers agricoles," Corporation Nationale Paysanne, Service Social, Comité d'Etudes des Questions Ouvriers, 1 April 1942. All of these documents can be found in AN F10 4970.

[48] Chalmin, *Les Assurances mutuelles agricoles*, p. 206. See chapter 5 for the conflict between UNSA and prorepublican *syndicats agricoles*.

[49] Caziot, *Au service de la paysannerie*. Also see Cleary, *Peasants, Politicians, and Producers*, pp. 99–103. Caziot served as Minister of Agriculture from July 1940 to April 1942. He was succeeded by Jacques Le Roy Ladurie. Paxton details the process by which the new peasant corporation was used by the state as machinery to manage the agricultural market and avoid food shortages. See Paxton, *Vichy France*, pp. 206–209. Also see Pierre Barral and Isabel Boussard, "La Politique agrarienne," *Colloque sur le Gouvernement de Vichy et la Révolution Nationale*, Fondation Nationale des Sciences Politiques, 6–7 March 1970 (Paris: Armand Colin and Fondation Nationale des Sciences Politiques, 1972), pp. 210–233.

[50] W.D. Halls, *Politics, Society and Christianity in Vichy France* (Providence: Berg 1995), pp. 256–257.

[51] See chapter 5.

[52] "Note sur le Fonds National de Solidarité Agricole" by H. Buffandeau, 3 July 1943; Memo, Pierre Cathala, Ministère de l'Economie Nationale et des Finances, Direction du Budget, 1 er Bureau, to Ministre Secrétaire d'Etat d'Agriculture, 10 July 1943, both in AN F10 5108.

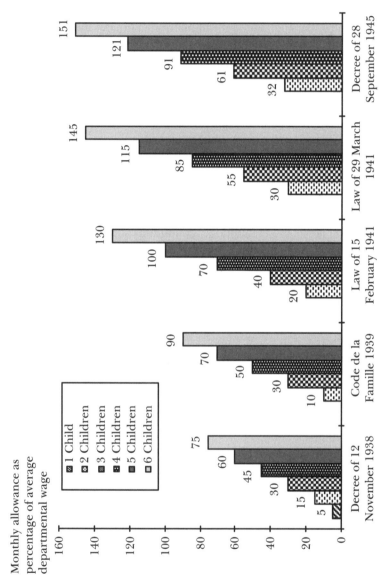

Monthly allowance as
percentage of average
departmental wage

1 Child
2 Children
3 Children
4 Children
5 Children
6 Children

Decree of 12
November 1938

Code de la
Famille 1939

Law of 15
February 1941

Law of 29 March
1941

Decree of 28
September 1945

Figure 12 Increases in family allowance rates 1938–1945. *JO*, Lois et décrets, 30 July 1939, p. 9610; Ceccaldi, *Histoire des prestations familiales en France*, p. 92.

Between 1942 and 1944, Vichy extended the Agricultural Solidarity tax to most other farm products, and nearly doubled its rates. The tax increases were necessitated by the regime's repeated hikes in family allowance payments. Beginning in 1938, allowances were calculated according to an administratively determined average male monthly departmental wage of about 1,000 francs.[53] Yet Vichy administrators, who were charged with holding inflation in check, resisted pegging official departmental wages to rapidly rising prices. As a result, even the large monetary increases in allowances reported in figure 12 lagged behind the cost of living under occupation.

Inflation was especially hard felt in the countryside where price hikes in agricultural inputs outpaced officially sanctioned prices for farmers' produce. In Puy-de-Dôme, for example, a Légion Française des Combattants study revealed that officially sanctioned prices for the department's principal farm products rose 217 percent between 1939 and 1943 while the cost of agricultural inputs had risen 308 percent.[54] Such discrepancies fueled a large black market in food products, causing tension between rural and urban residents, with each blaming the other for unfair prices of agricultural supplies and food.

Despite these difficulties, Vichy labored to support peasant families as symbolic of national renewal. Shortly after its accession, the regime extended the newly created single-wage allowance (*allocation de salaire unique*) to the agricultural sector. This payment replaced the home-mother allowance (*allocation de la mère au foyer*) that had been paid in commerce and industry since 1938. Eligibility for the home-mother allowance had required the presence of dependent children and prohibited the employment of the mother. The new single-wage allowance permitted wives whose spouses were confined to POW camps or conscripted for labor in Germany to collect family support even if they were employed outside the home.[55] Together, increased agricultural family allowances, even though eroded by inflation, and the extension of the single-wage allowance to peasant families further bolstered the state's direct role in family welfare.[56] By 1945, agricultural family allowances totaled approximately

---

[53] "Les Allocations familiales en agriculture: Résultats statistiques pour les années 1940 à 1945," Caisse Centrale d'Allocations Familiales Mutuelles Agricoles, AD Meuse 415 Mp 4. On the average monthly male departmental wage, see chapter 5.

[54] "Enquête sur les bases du ravitaillement," Légion Française des Combattants, Commission Agricole, Archives départementales de Puy-de-Dôme M05755, cited by Sweets, *Choices in Vichy France*, p. 78.

[55] Pedersen, *Family, Dependence, and the Origins*, p. 408.

[56] François Jourdain, *Les Allocations familiales en agriculture: vos droits et vos devoirs* (Paris: Publications Sociales Agricoles, 1940).

8 billion francs annually. Of this total, 2.7 billion came directly from state coffers, 3.6 billion were collected in agricultural taxes, and 1.7 billion were provided by the *caisse* premiums of agricultural employers.[57] Such an auspicious commitment of tight fiscal resources matched the Third Republic's earlier initiative to subsidize agricultural social insurance. Gaullist officials in London, who were planning France's postwar system of social welfare, could not help but sit up and take notice.

PLANNING FOR *LA SÉCURITÉ SOCIALE*

After February 1942, a distinguished group of French social reformers held regular meetings at 3 St. James Square, London, to prepare welfare reforms for a liberated France. The group included the left wing Gaullist Henry Hauck, who held the position of Directeur du Travail à la France Combattante. Hauck was joined by Pierre Maisonneuve, Jean Gendrot, and after his arrival in late 1942 to work for de Gaulle's Comité Général d'Etudes, Pierre Laroque.[58] Known officially as the Section Sociale de la Commission pour l'Etude des Problèmes d'après Guerre d'Ordre Economique et Social, the group constituted the first official resistance efforts at preparing a social welfare system for postwar France. The Section Sociale considered not only social insurance and family welfare issues but also broader questions that the group deemed relevant to their task and likely characteristics of a postliberation society. These included the state's role in economic planning, the nationalization of industries, worker participation in industrial management, and government regulation of wages, including minimum levels as well as wage equity between men and women. The scope of these discussions were influenced by reports on foreign social programs, including the Tennessee Valley Authority and the newly released British welfare proposal, the Beveridge Report. Not surprisingly, there was no mention of German social insurance, which had played such an important role in post Great War discussions of French social reform. However, the Section Sociale expressed a keen interest in Vichy social policy and received regular intelligence reports on it.[59]

[57] "Les Allocations familiales en agriculture: résultats et statistiques pour les années 1940 à 1945," p. 11, AD Meuse 415 Mp 4.
[58] After his expulsion from the Vichy government in October 1940, Laroque was given a job in the Lyon silk industry by an old friend. In December 1942 he was recruited by resistance leaders Jean Moulin and Alexandre Parodi and persuaded to join efforts underway in London. See Laroque, *Au service de l'homme et du droit*, pp. 127–131.
[59] AN 72 AJ 546 contains several reports that were completed by the Section Sociale. For more on wartime planning among Resistance leaders, see Andrew Shennan, *Rethinking France: Plans for Renewal 1940–1946* (Oxford: Clarendon, 1989).

Participants in the Section Sociale regarded various Vichy social reforms in different ways. On the one hand, comments a Section report, "some among them, had they been enacted during a different era, would have undeniably constituted a step forward. However, certain others are so imbued with reactionary thinking that it is difficult to lend the least confidence in the entire edifice that has been so painstakingly created by the 'hinterland' authorities at Vichy." The Labor Charter came in for especially harsh criticism, being called an "indescribable muddle of medieval rules that challenges all good sense and logic . . . the Charter's entire construction is based uniquely on force and therefore doomed in advance."[60] But on issues of rural family welfare, where Vichy had expended considerable energy, both in implementing the Code de la Famille and through its own initiatives, the Section Sociale embraced Vichy's goals and methods. Indeed, a Section Sociale report on France's demographic circumstances bears a strong resemblance to Vichy documents on the same subject. The Section singled out five areas for action, including a "battle against the rural exodus" and persuading citizens to "return to the land." Also included are increases in family allowances and birth primes. In fact, an intelligence report praises the work of Vichy's last minister of industrial production and labor, Jean Bichelonne, for achieving a long overdue raise in family allowances.[61] These reports, coupled with the early actions of the Provisional Government, suggest that Vichy initiatives provided a momentum for state intervention in social welfare that had been launched by the Code de la Famille of 1939. In so doing, the wartime regime provided postliberation reformers with a powerful model of state-centered change that would influence reforms in the strife-ridden system of urban family allowances. Gaullist planners, however, viewed Vichy's stewardship of social insurance much more critically.

Most of the criticisms that the London-based reformers leveled at social insurance were well known before the war. Patients' difficulties in obtaining reimbursement for medical treatment due to the conflict between mutual society *caisses* and doctors topped their list of concerns. The scant unemployment coverage provided by the law of 1930 also raised unanimous condemnation, especially the law's stipulation that in order to collect benefits, a social insuree had to have made uninterrupted contributions during the previous year. As for Vichy, Gaullist planners

---

[60] Chauvet, "Rapport sur les lois sociales de Vichy," 10 May 1942, AN AJ 546.
[61] "Algiers, Note du Centre de Documentation, Renseignement tiré d'une lettre du 16 février 1944 du directeur d'une agence d'information de la Métropole, de tendances collaborationnistes," AN F22 2030.

denounced the legislation of March 1941 that granted retirement pensions to workers who had not previously contributed to social insurance *caisses*. They were outraged because law failed to furnish revenue for the extension of coverage. Instead, the government simply authorized the use of workers' capitalized accounts to pay for the newly encompassed retirees. Vichy's minister of labor, René Belin, authored the legislation, claiming that "[w]hat a false democracy couldn't enact, but had so often promised, the government of Marshal Pétain has done . . . believe in him. He has hope for you."[62] One Section Sociale participant noted with horror that Belin's "so-called law of 14 March 1941 for the benefit of retired workers . . . was created without foreseeing any financial resources . . . the entire annual receipts of retirement insurance and ten-years' worth of reserves of the caisse générale de garantie have been expended to pay these pensions." Gaullists viewed the law for what it was, a reckless method of winning support for the regime. After the liberation, reformers faced depleted pension accounts, virtually forcing them to adopt a pay-as-you-go (as opposed to a capitalized account) retirement system.[63] But Gaullist planners were not solely driven by modifications enacted by Vichy. Their wartime analysis of the 1930 social insurance law resulted in a set of principles by which they hoped to build a new, comprehensive social security system.

London-based planners identified four principles according to which postwar social protections would be expanded: (1) Insurance must protect workers against unforeseen disruptions of income of all kinds; (2) Cost will be shared by workers, employers, and society (*la collectivité*); (3) Social welfare should create solidarity between the insured, in particular, and among the entire society in general; (4) Compulsory participation should extend to all members of society. These principles demonstrate a willingness to go well beyond the interwar social insurance and family welfare systems. A close examination of specific program proposals indicates the visionary boldness of the Section Sociale. For example, principle one was defined broadly so as to include not only protections against accidents, maternity, and illness but also a comprehensive unemployment insurance as well as job training, retraining, and placement services. Similarly, principle two, in its call for employers to share in the costs of worker welfare, did not only mean payment of insurance premiums or

---

[62] Agence Française d'Information de Presse, 14 March 1941, "Un Discours de M. Belin," AN 72 AJ 1858.
[63] "Projet d'Ordonnance relative au financement des assurances sociales," 26 December 1944, AN F60 897/47.

family allowances, as during the interwar period, but also the acceptance of a minimum wage, a *salaire minimum national*. In an interesting discussion of how such a minimum wage could be calculated, planners settled on a two-part definition, which exemplified the diverse views present at the London planning sessions. The first clearly drew upon a Marxist concept of surplus labor value, stating that the wage should "express the worker's portion of return on the wealth produced by the national community." A second, more technocratic part, defined the new minimum wage in almost identical terms as William Oualid and Charles Picquenard had referred to the base wage of the *salaire vital* during the First World War.[64] As we saw in chapter one, the family allowance component of the *salaire vital* had been used by employers during the 1920s to hold down base wages. In a splendid example of how postliberation social reformers closed the wounds of interwar strife without abandoning the precepts of liberal economics, the final clause on the minimum wage notes that the "economy minister will fix for each place and class of employment a base wage . . . considering the equity of national riches."[65] What is more, the planners also insisted that the minimum wage apply equally to men and women. Reflecting on the interwar years, they noted that gender inequality in wages had "denied a woman her financial equality, encouraged immorality, reduced women's health . . . caused a desertion of so-called woman's work, thereby devaluing men's work." Planners' over-broad assertion that low-paid women turned to prostitution – thereby encouraging immorality – was accompanied by a striking condemnation of the "sociological conception of 'man, *chef de famille*'."[66] As we saw earlier, a construction of gender that presumed men's monopoly of this distinction resulted in widespread wage inequities and the denial of family allowances to deserving women.[67]

Reforms formulated by the London-based Section Sociale were backed by a belief that a strong *dirigiste* state would be necessary to carry out its plans after liberation. In the words of one participant, "the advantages obtained by the working class in 1936 were essentially annulled by the rising cost of living and the government was completely disarmed in the face of a *grand patronat* who refused to reduce their profits or accept new social legislation . . . In a planned economy, things would proceed along very different lines."[68] Indeed, state social and economic planning

---

[64] See chapter 1.
[65] Section sociale, "Salaire minimum," Articles 23–24, 1 June 1943, AN 72 AJ 546.
[66] Section Sociale, "Salaire minimum et salaire féminin," 18 June 1943, AN 72 AJ 546.
[67] See chapter 3.   [68] Section sociale, "Rapport de P. Chauvet," no date, AN 72 AJ 546.

was widely viewed by virtually all resistance groups as both the antidote for the humiliating end of the Third Republic and the most effective tool for rebuilding the war-shaken nation. Their intelligence services indicated that a return of the republic would be welcomed but only if it were a "strong Republic" capable of offering "order, justice, and work."[69] Although many of the programs outlined by the Section Sociale would not be adopted until several years after the war, its planning facilitated the Provisional Government's bold restructuring of French social welfare. Before turning to the Provisional Government's *ordonnance* of 4 October 1945, which marked the birth of France's postwar system of social welfare (*la sécurité sociale*), let us first appreciate a foreign influence on the Section Sociale.

Just as the First World War had injected German social policy into the politics of the Third Republic through the recovery of Alsace-Lorraine, so the presence of France's government-in-exile in London during the Second World War meant an unavoidable consideration of British reforms. Moreover, their stay in the British capital coincided with historic developments in that country's social welfare. In December 1942 William Beveridge unveiled his *Social Insurance and Allied Services*. The Beveridge report, as it was quickly dubbed, laid the basis for Britain's postwar social insurance, health, and poverty assistance institutions. Not surprisingly, the report received keen attention by members of the Section Sociale. Although the French found much to their liking in the report, they also rejected many provisions as wholly inappropriate for their homeland. For example, they noted one of the great innovations of the report was the improvement of family welfare, but that France had long enjoyed a system of family allowances, albeit under employer administration. They also rejected the Anglo-Saxon approach to family welfare, which relied on the notion of a *family wage*. Maintenance of a family wage involved adjusting wages and social welfare benefits so that the income of a single male breadwinner could provide an adequate standard of living for a wife and at least one dependent child. Interestingly, the family wage had once attracted support in France. During the nineteenth century, social Catholics, led by Pope Leo XIII had argued for a *just wage*, whose definition was essentially identical to the family wage. However,

---

[69] Direction Générale des Services Spéciaux, Rapport sur l'Etat d'Esprit en France au regard d'une forme de gouvernement pour l'après guerre, Alger, 23 February 1944, F22 2059. Also see Jacquier, *Refaire la France: l'effort d'une génération* (Paris: Plon, 1945) and Peter Hall, *Governing the Economy: The Politics of State Intervention in Britain and France* (Oxford University Press, 1986), pp. 140–141.

as we have seen, French social Catholic industrialists in Grenoble were among the innovators of family allowances. During the interwar years, proponents of a family wage continued to be found in social Catholic circles such as the UFCS. But they too acquiesced and ultimately supported the home-mother allowance (*allocation de la mère au foyer*), which provided an additional supplement for male workers with wives who stayed at home to care for children. In short, the French concept of the *salaire vital* proved far too entrenched to cast off. It justified a distinct treatment of family allowances and was viewed as a foundation for a new minimum wage.[70] However, two other aspects of the Beveridge Report appear to have deeply influenced the course of French social reform.

Members of the Section Sociale were especially interested in the reception Beveridge would receive from the British populace. Their principal question, the answer to which they believed might also apply to France, concerned whether grand social reforms should precede or follow the return of economic prosperity. Within weeks after the report's publication, the French observers believed that they had an answer: "For them [*les Anglais*] the Beveridge Plan is an act of faith while at the same time it serves as a gauge of national and universal prosperity. That's why they will follow Beveridge who, when he is asked if the country has the means to undertake his plan, responds that the country does not have the wherewithal not to adopt it."[71] This perception of British opinion fortified those in the Section Sociale who believed that the most opportune moment to launch a major reform would be during the first year after liberation. One member even quoted Beveridge, exclaiming that "a revolutionary moment in the world's history is a time for revolution, not for patching."[72]

A second, more demonstrable effect that Beveridge had on French planners concerned the ideal structure of social welfare institutions. In

[70] Secrétariat des Commissions, Rapport du Lieutenant Loubere sur le salaire minimum nationale, Section Sociale, 3 December 1942, AN 72 AJ 546. Loubere refers to the "family wage" as an Anglo system, practiced in Australia and New Zealand as well as Britain. An example of the application of the family wage approach can be found in Beveridge's discussion of social insurance benefits. He explains "For the purpose of the Social Insurance scheme housewives form a special Class ... Every woman on marriage will become a new person, acquiring new rights and not carrying on into marriage claims to unemployment or disability in respect of contributions made before marriage." See William Beveridge, *Social and Allied Services: A Report by Sir William Beveridge* (New York: Macmillan, 1942), paragraph 339, p. 131.

[71] Section sociale, "L'Opinion anglaise devant le Plan Beveridge," January 1943, AN 72 AJ 546.

[72] Section sociale, Secrétariat des Commissions, "Rapport du Lieutenant Loubere," 3 December 1942, 72 AJ 546.

a passage that must have struck the Gaullist planners as an echo from their own country, Beveridge bemoans the fragmented nature of social welfare "... social insurance and allied services, as they exist today, are conducted by a complex of disconnected administrative organs, proceeding on different principles, doing invaluable service but at a cost in money and trouble and anomalous treatment of identical problems for which there is no justification."[73] Beveridge's solution was an entirely unified system, "enabling each insured person to obtain all benefits by a single weekly contribution on a single document."[74] The Section Sociale identified Beveridge's unified scheme as "meriting our special attention," and agreed that its enactment in France would improve the efficiency of welfare protections there too. Also, in an indication of their belief in state power, the French appreciated Beveridge's recommendation for a "ministry of social insurance that would direct and administer the reforms and their implementation."[75] As we saw earlier, a proposal for a unified system of social welfare had been briefly circulated by René Belin and Pierre Laroque during their service for Vichy. But their proposal had run into staunch opposition from employers, many of whom were key Vichy supporters. In their second attempt, proponents of a comprehensive system of social security would find their previous adversaries in retreat before an irresistible Gaullist coalition.

THE PROVISIONAL GOVERNMENT OF THE REPUBLIC RECASTS SOCIAL WELFARE

Astute planning and savvy political calculation permitted the de Gaulle-led Provisional Government to quickly assume the position of sole legitimate replacement for the Etat Français based in Vichy. Within weeks of Paris' liberation by Allied forces, de Gaulle preempted potentially divisive conflict among the resistance by creating a cabinet of national unanimity. The new group included two communists, four socialists, three social Christians, three Radicals, one conservative, and nine ministers who professed no party allegiances.[76] De Gaulle's invitation to only one avowed conservative indicated the enfeebled condition of the right in postliberation reconstruction. Although some prominent members of the *patronat*, such as Marcel Michelin, emerged after the war with a list of patriotic feats, many more industrialists were implicated in outright

---

[73] Beveridge, *Social and Allied Services*, p. 6.   [74] *Ibid.*, p. 15.
[75] Section sociale, "Observations sur l'envoi du Rapport Beveridge," Mélamède, 6 January 1943.
[76] Shennan, *Rethinking France*, p. 2.

collaboration with German forces and the Nazi regime. As one planning document put it, "Some employers conducted themselves admirably. But collectively, the *patronat* was absent from the resistance . . . the state should substitute itself for the defunct employer confederation and take charge of purifying the governing boards of employer associations."[77] To a lesser extent, rural corporatists and the mutual movement were also politically disabled by the liberation. Their legacy stood in stark contrast to the celebrated role of the left in the most dangerous efforts at resistance. The Provisional Government thus seized an auspicious moment to announce that it would propose massive reforms to the country's social welfare system. Moreover, due to both Vichy and Gaullist propaganda, any and all institutions of the Third Republic – not just the military – had become associated with moral decline and the catastrophe of defeat in 1940. In this context, the planners who had been busy in London faced little burden of justification for their proposals. The Conseil National de la Résistance (CNR) included a call for a comprehensive social security plan in its Common Program. And, although many reformers viewed economic restructuring as their principal goal, they also stressed France's need for a thorough revolution in social policy in order to repair a society torn apart by strife during the 1930s and German occupation during the war. The need for such a task appeared even more imperative because France now confronted threats of hegemony from both the United States and the Soviet Union.[78] Reformers' ambitious plans could not be fully realized during the immediate postliberation year due to new and old obstacles. Nevertheless, their work led to wholesale changes in family welfare and social insurance that, in time, would evolve into one of Europe's most comprehensive and generous welfare states.

In early 1945, Pierre Laroque assumed leadership of the newly created Direction Générale de la Sécurité Sociale. The Direction Générale corresponded to the special ministry for social welfare that London planners had admired in the Beveridge Report three years earlier. Although technically under the control of the minister of labor, Alexandre Parodi, Laroque enjoyed significant freedom of action due to his personal rapport with de Gaulle and several other important members of the

---

[77] Commission des Affaires économiques et sociales, Comité sur les Problèmes sociaux de la France libérée, "Rapport sur les principales mésures sociaux à prendre dès la libération, rapporteur: Albert Gazier," January 1944, AN F22 2050. On Michelin, see Sweets, *Choices in Vichy France*, p. 194.

[78] Shennan, *Rethinking France*, pp. 2–3, 212–214; Pierre Laroque, in preface to Henry C. Galant, *Histoire politique de la sécurité sociale française, 1945–1952* (Paris: Armand Colin), p. xiv.

Provisional Government. Moreover, Laroque did not depend on the labor ministry for staff, either in Paris or in the provinces. Indeed, Laroque commanded his own small army of social policy experts and support staff that totaled over 400 in Paris alone. He also controlled sixteen regional offices that, in turn, had assumed administrative supervision of several hundred social insurance and family allowance *caisses* nationwide. During the first months after the liberation, Laroque reported a profound *esprit de corps* among his staff as they set about preparing a comprehensive social welfare system. Laroque was well acquainted with the complex workings of the 1930 social insurance law and with the family allowance *caisses* that had evolved under employer control between the wars.[79] Laroque's knowledge of and, in many cases, intimate involvement with, the compromises and shortcomings of interwar and Vichy social protections clearly informed the audacious reforms that together would become the *ordonnance* of 4 October 1945, which launched France's postwar welfare state.

Laroque's reforms, which were first unveiled to the government's consultative assembly in July 1945, professed three goals for the country's social welfare system: democratization, national solidarity, and rationalization. The first, democratization, meant that local family allowance and social insurance *caisses* were to be managed by representatives of beneficiaries. In most cases, the plan called for a predominant role for the locally most powerful workers' union. Employers and state officials also gained an administrative role, but most powers were given to organized labor. Second, Laroque envisioned a consolidation of national solidarity through the eventual extension of the system to all citizens, including the self-employed, professionals, and management. Revenues were provided, as under the old social insurance regime, through payroll levies on workers and employers, which were supplemented by state subsidies. Total contributions for social insurance rose to 16 percent. Of this total, employers paid 10 percent and the remaining 6 percent was withheld from workers' paychecks. Employers remained entirely responsible for a dramatically higher family allowance bill of 14 percent of wages. The hike in allowances owed primarily to the lagging value of family support during Vichy and the continued popularity of pronatalist policies after the liberation. Employers also remained responsible for worker accident insurance, about 3.5 percent of wages, but instead of purchasing coverage from private firms, Laroque folded this social protection into

[79] See above and chapter 4.

the newly reorganized social security system.[80] Thus, the sum total of different contributions – social insurance, family allowances, and accident insurance – amounted to approximately one third of the total national income from wages. However, Laroque viewed employer contributions through a wholly different lens than social reformers of the 1930s. They had insisted that social insurance premiums were essentially a tax on wages. But with the creation of *comités d'entreprise* after 1945 workers were promised significant influence over industrial management. Thus, the employer contribution, argued Laroque, must be viewed as a contribution from the firm, which was to a great extent he assumed, under worker control.[81]

Under the headings of national solidarity and rationalization, Laroque called for the creation of a single Caisse Nationale de Sécurité Sociale in order to rationalize the disparate institutions of social welfare that had evolved between the wars.[82] Benefits from the new system were to be more generous than previous social insurance and family allowances. But the cost of national rebuilding which lay before the country led Laroque to avoid too many specifics. He spoke in generalities, promising to protect workers against the "uncertainty of tomorrow," to provide all with "sufficient resources for the maintenance of their families," and a just compensation for all work.[83] Laroque believed that social security should be closely coordinated with fiscal and monetary policies which assured full employment and income redistribution.[84] In fact, his plan lacked unemployment insurance. Laroque was convinced in 1945, rightly as it turns out, that full employment would be easily attained as the nation set about the task of reconstruction. Indeed, France attracted a substantial number of foreign workers during its postwar economic boom. Laroque's plan provoked considerable lobbying efforts from employers, labor unions, pronatalist groups, mutual leaders, and doctors' associations. But unlike the previous conflict over social insurance during the 1920s virtually no voices condemned the endeavor outright.[85] The benefits of social insurance and the importance of family welfare for a still

---

[80] Pierre Laroque, "From Social Insurance to Social Security: Evolution in France," *International Labour Review* 57: 6 (June 1948), 565–590, especially p. 583.
[81] Pierre Laroque, "Le Plan français de sécurité sociale," *Revue Française du Travail* 1 (April 1946), 9–20, especially p. 19.
[82] Laroque, *Au service de l'homme et du droit*, pp. 210–214.
[83] Laroque, "Le Plan français de sécurité sociale," p. 10.
[84] Laroque, "From Social Insurance to Social Security," pp. 569–570.
[85] Laroque, *Au service de l'homme et du droit*, p. 219.

demographically troubled nation were beyond question. What remained to be settled was the nature and structure of welfare institutions.

Laroque encountered his first major setback in the area of family welfare where he proposed integrating employer *caisses de compensation* into the Caisse Nationale de Sécurité Sociale. In the postliberation political climate, a weakened *patronat* could not prevent the appropriation of their *caisses*, but pronatalist and familial groups, which had long supported a distinct family allowance system, mounted a successful campaign to stop the amalgamation. Pronatalists and familial groups, such as the Alliance Nationale and La Plus Grande Famille, remained powerful after the liberation despite their association with Vichy because of enduring anxieties over depopulation. Indeed, the Gaullist planners in London gave considerable credence to France's continuing demographic crisis and suggested that the government of liberation enact strong family policies.[86] Also, just after the liberation, Georges Pernot, who had headed the High Committee on Population before the war, launched a successful propaganda effort. In July 1945, Pernot began publication of *Pour la vie*, a journal whose early issues were devoted to distancing the pronatalist movement from Vichy. Pernot emphasized the interwar sources of pronatalism and portrayed the Code de la Famille as the movement's principal service to the nation, not its collaboration with Vichy.[87] The exact influence of Pernot's efforts are hard to gauge, yet a 1947 poll indicated that government policies to increase population growth garnered a 73 percent approval.[88] Pronatalism thus emerged strong after the war, harbored in great measure by the social Catholic-inspired Mouvement Républicain Populaire (MRP) but also supported by all major parties, including the communists. Indeed, resistance leaders from diverse camps openly recognized specific achievements of Vichy's Commissariat Général à la Famille in the areas of maternity, infant protection, and rural family allowances. Much of the Commissariat's administrative structure was retained under the Provisional Government although it was renamed the Secrétariat Général à la Famille et à la Population. De Gaulle himself trumpeted the nation's pronatalist cause in March 1945 by calling for "twelve million beautiful babies" to restore the *grandeur* of France.[89] The general also resurrected the Third Republic's High Committee on Population that

---

[86] Comité des Problèmes sociaux de la France liberée, "Note sur l'orientation future de la politique familiale," January 1944, AN F22 2059.

[87] Georges Pernot, "D'où vient, où va le mouvement familial?," *Pour la Vie* 1 (July 1945), 83–86.

[88] Antoine Prost, "L'Evolution de la politique familiale en France de 1938 à 1981," *Le Mouvement Social* 129 (October–December 1984): 8–12.

[89] Cited by Shennan, *Rethinking France*, p. 208.

had drafted the Code de la Famille and personally chaired many of its meetings.[90] Pronatalist organizations used the popularity of their cause and their own proximity to power in order to rewrite Laroque's plan for family allowance *caisses*. Specifically, pronatalists gained de Gaulle's backing for a temporary separation of family allowance *caisses*, at both the regional and national levels, from the Caisse Nationale de Sécurité Sociale. Laroque had little choice but to amend his proposal, knowing that the so-called temporary separation would be difficult to reverse.

De Gaulle also decided to maintain the Vichy notion of rural interests looking after their own social welfare. To be sure, the National Peasant Corporation had been promptly abolished by the Provisional Government, but de Gaulle left responsibility for agricultural family allowances and social insurance in the hands of the minister of agriculture. This permitted UNSA officials, who had been highly influential in the Vichy agriculture ministry to maintain their sway over rural social policy. Although UNSA itself did not survive the liberation, its ideals and much of its personnel shifted to the newly founded Fédération Nationale des Syndicats d'Exploitants Agricoles (FNSEA). The loss of agricultural social insurance and family allowances severely undermined Laroque's plan for a fully unified and rational social security system under a single Caisse Nationale. Yet these defeats should not overshadow Laroque's important victories in the democratization of welfare institutions.

After 1945 commercial and industrial employers were stripped of their control of family allowance *caisses de compensation* and replaced, in most instances, by the CGT. This turnabout marked a democratization of social welfare that union leaders had awaited for over two decades. Interestingly, Adolphe Landry, the Radical proponent of the 1932 law that consecrated employer control of family allowances, authored the legislation which effectively turned employer *caisses* over to workers' unions.[91] Although separated from Laroque's proposed Caisse Nationale, agricultural family allowance *caisses* too came under the direct control of local beneficiaries while receiving further financial support

---

[90] Prost, "L'Evolution de la politique familiale," p. 11; Shennan, *ibid.*, p. 208–210. Also see Alfred Sauvy's memoirs, *De Paul Reynaud à Charles de Gaulle* (Tournai: Casterman, 1972). Pronatalism remains a salient force in French society and among social policymakers. See Hervé le Bras, *Marianne et les lapins: l'obsession démographique* (Paris: O. Orban, 1991). Also, Andrés Horacio Reggiani argues that the crisis of defeat and occupation convinced the governing classes that national recovery depended on a demographic revival. See his article, "Procreating France: The Politics of Demography, 1919–1945," *French Historical Studies* 19:3 (Spring 1996): 725–754.

[91] Author's interview with Laroque, 2 December 1995. Also see Laroque, *Au service de l'homme et du droit*, p. 214; The Caisse Nationale des Allocations Familiales and its regional offices remain distinct administrations within France's welfare state to this day.

from the state. In fact, the minister of agriculture recommended to the Secrétariat Général du Comité Economique that Vichy's intervention in rural family allowances be treated as a *fait accompli* and that state funds be promptly approved to maintain the system.[92] A new law on state finances subsequently increased annual state subsidies to 3.45 billion francs and offered a generous bail out to family allowance *caisses* that suffered from financial difficulty due to the war.[93]

For Laroque, the democratization of social insurance necessarily meant dispossessing mutual societies of the predominance they enjoyed under the 1930 law. While workers' unions and employers also lost *caisses*, mutual societies laid claim to by far the largest number. The FNMF responded by charging that "the government of national liberation [proposes] a plan which the Vichy regime twice attempted whose consequence is the suppression of one of the citizen's most fundamental liberties... that of free association." The FNMF launched a massive effort to rally mutual society social insurees against Laroque's plan. Thousands of posters and handbills were distributed throughout the country which accused the government of "wanting to institute in each department a system of unified *caisses*, cold and bureaucratic, where social insurees will be integrated *pêle-mêle*, without their consent." Mutual leaders further warned their members that Laroque's plan would be "a brutal transformation" which would "rashly provoke a catastrophic disorganization whose victims will be social insurees."[94] Yet despite the hyperbole and the real dangers presented by massive reform, the appeals of the FNMF fell mostly on deaf ears, both within ruling circles and among the populace.[95] In his memoirs, Laroque professes a certain sympathy for mutual leaders at this time. Yet he insists that the mutual movement's central role in social protection simply had to be abolished. Laroque viewed the FNMF's challenge to the proposed Caisse Nationale as potentially much more damaging than pronatalist leaders' demand for a separate family allowance administration. For although the separation of family allowances violated Laroque's design of a fully unified system, it nonetheless permitted a democratization of family welfare *caisses*. In contrast, the FNMF wanted to preserve their control over a system that Laroque found inherently undemocratic. For Laroque, democratization

[92] "Rapport sur le financement des allocations familiales agricoles, Communication de M. le Ministre de l'Agriculture," 18 December 1944, AN F60 897/45.

[93] Commission des Allocations Familiales Agricoles, *procès-verbaux*, 5 February 1946, AD Meuse 415 Mp 8.

[94] Text of FNMF poster reprinted in Romain Lavielle, *Histoire de la Mutualité*, pp. 163–164.

[95] Galant, *Histoire politique de la sécurité sociale français*, pp. 33–34.

meant that the "chief administrative officers of *caisses* come, for the most part, from the beneficiaries." While he never called into question the cooperative nature and humanitarian goals of the mutual movement, Laroque noted that "mutual leaders most often belong to the professional, management, and executive classes from industry and commerce and rarely to the wage-earning workers."[96] Of course, a large enough pool of sufficiently experienced managers, who also had working-class origins, could only be found in the leadership of France's labor unions. Here too, Laroque faced resistance to his plan.

The country's leading workers' union, the CGT, stood as the unmistakable heir apparent to lead most regional social security and family allowance *caisses* as well as the Caisse Nationale under Laroque's plan. The CGT's predominance was virtually assured by a provision that permitted the locally most popular labor union to directly appoint administrators to *caisse* governing boards. The CFTC vehemently denounced this arrangement, arguing that it effectively excluded it from the management of social welfare even in regions where it represented a sizable minority. The Christian trade union eventually proved much more effective than the FNMF in obtaining changes to the law. They argued that governing boards should be elected by workers, which would allow a greater potential for CFTC representation on governing boards. Absent such a change, they refused the token participation that the appointment system offered them although they did take control of social security and family allowance *caisses* in the departments of the Moselle, Haut-Rhin, and Bas-Rhin where their membership justified it. The fact that the CFTC had a much wider audience than simply its union members aided their cause. They could appeal to sympathetic social Catholics and the MRP, which had a significant voice in the Provisional Government. Their incessant appeals for more democratic procedures finally prevailed in October 1946 when legislation that required the election of *caisse* governing boards was enacted. This law also permitted the FNMF to mount an electoral effort to regain control of some *caisses*. The first election, which was held on 24 April 1947, reconfirmed the preeminence of the CGT, but it also marked the entrance of the CFTC on social security and family allowance governing boards outside Alsace-Lorraine. Table 6.1 indicates the results of this election.

Of the 124 social security *caisses* nationwide, the CFTC won majorities on 7, primarily in Alsace-Lorraine. The CGT claimed 109 majorities

---

[96] Laroque, *Au service de l'homme et du droit*, p. 215.

Table 6.1. *Elections to social security and family allowance*
governing boards, 24 April 1947

	Number of votes	Percent	Seats awarded
CGT			
Social security	3,280,183	59.27	1,384
Family allowances	659,930	61.88	909
CFTC			
Social security	1,458,475	26.36	613
Family allowances	266,123	25	316
Mutual movement			
Social security	507,599	9.17	114
Family allowances	123,993	11.66	90
Independent / miscellaneous			
Social security	287,973	5.20	70
Family allowances	15,583	1.46	23

Source: statistics compiled from Galant, *Histoire politique de la sécurité sociale française*, p. 125.

while 2 went to independent or mutual coalitions and another 6 were evenly split. Of the 111 family allowance *caisses*, the CFTC emerged with a majority on only 1, the CGT controlled 101, 2 went to independent or mutual coalitions and another 7 were without any affiliated majority.[97]

Doctors were also concerned about their place in the new social security system. The Confédération des Syndicats Médicaux, whose recognition had been restored by the Provisional Government, announced its determination to "defend French medicine and doctors themselves... our liberal profession, and our tattered Charter. We hope for... a long and fruitful collaboration with Public authorities in the struggle ahead..."[98] Laroque had been a keen observer of the myriad difficulties encountered by patients under the 1930 social insurance law. Most social insurance *caisses* had sought contracts with professional medical associations (doctors, pharmacists, etc.), but varied fee schedules and the relatively small size of mutual society social insurance *caisses* had bedeviled the system. *Caisses* constantly attempted to undercut their commitments while disputes with doctors left patients with paltry reimbursements. Under the new national medical insurance system, the government took a major role in drawing up contracts between doctors

[97] *Ibid*, p. 126.   [98] *Le Médecin de France*, 20 July 1945.

and medical insurance *caisses* and oversaw what came to be called fee *conventions* that governed most common medical procedures. Also, agreements between *caisses* and doctors associations sometimes resorted to a *tarif opposable*, that is, an arrangement where *caisses* could reimburse the patient at 80 percent of costs. Doctors' associations set a maximum cost for such therapies and therefore limited, in advance, patients' out-of-pocket expenses. This arrangement marked an inversion of the system that had emerged in the 1930s where negotiated fee schedules became treated as minimum charges after which the patients' responsibility for payment could escalate without limit.[99] In this crucial area of social protection, a more powerful state role appeared to deliver on Laroque's promise of improved efficiency.[100]

The attempt to expand social security to all citizens of the Republic during the immediate postwar years proved an unobtainable goal, at least under the unified system foreseen by Laroque. Indeed, Laroque had not intended to extend the fledgling system beyond wage-earning or similarly employed workers until much later. This still meant that the plan reached about 60 percent of the active population or roughly 12 million of the country's 21-million-strong work force.[101] But in February 1946 key members that represented all the major parties of the first constituent assembly called for a prompt extension of social security to virtually all workers and their families.[102] Incapable of resisting such a powerful coalition and under pressure from communist Minister of Labor Ambroise Croizat, Laroque quickly drafted the necessary legislation, which was unanimously adopted by the Assembly. Despite the failure of the first Assembly to produce a constitution – a referendum on its work fell short in May – the second constituent Assembly set 1 January 1947 as the start date for pension contributions from all independent workers in commerce and industry, including the liberal professions. However, by this time, the enthusiasm for national solidarity that had permeated the postliberation months, suffered from the acrimony aroused by the Fourth Republic's failed first constitution. The politics of social reform registered the new mood.

Charles Viatte, a prominent member of the MRP, began a campaign on behalf of the self-employed to prevent extension of social security. The Confédération des Classes Moyennnes let it be known that its

---

[99] See chapter 4.   [100] Laroque, *Au service de l'homme et du droit*, p. 219.
[101] Laroque, "From Social Insurance to Social Security," p. 576.
[102] These included Gabelle (MRP), Jean Moreau (Independent) Musmeaux (Communist), and Segelle (Socialist). Laroque, *Au service de l'homme et du droit*, pp. 221–222.

leaders viewed the extension of social security as an erosion of their status that threatened to lower them to the level of wage earners. But not only status was at stake. Opponents of the extension argued that enrollment of several million self-employed workers was a financing ploy, pure and simple, meant to subsidize lower premiums for the working class. Proponents responded that not only was national solidarity at stake, but that many independent workers, such as precarious independent artisans, would be aided, not harmed, by extension. Nevertheless, when the deadline for enrollment came, large numbers of the self-employed refused to comply. By March 1947, the government had capitulated with Croizat saying that he was unwilling to force participants into a social security system against their will. Croizat's successor at the ministry of labor, socialist Daniel Mayer, accepted the work of a special commission chaired by Frédéric Surleau. The Surleau commission conceded the impossibility of a unified social security system, calling for the creation of four separate regimes to service professionals, industrial and commercial independents, artisans, and agriculture. The law of 17 January 1948, which closely followed the Surleau commission's recommendations, permitted the creation of separate social insurance regimes based on socioprofessional categories.[103]

The unwillingness of self-employed middle-class workers to accede to a unified social security system exacerbated the segmentation that had already been accepted by government planners in family allowances and some working-class professions. Railroad workers, miners, gas and electric workers, and merchant sailors had long enjoyed well-established separate social welfare agencies. In 1945 they had adopted a wait-and-see attitude about social security. Laroque hoped that these workers would eventually find their separate regimes superfluous and that, in time, they would join social security. But the failure of Laroque's social security administration to enroll middle-class workers meant a hardening of attitudes among working-class participants in specialized regimes. As with the earlier separation of family welfare from the Caisse Nationale, Laroque realized that abolishing the distinct social insurance *caisses* which served particular socioprofessional groups would be very difficult. Over time, political lobbies would evolve to insure their continued existence, regardless of unfortunate turns in their

---

[103] Peter Baldwin provides an excellent account of the attempt to enroll independent workers in social security. See *The Politics of Social Solidarity: Class Bases of the European Welfare State, 1875–1975* (Cambridge University Press, 1990), pp. 172–178, 183–184. For a detailed account of social security during the immediate postwar years, see Galant, *Histoire politique de la sécurité sociale.*

demographic or economic circumstances and despite their lack of efficiency.[104] The reluctance of more affluent workers to participate in a system where their incomes were vulnerable to perceived redistributive designs by the left presented a major obstacle to reform.

As one historian has put it: "Universalist reforms in France . . . were motivated by ambitions to aid the poorest directly at the expense of the better-off. The resistance marshaled by those negatively affected was more than a match for the political muscle of reformers . . ."[105] This is no doubt true. But the reformers of 1945 faced more than just a politically influential middle class. They faced the irremovable foundations of a social welfare system that had been laid by employers, mutual society leaders, pronatalists, and others between the wars. Laroque and his successors had little choice but to build their edifice on top of these foundations. They could use new materials, build higher, and add many rooms, but the outlines of the old structure would always be visible.

[104] Author's interview with Laroque, 2 December 1995; Laroque in preface to Galant, *ibid.*, p. xvi.
[105] Baldwin, *Politics of Social Solidarity*, pp. 185–186.

Conclusion

Disparate historical forces have been at work on social welfare in France since the nineteenth century. Louis Napoleon's boost to the mutual movement and the 1898 Charte de la Mutualité launched a highly resilient regime of voluntary social protections that closely matched France's liberal temperament up to the First World War. The mutual movement dutifully respected the distinction between social insurance and *assistance*, a separation that held credence across political affiliation and class. This distinction was also important in family welfare. Even during the 1920s when they enjoyed complete freedom from government regulation, employers rarely justified their voluntary family allowances as charity. Rather family allowances became part and parcel of the scientific rationalization of industry, labor pacification, and the fight against depopulation. The 1920s also witnessed a convergence of forces that instigated state efforts to expand and mandate social insurance. France's recovery of its territories in Alsace and Lorraine, where Germany had developed a successful form of compulsory social insurance, served as an immediate impetus to reform. The mutual movement too, although initially divided over the issue of obligation, served as a proximate cause for the creation of France's interwar social insurance protections. Mutual leaders recognized both the momentum of international developments in favor of compulsory insurance and the increasing power of the industrial working-class whose affinity with mutual assistance was weak at best. Meanwhile their own core constituency of independent artisans and shopkeepers was suffering a relative decline in the face of urbanization and industrialization. The FNMF successfully lobbied for a mutualized social insurance law and, as a result, its constituent societies captured a virtual monopoly on insurance *caisses* during the 1930s. For all its problems, this system granted unprecedented benefits to approximately nine million workers, many of whom had never been protected against the hazards of modern urban and industrial life. The 1930s also witnessed the growing virulence of the pronatalist movement. By 1939 a national recognition of the depopulation crisis and avowals to combat it had attained the same status as respect for the distinction between social insurance and public assistance. The momentum of the pronatalist cause was sustained by Vichy and emerged after 1945 as a salient imperative in the minds of French social reformers.[1]

This study has attempted to examine the origins of France's welfare state and, in so doing, explain why the French became so attached to it. This I believe is because France's interwar institutions of social welfare, although hotly contested, demonstrated close continuities with the nation's past, its culture, and popular perceptions of national crisis. The mutual movement enjoyed a reputation of public service and integrity that permitted its leaders to play a central role in the creation of national social insurance. Similarly, employers used social Catholic and pronatalist arguments in the creation and perpetuation of their family welfare *caisses*. Just as the popularity of the mutual societies aided the FNMF in its bid to control the country's first social insurance system, a perception of national decline and demographic crisis was essential to the success of the industrial model of family welfare. As we have seen, working-class leaders, doctors, and others struggled to reform these models of social welfare throughout the interwar and Vichy years. But only rarely did they attack their founding appeal. Doctors fought against the preeminence that had been granted to mutual societies in the provision of medical care, but they never questioned that a "mutualized" social insurance system well befitted the French temperament. Likewise, union leaders used the rhetoric of national decline and pronatalism to attack the insufficiency and injustice of employer-controlled family welfare, but they never challenged the importance of family allowances in the struggle against depopulation. Thus, the contemporary opponents of the industrial and mutual models, through their willingness to accept the generative principles of these institutions, actually aided in their entrenchment. The struggle for social reform became less about fundamental structures and more about who controls, who administers, and the equity of benefits. As a result, important aspects of the industrial and mutual models enjoyed an almost unquestioned legitimacy and popularity among social reformers. In contrast to the case of Britain, where Beveridge launched

---

[1] There is no better example than Pierre Laroque in this regard. He contributed articles to the *Alliance Nationale – Population et Avenir*, the renamed journal of the postwar Alliance Nationale. Laroque was also a close collaborator of Alfred Sauvy, founder of the Institut National d'Etudes Démographiques (INED) in 1945.

a systematic rationalization of social welfare, Laroque could not entirely retrace the path that France had pursued since 1914. Quite by necessity, he ultimately accepted important aspects of the industrial and mutual models as a *fait accompli* and fashioned his own version of the welfare state after them. In so doing, he further contributed to the structural continuity of French social welfare, its alignment with national aspirations, and its popularity.

The post-1945 French welfare state is an intrinsic component of France's social democracy. It is also both the main agent and evidence of national solidarity and an important component of what it means to be French. In this light, the creation of family welfare and social insurance under the respective tutelage of industrialists and mutual leaders takes on a historical significance that extends beyond their indelible marks on the organization of today's *sécurité sociale*. Liberalism and employer paternalism played a formative role in French social reform, and not merely as an ideological foil against which leftists could exercise their wrath, but as a foundation on which welfare was constructed.

Indeed, a rundown of the protagonists in this study reveals a cast of many moderate but also several very conservative actors. In parliament, Radical and other centrist legislators who professed a mix of solidarism and pronatalist fervor led the way on social insurance and family welfare reform. Radical Adolphe Landry epitomized their cautious approach to social policy. These lawmakers eventually reached far-reaching compromises on social insurance with realist leaders in the mutual movement, such as Georges Petit and Raoul Péret. Realists rescued mutualism from demographic and social decline and succeeded at renovating the movement as a basis for national social insurance. Their actions virtually assured the initial success of compulsory social insurance, a deed that led to later progress even if the mutual movement itself was to play a greatly diminished role. Nowhere is the debt to mutualism greater for social protection than in the countryside. Even more than urban mutual leaders, which is saying a lot, agricultural syndicalists – especially conservative Catholic corporatists – parlayed their organizational strength into vast gains for rural inhabitants. In due course, they forced unprecedented fiscal commitments to social insurance and family welfare, an accomplishment that also served as a basis for state action after 1945. Similarly, the *grand patronat*, social Catholics, and pronatalists, each acted according to their own conservative scripts. However, the result was a strikingly well-coordinated, even sophisticated, system of aid to families with dependent children, which soothed popular concerns about moral decline and depopulation while it granted employers more leverage over their workers. Although in the 1970s feminists successfully advocated reforms to reverse discrimination against women, in the 1930s most granted qualified support to the family allowance movement's prescription of traditional gender roles.

Doctors, rural radicals, and workers' unions played the roles of antagonists in the drama. Doctors succeeded in checking a mutual movement that appeared bent on dominating the provision of medical care. Their role, and the abuse they suffered under Vichy for playing it, contributed to France's adoption of a national health insurance – as opposed to a national health service – system of medicine after 1945. Thus French doctors preserved at least some of the trappings of liberal medicine that, for example, British doctors do not enjoy. For their part, rural radicals failed to arouse a full-fledged rebellion in the countryside against welfare mandates in the 1930s. Dorgères suffered from his split with UNSA and achieved relatively little power in the Vichy government. He and his followers persisted in their resistance to the establishment of social security after 1945 but failed to elicit significant support. Yet despite Dorgères' personal failures, today's FNSEA employs his direct-action style tactics to fight developments they deem unjust to the rural ideal and their autonomy. When farmers arrive *en masse* in Paris today, a legacy of rural turmoil over social welfare is clear for all to see. The roles of workers' unions are diverse and difficult to encapsulate. When the CGT and CFTC supported the mutual model of social insurance, they won concessions regarding its requirements, benefits, and administration. On family welfare, however, union leaders of all groupings were much less successful. Their failure to rally the rank and file meant ineffectual resistance to employer control of family allowances until the Popular Front. Even then, the Popular Front's arbitration law and its attempt to extend family allowances to agriculture wreaked havoc instead of imposing constructive solutions. But the havoc turned out to be creative destruction. In a manner of speaking, the Popular Front blew a large hole in family welfare that succeeding governments, including Vichy, had no choice but to patch themselves.

Statist solutions to social welfare had been edging forward since 1930 when subsidies were granted to rural social insurees. The decree of 1938, the 1939 Code de la Famille, and Vichy's numerous edicts – each was a response to specific exigencies but together they laid the groundwork for large-scale, state-directed reform after the war. No one was more aware of this than Pierre Laroque whose vantage points included Paris, Vichy, and London. The immediate postliberation years gave leftist leaders an opportunity which they exploited to advantage. In Laroque, workers' unions and their allied political parties found a well-versed and well-connected *haut fonctionnaire* who wanted to use state power to unify and democratize social welfare and expand benefits. Much was accomplished. But 1945 represented only the latest in a series of conjunctures that began in the late nineteenth century. Although liberalism was in disrepute, having been replaced by Gaullist *dirigisme*, France's experience with employer-based welfare and socioprofessional mutual aid exerted an irresistible sway. Put differently, Laroque's appeal for all citizens to enroll in a single social security *caisse* for the sake of national solidarity had no history. Conversely, specialized associations for social protection, which proliferated after 1948, were entirely acceptable as long as they operated themselves in a sufficiently democratic fashion. In fact, the specialized regimes were, in a manner of speaking, a comforting element of the good ol' days which had been sufficiently democratized and rationalized to meet the demands of the postwar era. Mutual leaders themselves recognized the remaining pool of public enthusiasm for private and specialized social protection plans at their 1948 national conference in Aix-les-Bains.[2] By the late 1950s, the newly renamed mutualist societies (*sociétés mutualistes*) emerged as the principal providers of supplementary insurance to cover medical expenses that were not reimbursed by social security, a role in which they continue to thrive to this day. Mutuals also offered comprehensive coverage to individuals and socioprofessional groups who had not yet been incorporated into a specialized regime of social security.[3] Family welfare represented a somewhat different case. Its success after 1945 relied much more directly on popular support for national solidarity. The trauma of the interwar depopulation crisis ensured that national solidarity included intergenerational support for the French family and succor for a demographically troubled nation. Under this banner, a unified institution of family welfare, the Caisse Nationale des Allocations Familiales, could succeed as an important entitlement program and later as a principal tool in the battle against poverty. France's welfare state has undergone extensive modifications since 1947, most of which further contributed to the system's generosity and complexity.

[2] Lavielle, *Histoire de la mutualité*, pp. 186–187.
[3] Today over 80 percent of the French population belongs to a mutual society in order to insure themselves against risks and expenses that are not covered by social security or their professional social insurance fund.

Comprehensive commitments to family welfare and social insurance remain central to *la sécurité sociale* and touchstones in French social and political life.

When I left Pierre Laroque on that December morning in 1995, a resolution to the strike over Prime Minister Alain Juppé's plan to trim welfare benefits was nowhere in sight. We had talked for two hours about the formative decades of the welfare state, but as I turned for the door, to wend my way back through the rain and snarled traffic, we both knew that our parting words would be about the strike. In his friendly but magisterial voice, Laroque commented that, "there are some things that the government cannot and will not change."[4] He meant this simply as a reassuring observation about the future of the welfare state, wishing to condemn neither side in the ongoing conflict. As I walked home, I realized that Laroque's parting words were as much about the past as they were about the future.

4 Author's interview with Pierre Laroque, Paris, 2 December 1995.

Bibliography

MANUSCRIPT SOURCES

ARCHIVES DÉPARTEMENTALES DE L'AVEYRON, RODEZ

5 X	Allocations familiales et assurances sociales
6 M	Prix et salaires
7 M	Salaires agricoles
10 M	Travail

ARCHIVES DÉPARTEMENTALES DE L'EURE-ET-LOIR, CHARTRES

7 M	Allocations familiales agricoles
10 M	Travail
3 X	Préfet
4 X	Caisses mutuelles agricoles
5 X	Allocations familiales

ARCHIVES DÉPARTEMENTALES DE LA MEUSE, BAR-LE-DUC

236 Xp	Allocations familiales
415 Mp	Allocations familiales agricoles

ARCHIVES DÉPARTEMENTALES DE LA MOSELLE, METZ

4 X	Natalité
6 X	Allocations familiales et assurances sociales
301 M	Syndicats
310 M	Travail

ARCHIVES NATIONALES, PARIS

F 2	Ministère de l'intérieur
F 7	Police
F 10	Ministère de l'agriculture
F 12	Commerce

F 22	Travail et la sécurité sociale
F 60	Premier Ministre
2 AV	Comité d'histoire de la sécurité sociale
37 AS	Comité d'histoire de la sécurité sociale
39 AS	Groupe des industries métallurgiques, mécaniques et connexes de la région parisienne
72 AJ	Seconde Guerre

ASSEMBLÉE NATIONALE DE LA RÉPUBLIQUE FRANÇAISE, SERVICE DES ARCHIVES, PARIS

Procès-verbaux: Commission d'Assurance et de Prévoyance Sociales, Chambre; Commission du travail, Chambre.

BIBLIOTHÈQUE DU MUSÉE SOCIAL

Procès-verbaux: Conseil d'Administration et les Assemblées Générales de la Société de Secours Mutuels des Usines Renault.

CAISSE D'ALLOCATIONS FAMILIALES DE LA MOSELLE, METZ

Procès-verbaux: Caisse d'Allocations Familiales de la Moselle.

CAISSE D'ALLOCATIONS FAMILIALES DE PARIS, PARIS

Procès-verbaux: Caisse de Compensation de la Région Parisienne.

CAISSE NATIONALE DES ALLOCATIONS FAMILIALES, PARIS

Procès-verbaux and *Comptes rendus:* Comité Central des Allocations Familiales.

POPULATION ET AVENIR, ALLIANCE NATIONALE, PARIS

Procès-verbaux: l'Alliance Nationale pour l'accroissement de la population française.

SYNDICAT GÉNÉRAL DES ENTREPRENEURS DU BÂTIMENT DE LA MOSELLE, METZ

Procès-verbaux: Syndicat des Entrepreneurs de Bâtiment et Travaux Publics de Metz.

INTERVIEWS

Pierre Laroque, Former Official at the Conseil d'Etat, Former Chief of Staff for Minister of Labor, Adolphe Landry, Paris, 2 December 1995.

Jean-François Montes, Historian, Caisse Nationale des Allocations Familiales, Paris, 30 May 1996.
Philippe Steck, Director, Caisse Nationale des Allocations Familiales, Paris, 16 November 1995.

PUBLISHED MEETING RECORDS, NEWSPAPERS, AND JOURNALS

Almanach Encyclopédique de la Famille
Annuaire de la Famille Nombreuse
Annuaire statistique de la France
Assemblée Permanente des Présidents des Chambres d'Agriculture: *Comptes rendus*
Les Assurances Sociales
L'Aube
Bulletin de l'Académie de Médecine
Bulletin de la Fédération Nationale de la Mutualité Française
Bulletin Mensuel des Allocations Familiales (et des Assurances Sociales)
Bulletin du Ministère du Travail
Bulletin Officiel de la Fédération Nationale de la Mutualité Française
Bulletin des Sociétés de Secours Mutuels
Bulletin de la Statistique Générale de la France
Bulletin des Usines de Guerre
Cahiers du Bolchevisme
Cahiers du Redressement Français: Comptes rendus
Chronique Sociale de France
Comité Central des Allocations Familiales: *Annuaires*
Comité National d'Etudes Sociales et Politiques: *Comptes rendus, Les Assurances Sociales*
Conférences Nationales des Unions Régionales d'Assurances Sociales: *Comptes rendus*
Congrès Confédéral de la Confédération Générale du Travail: *Comptes rendus*
Congrès de la Fédération des Ouvriers des Métaux: *Comptes rendus*
Congrès de la Fédération Unitaire des Ouvriers et Ouvrières sur Metaux: *Comptes rendus*
Congrès National des Allocations Familiales: *Comptes rendus*
Congrès National de la Confédération Française des Travailleurs Chrétiens: *Comptes rendus*
Congrès National de la Confédération des Groupements Commerciaux et Industriels: *Comptes rendus*
Congrès National Corporatif de la Fédération Nationale des Travailleurs du Sous-Sol: *Comptes rendus*
Congrès National de la Natalité: *Comptes rendus*
Congrès du Parti Communiste Français: *Comptes rendus*
Congrès National du Parti Socialiste: *Comptes rendus*

Congrès National Unitaire des Travailleurs du Sous-Sol: *Comptes rendus*
Conseil Supérieur de la Natalité: *Procès-verbaux* and *Rapports*
Conseil Supérieur du Travail: *Comptes rendus, Annexes, Procès-verbaux*
Le Cri du Sol
La Croix Meusienne
Dossiers de l'Action Populaire
Le Droit des Femmes
Droit Social
L'Economiste Français
L'Elan Social
Etats Généraux du Féminisme
Etudes
Exselsior
Fédération des Ouvriers en Metaux, Congrès Fédéral: *Comptes rendus*
Fédération Unitaire du Textile-Vêtement et Parties Similaires, Congrès: *Comptes rendus*
La Femme dans la Vie Sociale
Le Figaro
La Française
La France Active
La France Economique
L'Humanité
Information Ouvrière et Sociale
Information Sociale
Journal Officiel de la République Française (JO)
La Journée Industrielle
Journée Internationale des Allocations Familiales: Comptes rendus
La Liberté
Le Lorrain
Lothringer Volkszeitung
Le Médecin de France
Le Messin
Minerva
Le Monde
Le Monde Ouvrier
Le Mutualiste Français
The New York Times
Les Nouveaux Cahiers
L'Œuvre
L'Ouvrière
Le Paysan Lorrain
Le Peuple
Le Populaire
Pour la Vie
Redressement Français

La Réforme Sociale
Revue de l'Alliance Nationale (prior to January 1922, *Bulletin de l'Alliance Nationale*)
La Revue de la Famille
Revue Internationale du Travail
Revue Politique et Parlementaire
Revue de la Prévoyance et de la Mutualité
Revue de Rouergue
Les Syndicats Paysans
Le Temps
Union des Industries Métallurgiques et Minières: *Annuaires*
Union Nationale des Caisses Primaires Mutualistes, Union Nationale des
    Caisses Autonomes Mutualistes, Assemblées Communes: *Comptes rendus*
L'Union des Syndicats
L'Usine
Vendredi
La Verité
La Victoire du Dimanche
La Vie Ouvrière
La Vie Syndicale
La Voix du Peuple
La Voix Sociale

CONTEMPORARY DOCUMENTS, SPEECHES, AND PAMPHLETS

Abeille, Elzéar. *Le Problème des allocations familiales en face des problèmes de la sous-consommation et de la denatalité.* Chambre de Commerce de Marseille, 28 April 1939.
Achard, F. "Le projet de loi sur les assurances sociales." *Revue Politique et Parlementaire* (May 1922), 259–275.
Ansari, Nasser. *La Natalité: influences des allocations sur la natalité, système français, système allemand.* Paris: J. Haumont (no date).
Antonelli, E. *Guide pratique des assurances sociales.* Paris: Payot, 1928.
Arendt, Joseph. *La Nature, l'organisation et le programme des syndicats ouvriers chrétiens.* Paris: Action Populaire, 1926.
Argentier, Clément. *Les Résultats acquis par l'organisation permanente du travail de 1919 à 1929.* Paris: Sirey, 1930.
Assurance maladie et les œuvres sociales dans les industries d'Alsace et de Lorraine. Metz: Imprimerie Paul Even, 1922.
Audouin, Louis. *Les Caisses de compensation et les allocations familiales dans l'industrie française.* Poitiers: H. Mansuy, 1928.
Auréjac, Intendent Général. "Les Allocations Familiales." *Revue Politique et Parlementaire,* no. 528 (10 November 1938).
Bastide, Etienne. "La Vie commerciele et industrielle, 1900–1950." *Revue de Rouergue,* no. 4 (October–December 1950), 567–591.

Batier, Gabriel. "Le Projet sur les assurances sociales jugé par un médecin d'Alsace." *Revue Politique et Parlementaire* (February 1926), 245–253.

Baudouin, Eve. *La Mère au travail et le retour au foyer.* Paris: Bloud et Gay, 1931.

Comment envisager le retour de la mère au foyer. Paris: Spès, 1933.

Belot, G. *Les Problèmes de la famille et le féminisme.* Paris: F. Nathan, 1930.

Berthelot, Cyriaque. *La Guerre de 1914, la gestion des loyers et des congés, les allocations familiales aux familles nécessiteuses.* Sievron: Documentations Officielles, 1915.

Bertillon, Jacques. *La Dépopulation de la France, ses conséquences, ses causes, et mesures à prendre pour la combattre.* Paris: Alcan, 1911.

Beveridge, William. *Social and Allied Services: A Report by Sir William Beveridge.* New York: Macmillan, 1942.

Bonvoisin, Gustave. *Allocations familiales et caisses de compensation, leur origine, leur raison d'être, leurs effets, leur fonctionnement dans la région parisienne.* Paris: Lang Blandrons, 1927.

Extrait du Bulletin de la Chambre de Négociants Commissionaires et du Commerce Extérieur. Paris, 1927.

La Loi sur les assurances sociales et les allocations familiales. Conférence faite à la Chambre de Commerce de Paris, 1 March 1928. Paris: Arrault, 1928.

L'Institution française des allocations familiales. Paris: Centre d'Information Documentaire, 1935.

La Dénatalité, ses causes, ses remèdes. Paris: Edition Sociale Française, 1937.

Les Allocations familiales en 1943. Paris, Edition Sociale Française, 1944.

and Georges Maignan. *Allocations familiales et caisses de compensation.* Paris: Sirey, 1930.

Boverat, Fernand. "Les Allocations familiales et l'émigration vers les villes." *Revue de l'Alliance Nationale,* no. 142 (May 1924), 141–144.

Comment nous vaincrons la dénatalité. Paris: Editions de l'Alliance Nationale, 1939.

Niveau d'existence et charges de famille: étude comparative. Paris: Librarie des Medicis, 1944.

Braibant, Marcel. *La Tragédie paysanne,* preface by Georges Monnet. Paris: Gallimard, 1937.

Brodier, Jean. *Capitalisme et travail.* Paris: CFTC, 1939.

Bruxelles, Aimé. *Nature juridique et caractères des cotisations d'assurances sociales dans la législation française.* Lyon: Bosc Frères, 1932.

Buisson, Georges. *Les Assurances sociales en danger.* Paris: Edition de la CGT, 1932.

Que disent les décrets sur les assurances sociales: entretiens sur les décrets-lois des 28 et 30 Octobre 1935 modifiant le régime des assurances sociales. Paris: Editions de la Fédération Nationale des Mutuelles Ouvrières, 1936.

Bureau International du Travail, "Les Allocations familiales." "Salaires et durée du travail." *Etudes et Documents,* Série D, no. 13. Geneva: A. Kundig, 1924.

"Les Problèmes généraux de l'Assurance Sociale." *Etudes et Documents,* série M, No. 1. Geneva: A. Kundig, 1925.

Caisse de compensation des allocations familiales de Loir-et-Cher. *Statuts et règlements.* Blois: Siège Sociale (no date).

Caisse de compensation de la région de Besançon. *Mémento pour l'application du Code de la Famille.* Besançon: A. Eblé, 1942.

Caisse Nationale Agricole d'Allocations Familiales. *Documentation générale*. Paris: Maison de l'Agriculture, 1940.

Cambon, Victor. *L'Industrie organisée d'après les méthodes américaines*. Paris: Payot, 1920.

Cann, Jeanne. *Les Allocations familiales, l'allocation de la mère au foyer et l'allocation de salaire unique dans le commerce et l'industrie*. Loudéac: Tranouil-Anger, 1944.

Caziot, Pierre. *Au service de la paysannerie*. Paris: Fernand Sorlot, 1942.

Cetty, Abbé. *La Famille ouvrière en Alsace*. Rixheim: A. Sutter, 1883.

Chatenay, Henry. *Les Allocations familiales en agriculture*. Poitiers: Imprimerie moderne, 1939.

Chauveau, Claude. *Loi sur les assurances sociales: commentaire juridique, financier, et administratif*. Paris: Librarie Générale de Droit et Jurisprudence, 1928.

Chenut, Christian. *Les Allocations familiales dans les marchés de travaux publics*. Paris: Recueil Sirey, 1931.

Cheysson, Emile. *La Famille, l'association, et l'état*. Paris: Guillaumin, 1904.

Comité Central des Allocations Familiales. *Manuel pratique des allocations familiales et commentaire de la loi du 11 mars 1932 et du règlement d'administration publique du 14 mars 1933*. Paris: Comité Central des Allocations Familiales, 1933.

Abrégé de la législation concernant les caisses de compensation. Paris: Edition Sociale Française, 1940.

Circulaires ministérielles concernant les allocations familiales: textes réglementaires. Paris: Edition Sociale Française, 1943.

Rapports présentés à l'assemblée générale. May 1943. Paris: Edition Sociale Française, 1943.

Statistiques 1944. Paris: Edition Sociale Française, 1945.

Réorganisation des caisses d'allocations familiales, conformement à l'ordonnance du 4 octobre 1945. Paris: Imprimerie de Moriamé, 1946.

Comité International Pour la Vie et la Famille. *Ier conférence internationale pour la vie et la famille*. Paris, 2–3 June 1928. Paris: Comité International Pour la Vie et la Famille, 1928.

IIIe conférence internationale pour la vie et la famille. Anvers, 8–19 August 1930. Paris: Comité International Pour la Vie et la Famille, 1930.

Compère-Morel. *Le Socialisme agraire*. Paris: Marcel Rivière, 1920.

Courau, R. *Les Assurances sociales dans les industries d'Alsace et de Lorraine, Code impérial d'assurance des employés, caisses minières de secours*. Strasbourg: Imprimerie Strasbourgoise, 1919.

Dassonville, J. *Un Cheminot d'Epernay – comment il élève ses 8 enfants avec 1,150 francs par mois*. Paris: Editions Spes, 1925.

Degas, M. *Les Assurances sociales*. Paris, Dunod, 1924.

"La Mutualité française," Speech delivered by, Directeur Général des Services de la Fédération Nationale de la Mutualité Française à la Fondation Française pour l'Etude des Problèmes Humains, 2 June 1943. Paris: Bernard Frères.

Delzons, Louis. *La Famille française et son évolution*. Paris: Colin, 1913.

Digard, Henri. *Les Assurances sociales et l'agriculture*, preface by Pierre Cathala. Paris: Recueil Sirey, 1931.

Dorgères, Henri. *Haut les fourches*. Paris: Les Œuvres Françaises, 1935.

Révolution paysanne. Paris: Jean Renard, 1943.

Drouhet, Pierre. *L'Evolution juridique des allocations familiales*. Paris: Edition Sociale Française, 1943.

Dubourg, Gabriel. *Nouvelles Allocations familiales*. Paris: Dumas, 1945.

Duporcq, Jean. *Les Œuvres sociales dans la métallurgie française*. Université de Paris, 1936.

Durand, Abel. *Une Etape des allocations familiales: discours prononcé a l'assemblée plénière du 22 juin 1945*. Paris: Edition Sociale Française, 1945.

Témoignage: l'institution française des allocations familiales, 1918–1946. Paris: Edition Sociale Française, 1946.

Erouart, Jean. *Evolution du régime des allocations familiales depuis la loi du 11 mars 1932*. Lille: Douriez-Bataille (no date).

Eylaud, Jean-Max. *Les Assurances sociales en France et la protection de la santé publique*. Bordeaux: Imprimerie de l'Université, 1929.

Fallon, Valère. *Les Allocations familiales en Belgique et en France*. Bruxelles: Dewit, 1926.

Fédération Française des Syndicats d'Employés Catholiques. *Notice et statuts*. 1923.

Fédération Nationale Catholique. *Natalité et les allocations familiales*. Paris: J. Alléon, 1934.

Fleury, Emile. *Commentaire pratique et critique de la loi du 5 avril 1928 sur les assurances sociales*, preface by Adolphe Landry. Paris: Recueil Sirey, 1929.

Fonvieille, André. *Etude critique du régime des allocations aux familles des militaires soutiens indispensables*. Montpellier: L'Abeille, 1919.

Forestier, H. *La Famille ouvrière dans sa maison: enquête sur les logements ouvriers*. Paris: Edition du Temps Présent, 1941.

Fougerol, Saillard. *Les Allocations aux familles des mobilisés, textes officiels avec commentaire pratique, modèles et formules*. Paris: Berger-Levrault, 1915.

Fouquet, J. *Les Pensions de l'Etat, les allocations provisoires d'attente et les allocations spéciales aux grandes invalides*. Bordeaux: Marcel Durand, 1924.

Frantzen, Paul. *Les Assurances sociales*, Les Cahiers du Redressement Français, no. 22. Paris: Editions de la SAPE, 1927.

Gony, Maurice. *La Situation de l'employeur au regard de la législation des assurances sociales*. Nimes: Albin Pujolas, 1932.

Grinda Edouard, (Deputy). *Rapport fait au nom de la Commission d'Assurance et de Prévoyance Sociales sur les Assurances Sociales*, no. 5505, Chambre des Députés, session de 1923, Annexe au procès-verbal de la séance du 31 janvier 1923. Paris: Imprimerie de la Chambre, 1923.

Guesdon, Victor. *Le Mouvement de création et d'extension des caisses d'allocations familiales*. Paris: Vie Universitaire, 1922.

Guibal, Jean. "Les Allocations familiales agricoles." *Bulletin de la Société Centrale d'Agriculture de l'Aude*, no. 122, April 1938.

Guyot, Yves. "Les diverses formes de la mutualité." *Journal des Economistes,* vol. 72 (1913), 8.

Helleu, Yves. *Les Caisses de compensation des allocations familiales depuis la loi du 11 mars 1932.* Paris, 1937.

Hubert, René. *Salaires, allocations familiales, et caisses de compensation.* Paris: Chaix, 1921.

"Revue de la presse." *Bulletin Mensuel des Allocations Familiales (et des Assurances Sociales),* vol. 19 (July 1929), 138.

"Les Assurances sociales et l'opinion publique." *Revue Politique et Parlementaire* (October 1929), 30–42.

Jacquier, *Refaire la France: l'effort d'une génération.* Paris: Plon, 1945.

Jeanin, Gabriel. *La Prime à la première naissance.* Paris: Publication Sociale Agricole, 1941.

L'Institution des allocations familiales: rapport général présenté à l'Assemblée plénière du 14 décembre 1944. Paris: CCAF, 1944.

Jourdain, François. *Les Allocations familiales en agriculture: vos droits et vos devoirs.* Paris: Publications Sociales Agricoles, 1940.

Keynes, John Maynard. "The Social Consequences of Changes in the Value of Money," first published 1923, *Essays in Persuasion.* New York: Norton, 1963.

Kula, P. "Salaires et budgets familiaux." *Les Nouveaux Cahiers* (15 November 1938), 4–9.

Labaume, Pierre de. *Les Allocations patronales aux familles nombreuses et les caisses mutuelles en vue de ces allocations.* Thèse pour le doctorat. Paris: Trévoux, 1922.

Laguarde, Georges de. *Les Caisses d'allocations familiales et les caisses d'assurance sociales.* Paris: Edition Sociale Française, 1942.

Lancelot, E. *Pour l'ordre familiale: un plan, une organisation à réaliser,* preface by Georges Pernot. Paris: Edition Marriage et Famille, 1934.

Landry, Adolphe. *La Politique sociale, rapport par le Congrès National de l'Alliance Démocratique.* Paris, 1929.

Laporte, Marie-Magdeleine. *Les Allocations familiales dans le commerce et l'industrie en droit français et étranger.* Paris: Dalloz, 1938.

Laroque, Pierre. *Les Conventions collectives de travail.* Paris: Imprimerie Nationale, 1934.

Les Rapports entre patrons et ouvriers. Paris: Fernand Aubier, 1938.

"Le Plan français de sécurité sociale." *Revue Française du Travail,* no. 1 (April 1946) 9–20.

"From Social Insurance to Social Security: Evolution in France." *International Labour Review,* vol. 57, no. 6 (June 1948), 565–590.

Lavielle, Romain. "L'Œuvre de la mutualité et des assurances sociales." Maison de la Mutualité, Paris, 15 March 1944. Paris: Imprimerie Municipale, 1944.

Lebas, Jean. *L'Assurance sociale et le Parti Socialiste.* Lille: Imprimerie Ouvrière, 1921.

Les Rapports entre patrons et ouvriers. Paris: Fernand Aubier, 1938.

Lebreton, André. *La Famille et les lois sur les allocations de guerre, les pensions militaires, et le pécule.* Saint-Brieuc: René Prudhome, 1921.

Lefebvre, Charles. *La Famille en France dans le droit et dans les mœurs.* Paris: Giard et Brière, 1920.

Léonard, Jacques. *La Médecine entre les savoirs et les pouvoirs.* Paris: Aubier Montaigne, 1981.

Le Play, Frédéric. *L'Organisation de la famille.* Third edition, Tours: Mame, 1884.

Liek, E. *Les Méfaits des assurances sociales en Allemagne et les moyens d'y remédier.* Paris: Payot, 1929.

List, Friedrich. *Das nationale System der politischen Okonomie.* Berlin: Academic-Verlag, 1982.

Marcadé, Paul. *Le Médecin français et la loi sur les assurances sociales.* Bordeaux: Imprimerie-Librarie de l'Université, 1933.

Martin, Henriette. *Les Assurances sociales et l'agriculture.* Paris: Editions Domat-Montchrestien, 1932.

Mascarel, Arnold. *La Famille et ses lois.* Paris: Gabriel Beauchesne, 1921.

Masui, Emile. *Organisation économique du Travail dans les usines.* Paris: Dunod, 1920.

Mazas, Pierre. *Le Fondement de l'obligation aux allocations familiales.* Paris: Sirey Recueil, 1936.

Maze, Hyppolyte. *La Lutte contre la misère.* Paris: La Cerf, 1883.

Meline, Pierre. *Morale familiale.* Paris: Bloud et Gay, 1928.

Michelin Cie. *Une Expérience de natalité.* Paris: de Cussac, 1929.

Michot, Hervé. *Une Politique fiscale et financière de la famille.* Rennes: de Oberthur, 1943.

Millerand, Alexandre. *Le Retour de l'Alsace-Lorraine à la France.* Paris: Charpentier, 1923.

Ministère de la Guerre. *Recueil des textes officiels concernant les allocations aux familles de mobilisés.* Paris: H. Charles-Lavauzelle, 1917.

Ministère de l'Intérieur, Direction du Personnel. *Décrets, arrêtés, et circulaires concernant l'application de la loi du 5 août 1914 sur les allocations aux familles de mobilisés.* Paris: Melun, 1915.

Molliard, André. *Les Allocations familiales et les caisses de compensation.* Paris: Marcel Giard, 1922.

Office général des assurances sociales d'Alsace et de Lorraine. *Les Assurances sociales d'Alsace et de Lorraine,* Second edition. Strasbourg: Imprimerie Strasbourg, 1922.

Oualid, William and Charles Picquenard. *Salaires et tarifs, conventions collectives et grèves: la politique du Ministère de l'Armement et du Ministère du Travail.* Paris: Presses Universitaires de France, 1928.

Parisot, Jacques. *Le Projet d'équipment national et les assurances sociales.* Paris: Editions Berger-Levrault, 1934.

Péricard, Jacques, ed. *Almanach encyclopédique de la famille française.* Paris, 1929.

Pernot, Georges. "D'où vient, où va le mouvement familial?" *Pour la Vie,* no. 1 (July 1945), 83–86.

Picard, Roger. *Le Salaire et ses compléments: allocations familiales et assurances sociales.* Paris: M. Riviere, 1928.

Pinte, Jean. *Les Allocations familiales.* Paris, Recueil Sirey, 1935.

Piquelle, Paul. *Vie à Metz pendant l'annexion.* Metz: P. Even, 1937.

Porte, Marcel. *Assurances sociales et traditions mutualistes.* Grenoble: Allier, 1923.

Prévost, Marguerite. *Pour l'éducation ouvrière – les jeudis de l'employé.* Bordeaux: 1923.

Recrutement de l'armée. *Allocations pour soutiens indispensables de familles.* Paris: H. Charles-Lavauzelle, 1912.

Renaud, Jean. *Les Devoirs du Front Populaire envers les paysans de France, 9ème Congrès du Parti Communiste Français*, Arles, 25–29 December 1937.

Rey A. *La Question des assurances sociales*, Paris: Félix Alcan, 1925.

Rhein, Roger. *Les Allocations familiales obligatoires: le régime de la loi du 11 mars 1932.* Paris: Recueil Sirey, 1932.

Ricardo, David. *The Principles of Political Economy and Taxation.* London: Dent, 1987.

Richemond, Pierre. "Allocations pour charges de familles et caisses de compensation." *Revue d'Economie Politique* (September–October 1920), 590–606.

Risler, Georges. "Les Assurances sociales en Alsace et en Lorraine: conférence faite au Conservatoire National des Arts et Métiers, le 10 février 1929." *Le Musée social*, no. 5 (May 1929), 200–228.

Romanet, Emile. *Le Salaire familiale.* Grenoble: Imprimerie Aubert, 1918.

Les Allocations familiales. Lyon: Chronique Sociale de France, 1922.

Salleron, Louis. *Un Régime corporatif pour l'agriculture.* Paris: Dunod, 1937.

"L'Agriculture et les allocations familiales." *Revue Politique et Parlementaire*, no. 521 (10 April 1938), 24–34.

Siegler, Jean. "Le Projet de loi sur les assurances sociales et les institutions d'initiative privée." *Revue Politique et Parlementaire* (September 1924), 399–409.

Tables analytiques des annales de la Chambre des Députés, 12th Legislature, 1919–1924, Tables de matières. Paris: Imprimerie de la Chambre des Députés. No date.

Taudiere, Henry. *Les Lois françaises contre la famille.* Paris: J. de Grigord, 1913.

Tessier, Gaston. *En face des assurances sociales.* Paris: Edition Spes, 1929.

Théry, E. *Les Richesses économiques de l'Alsace-Lorraine.* Strasbourg, 1920.

Toulemon, André. *Le Suffrage familial ou le suffrage universel intégral: le vote des femmes.* Paris: Recueil Sirey, 1933.

Vermont, Henri. "Reflexions sur le projet de loi contre les accidents du travail." *Extrait du Bulletin de la Société Industrielle de Rouen*, no. 1, 1896.

Bulletin des Sociétés des Secours Mutuels (September 1921), 133–136.

Vernhes, Marcel. *Les Allocations familiales dans les professions industrielles et commerciales, le régime légal, les extensions sociales, les projets de réforme.* Lyon: Bose Frères, 1938.

Weber, Anatole. *Les Errements des sociétés de secours mutuels.* Paris: 1913.

A travers la mutualité: étude critique sur les sociétés de secours mutuels. Paris: 1929.

Weil, Georges. *Histoire du mouvement social en France, 1852–1924.* Paris: Alcan, 1924.

BOOKS AND ARTICLES

Abbad, Fabrice. *La France des années 20.* Paris: Armand Colin, 1993.

Accampo, Elinor, Rachel G. Fuchs, and Mary Lynn Stewart. *Gender and the Politics of Social Reform in France, 1870–1914.* Baltimore: Johns Hopkins University Press, 1995.

Acker, Joan. "Class Gender, and the Relations of Distribution." *Signs*, vol. 13, no. 3 (Spring 1988), 473–497.

Ambler, John, ed. *The French Welfare State: Surviving Social and Ideological Change.* New York University Press, 1991.

Anderson, Benedict. *Imagined Communities: Reflections on the Origin and Spread of Nationalism.* New York: Verso, 1991.

Ashford, Douglas. *The Emergence of the Welfare States.* New York: Basil Blackwell, 1986.

"The Whig Interpretation of the Welfare State." *Journal of Policy History*, vol. 1, no. 1 (1989), 24–43.

"Advantages of Complexity: Social Insurance In France." *The French Welfare State*, ed. John Ambler, 32–57. New York University Press, 1991.

"Structural Analysis and Institutional Change." *Journal of the Northeastern Political Science Association*, vol. 19, no. 1 (Fall 1996), 97–123.

Ashley, Susan. "The Mechanics of Social Reform: Accident Insurance in France and Italy." *Proceedings of the Annual Meeting of the Western Society for French History*, vol. 18 (1991), 408–416.

Association Internationale de la sécurité sociale. *L'Évolution de la politique familiale à la lumière du développement démographique.* Geneva: l'Association Internationale de la Sécurité Sociale, 1990.

Baldwin, Peter. *The Politics of Social Solidarity: Class Bases of the European Welfare State 1875–1975.* Cambridge University Press, 1990.

Bard, Christine. "Les Femmes et la CFTC à travers le Nord social 1920–1936," mémoire de maîtrise d'histoire. Lille: Université de Lille III, 1987.

Les Filles de Marianne: histoire des féminismes 1914–1940. Paris: Fayard, 1995.

Barral, Pierre. *Les Agrariens français de Méline à Pisani.* Paris: A. Colin, 1968.

and Isabel Boussard. "La Politique agrarienne." *Colloque sur le gouvernement de Vichy et la Révolution Nationale*, Fondation Nationale des Sciences Politiques, 6–7 March 1970. Paris: Armand Colin and Fondation Nationale des Sciences Politiques, 1972, pp. 210–233.

Battais, Louisette. *Guide bibliographique CFTC et CFDT 1884–1987.* Paris: IRES, 1988.

Bedel, Henry. "La Vie agricole 1900–1950." *Revue du Rouergue*, no. 4 (October–December 1950), 592–609.

Bennet, Jean. *La Mutualité pendant la guerre de 1914–1918.* Etampes: Société d'Imprimerie et de Publicité, 1964.

La Mutualité française des origines à la révolution de 1789. Paris: CEIM, 1981.

Biographies de personnalités mutualistes, XIXe et XXe siècles. Paris: Mutualité Française, 1987.

Blum, Françoise. "Le Musée Social au carrefour?" "Autour de l'Année 1928, le social et l'urbain," eds. Françoise Blum, *et al.* 339–348, *Vie Sociale*, nos. 3–4 (May–June–July–August 1999).

and Colette Chambelland and Michel Dreyfus, eds. "Mouvements de femmes, 1919–1940." *Vie Sociale*, nos. 11–12 (November–December 1984).

et al., eds. "Autour de l'Année 1928, le social et l'urbain." *Vie Sociale*, nos. 3–4 (May–June–July–August 1999).

and Janet Horne, eds. "Feminisme et Musée Social." *Vie Sociale*, nos. 8–9, (August–September 1988).

Boswell, Laird. *Rural Communism in France, 1920–1939*. Ithaca, NY: Cornell University Press, 1998.

Bour, René. *Histoire de Metz*. Metz: Editions Serpenoise, 1979.

Caisse d'Allocations Familiales de Paris. *Guide des prestations familiales*. Paris: Caisse d'Allocations Familiales de Paris, 1958.

Rapport annuel d'activité. Paris: Caisse d'Allocations Familiales de Paris, 1994.

Callaghan, Hubert Curtis. *The Family Allowance Procedure: An Analysis of Family Allowance Procedures in Selected Countries*. Ph.D. thesis, Catholic University of America, Washington, DC: 1947.

Carlen, Claudia, comp. *"Rerum Novarum." The Papal Encyclicals, 1878–1903*. Wilmington, NC: McGrath, 1981.

Ceccaldi, Dominique. *Histoire des prestations familiales en France*, preface by Pierre Laroque. Paris: Union Nationale des Caisses d'Allocations Familiales, 1957.

Chagny, R. "La Mutualité française aux XIXème siècle: l'exemple de l'Isère." *Cahiers de l'Institut de Recherches Marxistes*, no. 33 (1988), 63–84.

Chalmin, Philippe. *Les Assurances mutuelles agricoles: de la cotise au groupe*. Paris: Economica, 1987.

Charbit, Yves. "Les Fondements idéologiques des politiques démographiques en France, 1850–1900." *La Fécondité dans les pays industrialisés*, ed. Yves Charbit, 263–272. Paris: Centre National de la Recherche Scientifique, 1986.

Chesnais, Jean-Claude. *The Demographic Transition: Stages, Patterns, and Economic Implications*. Oxford: Clarendon Press, 1992.

and Paul V. Dutton. "The Power of Numbers: Europe's Demographic Cycle Ends." *Global Affairs*, vol. 8, no. 2 (Spring 1993), 92–109.

Cleary, M.C. *Peasants, Politicians and Producers*. Cambridge University Press, 1989.

Clément, Juliette *et al. Eure-et-Loir*. Paris: Editions Bonneton, 1994.

Comité de l'histoire de la sécurité sociale. *La Sécurité sociale, son histoire à travers les textes*. Bordeaux: Association pour l'Etude de l'Histoire de la Sécurité Sociale, 1988.

Cova, Anne. "L'Assurance-maternité dans la loi de 1928–1930." Colloque sur l'histoire de la sécurité sociale, Paris: 1989, Actes du 114e Congrès National des Sociétés Savantes.

Crew, David F. *Germans on Welfare. From Weimar to Hitler*. Oxford University Press, 1998.

De Grand, Alexander. *Italian Fascism: Its Origins and Development*. Lincoln: University of Nebraska Press, 1989.

Delpa, François. "Les Communistes français et la sexualité, 1932–1938." *Le Mouvement Social*, no. 91 (April–June 1975), 121–152.

Demartini, Anne-Emmanuelle. "Le Clanisme politique en Corse: un cas particulier, le clan Landry," mémoire de maîtrise d'histoire. Paris: Université de Paris IV, 1988.

Dolléans, Edouard. *Histoire du mouvement ouvrier*. vol. III. Paris: Armand Colin, 1953.

Dorion, Georges. *La Sécurité sociale*. Paris: Presses Universitaires de France, 1994.

Downs, Laura Lee. "Les Marraines élues de la paix sociale? Les Surintendentes d'usine et la rationalisation du travail en France, 1917–1935." *Le Mouvement Social*, no. 164 (July–September 1993), 53–76.

Manufacturing Inequality: Gender Division in the French and British Metalworking Industries, 1914–1939. Ithaca, NY: Cornell University Press, 1995.

Dreyfus, Michel. "Mutual Benefit Societies in France: A Complex Endeavour." *Social Security Mutualism: The Comparative History of Mutual Benefit Societies*, ed. Marcel van der Linden, 209–224. Bern: Peter Lang, 1996.

"Mouvement ouvrier et mutualité: l'exception française?" Mémoire pour l'habilitation à diriger des recherches présenté sous la direction du professeur Antoine Prost. Paris: Université de Paris I, 15 January 1997.

"L. Mabilleau et le mouvement mutualiste français et international de 1895 à 1921." *Le Musée social en son temps*, ed. Colette Chambelland, 103–118. Paris: Presses de l'Ecole Normale Supérieure, 1998.

Dreyfus, Paul. *Emile Romanet: père des allocations familiales*. Grenoble: Arthaud, 1965.

Dumont, Jean-Pierre. *La Sécurité sociale toujours en chantier: histoire, bilan, perspectives*. Paris: Editions Ouvrières, 1981.

Dupâquier, Jacques. ed. *Histoire de la population française*, vols. I–IV. Paris: Presses Universitaires de France, 1988.

Dupeyroux, Jean-Jacques. *Sécurité sociale*, eighth edition. Paris: Editions Dalloz, 1994.

Durand, Paul. *Le Visage des nôtre, trente ans de petite histoire messine et lorraine, 1920–1950*. Metz: Editions de Lorrain, 1953.

Duriez, Bruno. "Mouvements familiaux et catholicisme social dans le Nord, 1919–1945." *Revue du Nord*, vol. 73, nos. 290–291 (April–September 1991), 445–454.

Ecole Nationale de la Santé Publique. *Protection sociale: historique et perspectives*. Rennes: Ecole Nationale de la Santé Publique, 1982.

Ehrmann, Henry W. *Organized Business in France*. Princeton University Press, 1957.

Elwit, Sanford. *The Making of the Third Republic*. Baton Rouge, 1975.

Ewald, François. *L'Etat providence*. Paris: B. Grasset, 1986.

Finlayson, Geoffrey. *Citizen, State, and Social Welfare in Britain, 1830–1990*. Oxford University Press, 1994.

Flora, Peter and Arnold Heidenheimer, eds. *The Development of Welfare States in Europe and America*. New Brunswick, NJ: Transaction, 1981.

Fridenson, Patrick, ed. *The French Home Front, 1914–1918*, trans. Bruce Little and Helen McPhail. Providence, RI: Berg, 1992.

Histoire des usines Renault, vol. 1: Naissance de la grande entreprise, 1898–1939. Paris: Seuil, 1972.

Fuchs, Rachel G. *Abandoned Children: Foundlings and Child Welfare in Nineteenth-Century France*. Albany: State University of New York Press, 1984.

Poor and Pregnant in Paris: Strategies for Survival in the Nineteenth Century. New Brunswick, NJ: Rutgers University Press, 1992.

Galant, Henry C. *Histoire politique de la sécurité sociale française, 1945–1952.* Paris: Armand Colin, 1955.

Garden, Maurice and Hervé Le Bras. "La Population française entre les deux guerres." *Histoire de la population française,* ed. Jacques Dûpaquier, vol. IV, pp. 83–141. Paris: Presses Universitaires de France, 1988.

Gibaud, Bernard. *De la mutualité à la sécurité sociale: conflits et covergences.* Paris: Editions Ouvrières, 1986.

Mutualité, assurances, 1850–1914: les enjeux. Paris: Economica, 1998.

Godfrey, John F. *Capitalism at War: Industrial Policy and Bureaucracy in France 1914–1918.* New York: St. Martin's Press, 1987.

Gordon, Linda, ed. *Women, the State, and Welfare.* Madison, WI: University of Wisconsin Press, 1990.

Grazia, Victoria de. *The Culture of Consent: Mass Organization of Leisure in Fascist Italy.* Cambridge University Press, 1981.

Guéneau, Emile-Pierre. *Le Pays messine: 2000 ans d'évolution urbaine et rurale.* Metz: Editions Serpenoise, 1994.

Gueslin, André, ed. *De la charité médiévale à la sécurité sociale.* Paris: Editions Ouvrières, 1992.

Gutman, Amy, ed. *Democracy and the Welfare State.* Princeton NJ: Princeton University Press, 1988.

Hall, Peter. *Governing the Economy: The Politics of State Intervention in Britain and France.* Oxford University Press, 1986.

Halls, W.D. *Politics, Society and Christianity in Vichy France.* Providence: Berg, 1995.

Hardach, Gerd. "Industrial Mobilization in 1914–1918: Production, Planning, and Ideology." *The French Home Front 1914–1918,* ed. Patrick Fridenson, 57–88. Providence, RI: Berg, 1992.

Hatzfeld, Henri. *Du Paupérisme à la sécurité sociale: 1850–1940,* second edition. Presses Universitaires de Nancy, 1989.

Hause, Steven C. and Anne R. Kenney. *Women's Suffrage and Social Politics in the French Third Republic.* Princeton University Press, 1984.

Hayward, J.E.S. "Solidarity: The Social History of an Idea in Nineteenth-Century France." *International Review of Social History,* vol. 4 (1959), 261–284.

"The Official Social Philosophy of the French Third Republic: Léon Bourgeois and Solidarism." *International Review of Social History,* vol. 6, (1961), 19–48.

Heclo, Hugh. *Modern Social Politics in Britain and Sweden: From Relief to Income Maintenance.* New Haven, CT: Yale University Press, 1974.

Helly, Dorothy O. and Susan Reverby, eds. *Gendered Domains: Rethinking Public and Private in Women's History.* Ithaca, NY: Cornell University Press, 1992.

Hochard, Jacques. *Aspects économiques des prestations familiales.* Paris: Union Nationale des Caisses d'Allocations Familiales, 1961.

Hong, Young-Sun. *Welfare, Modernity, and the Weimar State, 1919–1933.* Princeton University Press, 1998.

Humphreys, George G. *Taylorism in France 1904–1920: The Impact of Scientific Management on Factory Relations and Society*. New York: Garland, 1986.

Huss, M. "Pronatalism and the Popular Ideology of the Child in Wartime France." *The Upheaval of War: Family, Work, and Welfare in Europe, 1914–1918*, eds. Richard Wall and Jay Winter, 329–367. Cambridge University Press, 1988.

Jallade, Jean-Pierre. "Redistribution in the Welfare State: An Assessment of French Performance," in Jallade, ed., *The Crisis of Redistribution in European Welfare States*. Stoke-on-Trent, UK: Trentham Books, 1988, pp. 221–253.

Jeanneney J.-M. and E. Barbier-Jeanneney. *Les Economies occidentales aux XIXe–XXe siècles*. Paris: Presses de la FNSP, 1985, vol. I.

Jensen, Jane. "Gender and Reproduction: Or, Babies and the State." *Studies in Political Economy*, no. 20 (Summer 1986), 9–46.

Jolly, Jean-Claude, ed. *Dictionnaire des parlementaires français*. Paris: Presses Universitaires de France, 1970.

Kemp, Tom. *The French Economy, 1913–1939: The History of Decline*. London: Longman, 1972.

Kerber, Linda K. *Women of the Republic: Intellect and Ideology in Revolutionary America*. Chapel Hill NC: University of North Carolina Press, 1980.

Koonz, Claudia. *Mothers in the Fatherland: Women, the Family and Nazi Politics*. New York: St. Martin's Press, 1987.

Koos, Cheryl A. "Gender, Anti-individualism, and Nationalism: The Alliance Nationale and the Pronatalist Backlash against the *femme moderne*, 1933–1940." *French Historical Studies*, vol. 19, no. 3 (Spring 1996), 699–723.

Kott, Sandrine. *L'Etat social allemand: représentations et pratiques*. Paris: Belin, 1995.

Koven, Seth and Sonya Michel. "Womanly Duties: Maternalist Politics and the Origins of Welfare States in France, Germany, Great Britain, and the United States, 1880–1920." *American Historical Review*, vol. 95, no. 4 (October 1990), 1076–1108.

Kuisel, Richard. *Ernest Mercier: French Technocrat*. Berkeley: University of California Press, 1967.

Laing, Ronald D. *La Politique de la famille*. Paris: Stock, 1972.

Land, Hilary. "The Family Wage." *Feminist Review*, no. 6 (1980), 55–78.

Landes, Joan. *Women and the Public Sphere in the Age of the French Revolution*. Ithaca, NY: Cornell University Press, 1988.

Larkin, Maurice. *France Since the Popular Front*. Oxford University Press, 1988.

Laroque, Pierre, ed. *The Social Institutions of France*, trans. Roy Evans, New York: Gordon and Breach, 1983.

  Au service de l'homme et du droit: souvenirs et réflexions. Paris: Association pour l'Etude de l'Histoire de la Sécurité Sociale, 1993.

Lavielle, Romain. *Histoire de la mutualité*. Paris: Hachette, 1964.

Launay, Michel. *La CFTC: origines et développement 1919–1940*. Paris: Publication de la Sorbonne, 1986.

Le Bras, Hervé. *Marianne et les lapins: l'obsession démographique*. Paris: O. Orban, 1991.

Lepinay, Michel. *Sécurité sociale: faillite sur l'ordonnance*. Paris: Calman-Levy, 1991.

Lorwin, Val. *The French Labor Movement*. Cambridge MA: Harvard University Press, 1954.

Lygrisse, Jean. *La Caisse d'allocations familiales de Seine-et-Marne, 1921–1979*, preface by Pierre Boisard. Paris: Caisse Nationale des Allocations Familiales, (no date).

Macmillian, James F. *Housewife or Harlot: The Place of Women in French Society, 1870–1940*. Brighton, Sussex: Harvester Press, 1981.

Maignan, Georges. *Les Allocations familiales dans l'industrie et commerce*. Paris: CCAF, 1946.

Les Allocations dans l'industrie, commerce, et professions libérales. Paris: 1954.

Marec, Yannick. "L'Apôtre de la mutualité: Henri Vermont, 1836–1928." *L'Economie Sociale* (January 1987), 3–39.

Martin, Martine. "Ménagère: une profession? Les dilemmes de l'entre-deux-guerres." *Le Mouvement Social*, no. 140 (July–September 1987), 89–106.

Massard, Marcel. "Syndicalisme et mileu social, 1900–1940." *Le Mouvement Social*, no. 99 (April–June 1977), 23–33.

Mathis, Martine. *Metz, d'un siècle à l'autre*. Metz: Editions Trajectoires, 1991.

Metzger, Chantal. "Relations entre autonomistes lorrains et alsaciens de 1919 à 1932." 103e Congrès national des sociétés savantes, Nancy-Metz 1978, Histoire-Moderne, vol. II, pp. 155–170.

Michaux, Laurette. *Metz et la Moselle pendant la grande guerre: 1914–1918*. Metz: Archives de la Région de Lorraine, 1978.

Ministère de l'Education Nationale. *Lorraine Sidérurgique*. Paris: Ministère de l'Education Nationale, 1959.

Les Houillères lorraines et leur région. Paris: Ministère de l'Education Nationale, 1965.

Mitchell, Allan. *The Divided Path: The German Influence on Social Reform in France after 1870*. Chapel Hill: University of North Carolina Press, 1991.

"The Function and Malfunction of Mutual Aid Societies in Nineteenth-Century France." *Medicine and Charity Before the Welfare State*, eds. Jonathan Barry and Colin Jones, 172–189. London: Routledge, 1991.

Moine, Jean-Marie. *Les Barons de fer: les maîtres de forges en Lorraine du milieu du XIX siècle aux années trente*. Presses Universitaires de Nancy, 1989.

Montes, Jean-François and Brigitte Schmitt. *Les Organismes d'allocations familiales dans le département du Haut-Rhin (1918–1950)*. Paris: Caisse Nationale des Allocations Familiales, 1995.

Moulin, Annie. *Peasantry and Society in France since 1789*, trans. M.C. and M.F. Cleary. Cambridge University Press, 1991.

Mouré, K. *La Politique du franc Poincaré, 1926–1928*. Paris: Albin Michel, 1998.

Moutet, Aimée. "Patrons de progrès ou patrons de combat? La Politique de rationalisation de l'industrie française au lendemain de la première guerre mondiale." *Recherches*, nos. 32–33 (September 1978), 449–489.

"La Rationalisation industrielle dans l'économie française au XXe siècle: étude sur les rapports entre changements d'organisation technique et problèmes sociaux, 1900–1939," thèse de doctorat d'état. Université de Paris I, 1984.

Muel-Dreyfus, Francine. *Vichy et l'éternel féminin: contribution à une sociologie politique de l'ordre des corps.* Paris: Editions du Seuil, 1996.

Mutelet, Marius. *Metz annexée, 1870–1918, ou un demi-siècle de vie messine.* Metz: R. Gueblez, 1962.

Nada, Nadine, *Bibliographie sur les prestations familiales, 1911–1965.* Paris: UNCAF, 1966.

Bibliographie pour servir à l'histoire de la sécurité sociale, de l'assistance et de la mutualité en France de 1789 à nos jours. Paris: Comité d'Histoire de la Sécurité Sociale, 1987.

Navarro, J.P. *La Naissance des sociétés de secours mutuels dans le Tarn.* Union Mutualiste Tarnaise, 1985.

Noiriel, Gérard. "Du 'patronage' au 'paternalisme': la restructuration des formes de domination de la main-d'œuvre ouvrière dans la métallurgie française." *Le Mouvement Social,* no. 144 (July–September 1988), 19–35.

Nord, Philip. "The Welfare State in France, 1870–1914." *French Historical Studies,* vol. 18, no. 3 (Spring 1994), 821–838.

Nye, Robert A. *Crime, Madness, and Politics in Modern France: The Medical Concept of National Decline.* Princeton University Press, 1984.

Offen, Karen. "Defining Feminism: A Comparative Historical Approach." *Signs,* vol. 14, no. 1 (Autumn 1988), 119–157.

"Depopulation, Nationalism, and Feminism in Fin-de-Siècle France." *American Historical Review,* vol. 89, no. 3 (1989), 648–676.

European Feminisms, 1750–1950. Stanford University Press, 2000.

Paxton, Robert O. *Vichy France: Old Guard and New Order.* New York: Knopf, 1972.

French Peasant Fascism: Henry Dorgères's Greenshirts and the Crisis of French Agriculture, 1929–1939. New York: Oxford University Press, 1997.

Pedersen, Susan. *Family, Dependence, and the Origins of the Welfare State: Britain and France, 1914–1945.* Cambridge University Press, 1993.

"Catholicism, Feminism, and the Politics of the Family during the Late Third Republic." *Mothers of a New World: Maternalist Politics and the Origins of Welfare States,* eds. Seth Koven and Sonya Michel, 246–276. New York: Routledge, 1993.

Pindyck, Robert S. and Daniel L. Rubinfeld. *Microeconomics.* New York: Macmillan, 1989.

Pine, Lisa. *Nazi Family Policy, 1933–1945.* Oxford University Press, 1997.

Pollard, Miranda. *Reign of Virtue: Mobilizing Gender in Vichy France.* University of Chicago Press, 1998.

Prost, Antoine. "L'Evolution de la politique familiale en France de 1938 à 1981." *Le Mouvement Social,* no. 129 (October–December 1984), 7–28.

Prost, Auguste. *Etudes sur l'histoire de Metz.* Metz: Rousseau-Pallez, 1965.

Reggiani, Andrés Horacio. "Procreating France: The Politics of Demography, 1919–1945." *French Historical Studies*, vol. 19, no. 3 (Spring 1996), 725–754.

Reid, Donald. "Industrial Paternalism: Discourse and Practice in 19th-Century French Mining and Metallurgy." *Comparative Studies in Society and History*, vol. 27, no. 4 (October 1985), 579–607.

Robert, Jean-Louis. "La CGT et la famille ouvrière, 1914–1918." *Le Mouvement Social*, no. 116 (July-September 1981), 47–66.

Roberts, Mary Louise. "Rationalisation, Vocational Guidance and the Reconstruction of Female Identity in Post-war France." *Proceedings of the Annual Meeting of the Western Society for French History*, vol. 20 (1993), 367–381.

Civilization without Sexes: Reconstructing Gender in Postwar France, 1917–1927. University of Chicago Press, 1994.

Rollet, Henri. *Andrée Butillard et le féminisme chrétien.* Paris: Spes, 1960.

Rondeau, Daniel. *Chagrin Lorrain: la vie ouvrière en Lorraine, 1870–1914.* Paris: Seuil, 1979.

Rondel, Charles. "Nature et portée de l'arbitrage obligatoire." *Le Droit Social* (February 1938), 121.

Ronsin, Francis. *La Grève des ventres: propagande néo-malthusianne et baisse de la natalité en France 19e–20e siècles.* Aublier: Paris, 1980.

Rousselier-Fraboulet, Danièle. "Un syndicat patronal face à la seconde guerre mondiale: le groupement des industriels métallurgiques et minières de la région parisienne." *Bulletin du Centre d'Historique de la France Contemporaine*, no. 13 (1992), 45–60.

Rueff, Jacques. *Souvenirs d'un gouverneur de la Banque de France: histoire de la stabilisation du franc, 1926–1928.* Paris: Génin, 1954.

Sahlins, Peter. *Boundaries: The Making of France and Spain in the Pyrenees.* Berkeley: University of California Press, 1989.

Sauvy, Alfred. *De Paul Reynaud à Charles de Gaulle.* Tournai: Casterman, 1972.

Sérieys, Gilbert. *La Longue Marche de l'agriculture aveyronnaise.* Rodez: Chambre d'Agriculture, 1989.

Shalev, Michael. "The Social Democratic Model and Beyond: Two 'Generations' of Comparative Research on the Welfare State." *Comparative Social Research*, no. 6 (1983), 315–351.

Shennan, Andrew. *Rethinking France: Plans for Renewal, 1940–1946.* Oxford University Press, 1989.

Simon, Dominique. "Le Patronat face aux assurances sociales." *Le Mouvement Social* no. 137 (October–December 1986), 7–27.

"Les Assurances sociales et les mutualistes, 1920–1932." *Revue d'Histoire Moderne et Contemporaine*, no. 34 (October–December 1987), 587–615.

Skocpol, Theda. "Bringing the State Back In: Strategies of Analysis in Current Research." *Bringing the State Back In*, eds. Peter Evans, Dietrich Rueschemeyer, and Theda Skocpol, 44–77. Cambridge University Press, 1985.

Spengler, Joseph J. *France Faces Depopulation: Postlude Edition 1936–1976.* Durham NC: Duke University Press, 1979.

Stone, Judith. "The Republican Brotherhood: Gender and Ideology." *Gender and the Politics of Social Reform in France, 1870–1914*, eds. Elinor Accampo, Rachel G. Fuchs, and Mary Lynn Stewart, 28–58. Baltimore: Johns Hopkins University Press, 1995.

Sweets, John F. *Choices in Vichy France: The French under Nazi Occupation*. Oxford University Press, 1994.

Talmy, Robert. *Histoire du mouvement familial en France, 1896–1939*, vols. I–I Paris: Union Nationale des Caisses d'Allocations Familiales, 1962.

Thalmann, Rita, ed. *Femmes et fascismes*. Paris: Tierce, 1986.

Thébaud, Françoise. "Le Mouvement nataliste dans la France de l'entre-deux-guerres: l'Alliance Nationale pour l'accroissement de la population française. *Revue d'Histoire Moderne et Contemporaine*, vol. 32 (1985), 276–301.

Ticheur, Marcel. *Le Petit Lorrain*, 1920–1995. Metz, 1992.

Titmuss, Richard M. *Social Policy: An Introduction*. New York: Allen and Unwin, 1974.

Tomlinson, Richard. "The Politics of 'Dénatalité' during the French Third Republic 1890–1940," Ph.D. thesis, Christ's College. Cambridge, 1984.

"The 'Disappearance' of France, 1896–1940: French Politics and the Birth Rate." *Historical Journal*, vol. 28, no. 2 (1985), 405–415.

Toucas-Truyen, Patricia. *Mutualité au sein des populations littorales en Charente-Inférieure, 1850–1945*. Paris: Librarie de l'Inde, 1998.

Triby, Raymond. *Les Assurances sociales dans les départements des Haut-Rhin, Bas Rhin, et la Moselle: naissance et évolution, 1883–1984*. Strasbourg: Caisse Régionale d'Assurance Maladie Alsace-Moselle, 1984.

Trist, Suzanne Margaret. "Winning Hearts and Minds: The Organization of Worker Leisure in Inter-war French Industry." Ph.D. thesis. University of Melbourne, 1993.

Union des Industries Métallurgiques et Minières, *Sécurité Sociale*. Paris: UIMM, 1985.

Villey, François. *Le Complément familial du salaire: étude des allocations familiales et leurs rapports avec le salaire*. Paris: Edition Sociale Française, 1946.

Voirin, Roger. *Les Régimes de prévoyances des salariés*. Paris: Edition de Verneuil, 1989.

Wall, Richard and Jay Winter, eds. *The Upheaval of Work: Family, Work, and Welfare in Europe, 1914–1918*. Cambridge University Press, 1988.

"Pronatalism in the Interwar Period in France." *Journal of Contemporary History*, vol. 25 (1990), 39–68.

Weiss, John. H. "Origins of the French Welfare State: Poor Relief in the Third Republic, 1871–1914." *French Historical Studies*, vol. 13, no. 1 (Spring 1983), 47–78.

Wilson, Elizabeth. *Women and the Welfare State*. London: Tavistock, 1977.

Wright, Gordon. *Rural Revolution in France: The Peasantry in the Twentieth Century*. Stanford University Press, 1964.

Yagil, Limore. "La Politique familiale de Vichy et la conception de la 'femme nouvelle.'" *Guerres Mondiales et Conflits Contemporains*, no. 188 (1997), 27–49.

Index